Metapoesis

- Sound and Meaning: The Roman Jakobson Series in Linguistics and Poetics

C. H. van Schooneveld, Series Editor

Michael C. Finke

Metapoesis

The Russian Tradition from Pushkin to Chekhov

Duke University Press Durham and London 1995

Printed in the United States
on acid-free paper ∞
Designed by Cherie Holma Westmoreland
Typeset in Times Roman with Gill Sans display
by Keystone Typesetting, Inc.
Library of Congress Cataloging-in-Publication Data
appear on the last printed page of this book.

To the memory of my mother,

Carol Rae Bachrach Finke

Contents

Acknowledgments

Earlier versions of chapters 2 and 5 appeared in *Russian Language Journal* (respectively, vol. 43, no. 144; and vol. 39, nos. 132–34); chapter 5 was reprinted in *Anton Chekhov Rediscovered* (East Lansing, Mich.: Russian Language Journal, 1987).

The writing of this book was facilitated by two Faculty Research Grants from the Graduate School of Arts and Sciences at Washington University in St. Louis, for which I am grateful.

So much for institutions; my sense of debt to the extraordinarily generous teachers and colleagues who have assisted me over the years will not be discharged so easily. Those who read parts or all of the manuscript at some stage and made helpful suggestions include: Milica Banjanin, Henry Cooper, Aileen Douglas, Andrew Durkin, Sibelan Forrester, Iurii Mann, Judith Robey, Marc Silver, Anatoly Vishevsky; Caryl Emerson's very kind efforts to make this a better book deserve extra note. Special thanks to Reynolds Smith and Pamela Morrison of Duke University Press for seeing this project through. Thanks also to the folks at Educational Computing Services at Washington University for their assistance.

Marena and Savely Senderovich got me started on this path when I was an undergraduate and have been helping me along ever since. Vadim Liapunov directed the dissertation in which this book originated, and has assisted with every sort of problem, intellectual and otherwise, since the beginning of my graduate career. Nina Perlina's profound scholarship and good cheer have been invaluable. I found a brief period of study with Michael Holquist at Indiana University very stimulating. All have contributed more than the footnotes acknowledge; weak links, errors, and omissions are uniquely mine.

Preface

It is surely appropriate to preface a book bearing such a title with a "meta" statement of my own. This book offers a series of studies unified above all by a single, persistent angle of vision: it investigates how five major Russian authors spanning the nineteenth century included commentaries on their own poetics in their fictional works. I would claim a value for this perspective in measure with the depth of penetration and richness of reading it affords, rather than its relative success in deploying Pushkin, Gogol, Dostoevsky, Tolstoy, and Chekhov to articulate itself as a theory. Nevertheless, even a heuristic approach is selected on the basis of certain theoretical presuppositions, which ought, so far as possible, to be rendered manifest. And one is after all curious *why* a critical approach focusing on the metapoetic proves particularly fruitful in each reading. No single answer to this question is advanced, but instead a whole set of possibilities whose theoretical horizons range from a synchronic, formal understanding of metapoesis, to the specific literary-historical situations of each author under study, as well as our own situations as readers schooled in a patently self-reflexive era.

The introduction situates the term *metapoesis*—whose deployment in the inflationary economy of critical discourse needs some justification—with respect to the other similar (and far more common) usages of metaliterature, metafiction, *mise en abyme*, Romantic irony, and parody. Since the term *metapoesis* and the studies here have been conceived within the broad framework of Roman Jakobson's theoretical model of communication situations, this model will also be discussed in some detail. From it derives this book's guiding principles: that the significance of metapoetic discourse cannot be understood, first, in isolation from other communicative functions at play in the writing and reception of a given literary text, nor, second, without a general and historical understanding of the role of metapoesis in the broader arena of discourse to which it belongs. Whereas the varieties of autocommentary that can be called metapoetic have most often been adduced as proof of the radical disengagement of text from context, the present approach brings context back into the interpretive process precisely where its introduction would appear to be foreclosed: it offers a way out of the "double mirror" effect of the infinite regression of meaning—*mise en abyme*—celebrated in so many deconstructive treatments of textual self-reflection. The introduction opens with a brief discussion of Chernyshevsky's *What Is to Be Done?* (1863), a text in which the contextual significance of metapoesis is rather manifest.

Chapter 1 takes up Gogol's "Leaving the Theater after the Presentation of a New Comedy" ("Teatral'nyi raz"ezd posle predstavleniia novoi komedii," 1842), a one-act play which, from start to finish, stands explicitly in a "meta" relationship to another text, Gogol's own *The Government Inspector* (*Revizor*). I begin by situating "Leaving the Theater" in respect to *The Government Inspector.* Past readers have tended to dismiss the playlet as Gogol's marginally artistic, or even non-artistic, attempt at explaining his controversial dramatic masterpieces. I show that "Leaving the Theater" is a continuation of and complement to the full-length comedy which, nonetheless, deserves to be handled as an integral work of verbal art with its own peculiar dramatic movement. Moreover, the playlet's metapoetic thrust is not directed entirely outside of the text, but toward itself as well. I discuss "Leaving the Theater" in the context of the dominant one-act genre of the day, *vaudeville*, and conclude that Gogol fashioned the work as a kind of anti-*vaudeville.* In the end I suggest that the play serves the active, conative function of asserting its author's higher consciousness, and thereby helps lay a foundation for the didacticism of Gogol's subsequent writings. As a play about a play, "Leaving the Theater" is remarkable in its attempt to depict the full range of communicative factors involved in literary reception.

In Pushkin's "The Little House in Kolomna" ("Domik v Kolomne," 1830), it appears that metapoesis—explicit in the narrative poem's prefatory stanzas—is left behind once the frivolous tale about a young maiden

(Parasha) and her widowed mother is well under way. However, chapter 2 demonstrates that the poem's lyric hero actually continues a wry meditation on his own poetics and situation as a poet at an allegorical level in the Parasha tale. This revelation emerges from reviewing the literary polemic in which the metapoetic stanzas so clearly play a part, examining further Pushkin's ambivalent dialogue with Pavel Katenin (noted by Iurii Tynianov some sixty years ago), and situating the tale within its generic tradition. I suggest that the poem is chiefly addressed to Katenin, and that its particular combination of polemic, parody, and fable comprises a kind of game of one-upsmanship in the arena of literary genre.

In Dostoevsky's *The Idiot* (1869), an explicitly metapoetic dimension surfaces in two chief ways: in the latter part of the novel there are digressions in which the narrator despairs of telling his story fully, thereby introducing the narration of the novel as a theme in the novel; and the theme of storytelling is also elaborated throughout the novel by the proliferation of characters who tell stories, that is, by the function of inserted narratives in *The Idiot.* Chapter 3 focuses on the way this concern about poetics is expressed below the surface, however, and concludes that Dostoevsky presents Myshkin in the active role of an author who fails because of the genre in which he has conceived his activities. *The Idiot* can be read as a meditation on the practice and pitfalls of authoring, that is, in the terms of Mikhail Bakhtin's "Author and Hero in Aesthetic Activity," of taking the attitude of an author toward others. Two extreme possibilities for the nature or composition of such an attitude toward others are implicit in the novel, and Myshkin is the site of their competition. The first is associated with the corporeal Christ and, less obviously, with the figure of St. Francis of Assisi; the second, with Jean-Jacques Rousseau. If the positive attraction of Myshkin as a character issue from his similarities to Christ, the failure of Myshkin's poetics can be attributed to their Swiss, Rousseauean derivation.

My reading of Tolstoy's *Anna Karenina* (1877) in chapter 4 examines the novel's systematic treatment of questions of art, chiefly in regard to the pictorial arts. I suggest that Tolstoy has obliquely commented on the making of his own novel through his treatment of the "sister art" in the novel; I focus in particular on the episode, near the center of the work, where Anna and Vronsky visit the artist Mikhailov in Rome. Tolstoy's portrait of the artist at work invites interpretation as a self-portrait (Mikhailov does, after all, depict Anna Karenina), and the semantic field set up by the artist's masterpiece depicting Christ before Pilate reflects that of the novel as a whole. The Mikhailov episode has in fact received deserved notice from a number of interpreters of the novel; some have even viewed it as a key to the entire work. But readers have tended to be satisfied with pointing out a metaphoric association between the authoring of *Anna Karenina* and the authoring of Anna's portrait in the novel without exploring the implications of this self-reflexive moment in depth. The one does not simply stand for the other: there is an implicit comparison of Anna's various renditions in portrait painting and in the novel that cannot help but lead to reflections on the semiotic capabilities and limitations of the respective art forms.

The last chapter takes up Chekhov's first serious lengthy work, the first of his long works to appear unserialized, and the first to appear in a prestigious "thick journal." "The Steppe" (1888) was the story Chekhov wrote to create a turning point in his career. Critical evaluations of the story have tended to make three points: its overall shape or surface is irregular and flawed; its discourse works in a poetic, even musical fashion, lending the story a sense of unity which, however, defies precise articulation; and—perhaps in spite of Chekhov's intentions—the story not only reflects the beauty of the steppe while telling the story of a young child in crisis, but is symbolic of something greater as well. I show that the dominant structural principle of "The Steppe" is the figuration of its own structure, and that through the articulation of a series of metapoetic images, the steppe becomes a metaphor for literary space.

Each chapter offers a substantively new reading, in three cases ("Leaving the Theater," "Little House," and "The Steppe") of works that have not received their fair share of study; and in every case this has been made possible by attending to a metapoetic plane of meaning. Implicit in the selection of a chronologically and generically disparate group of texts by five different authors is the possibility that metapoesis represents a kind of tradition within Russian literature. This would be a tradition that was transported across the boundaries between various, at times mutually hostile, literary systems; it would be a tradition in which, as the instances of *Anna Karenina* and "The Steppe" suggest, even authors operating under the norms of what is conventionally called realism—that is, even those who on the face of it seek to render transparent the conventional nature of the form of communication in which they are engaged and all concomitant problems of poetics—desired or felt compelled to participate. That Russian literature of the nineteenth century was relentlessly self-reflexive has in fact become something of a critical commonplace. The key issue, of course, is *why*, what it meant in each of the cases presented here to wield the metapoetic pen, and in the end this must be discovered through careful readings of the texts involved. As we shall see, although all five authors engage in self-reflexive literature, their reasons for doing so are not shared. My introduction to metapoesis begins and ends with this last point.

A Note on Transliteration

The method of transliteration used in this book is deliberately dualistic. In my text the names of authors, their characters, and the titles of their works are rendered in familiar English formulations (Tolstoy, Dostoevsky, Vronsky, Nastasya, etc.). The titles of texts unavailable in English, quotations where the Russian sound or meaning is under discussion, and all reference matter have been transliterated into English according to the Library of Congress method, System II as described in J. Thomas Shaw, *The Transliteration of Modern Russian for English Language Publications* (Madison: University of Wisconsin, 1967). Although in citations I have occasionally adjusted the transliteration of a previous scholar to comply with my own, all bibliographic entries remain faithful to their published format. This method should satisfy the technical demands of scholars of Russian literature while making the text more readable for a wider audience.

Introduction

As both a feature grouping a series of texts into a subtradition in nineteenth-century Russian literature and a communicative process shaping the larger tradition, metapoesis reaches one of its most distinguished culminations, in the twentieth century and in exile, with Vladimir Nabokov's *The Gift*: "Its [*The Gift*'s] heroine is not Zina, but Russian Literature," wrote Nabokov in the author's foreword" (*The Gift*, 8). But the "Russian Literature" spoken of here is already literature about literature: even Nabokov's unfortunate object of parody, the nineteenth-century radical thinker, critic, and novelist, Nikolai Chernyshevsky, himself pursued a relentlessly self-reflexive narrative strategy in his outstanding literary effort, *What Is to Be Done?* (1863).

Nabokov and Chernyshevsky are two authors separated by multiple literary generations and a social, ideological, and aesthetic abyss; but it is the kind of abyss across which the literary word travels with particular force, as demonstrated by Nabokov's apparent wish to "purge" his predecessor from Russian literature through a devastating parody (Davydov). *What Is to Be Done?* itself manifests a certain purging activity, and both authors can be said to achieve this objective by means of self-reflexivity—an exemplary point of coincidence from which some far more important distinctions could be drawn.[1] As an introduction to my theoretical perspective, and as something of a paradigm for the way I proceed in the following chapters, let me discuss briefly the preface of Chernyshevsky's novel.

The narration of his preface is overtly self-reflexive:

> Yes, the first pages of my story reveal that I have a very poor opinion of my public. I employed the conventional ruse of a novelist: I began my tale with some striking scenes taken from the middle or the end, and I shrouded them with mystery. You, the public, are kind, very kind indeed, and therefore undiscriminating and slow-witted. You can't be relied upon to know from the first few pages whether or not a book is worth reading. You have poor instincts that are in need of assistance. (Chernyshevsky, 47)

The above excerpt is but one of many metaliterary passages sprinkled throughout the book, often addressing "my perspicacious reader." No wonder that a truly perspicacious reader of Nabokov is "tempted to say that even the device of autocriticism which Fëdor [the central hero of *The Gift*] employs throughout *The Gift* comes courtesy of Chernyshevsky" (Davydov, 365).[2]

Chernyshevsky's bantering preface, which in Sternean fashion is placed after the novel's beginning, makes doubly odd reading when one recalls the conditions under which it was written (in prison at the Peter and Paul Fortress), the relentless seriousness of the man who wrote it, and the time when it was written. Two decades had passed since Lermontov composed the comparably ironic prefaces to his *A Hero of Our Time.* New norms were at work in the Russian novel, norms on the face of it not congenial to the self-referential play characteristic of the century's second quarter, indeed, codified in that period as what would become designated "Romantic irony" (to which we will return). Nor could it be argued in this instance—as it has been regarding the novels published decades earlier by Pushkin, Lermontov, and Gogol—that the lack of critics to mediate between writer and public necessitated the incorporation of guidelines for reading into the narrative itself.[3] Even if the above passage appears to make such an assertion when it decries its uneducated reader, the fact of the matter is that this novel appeared at a time when the discourse of literary criticism had arguably gained the upper hand in Russian culture over literature itself; and this was especially true in the milieu where *What Is to Be Done?* had its greatest effect.[4] How are we to understand the deployment of such speech in *What Is to Be Done?*

Chernyshevsky's preface offers a couple of answers. "I possess not one bit of artistic talent," the author explains further, ". . . if I hadn't warned you, you might well have thought that this tale was being told artistically and that its author possessed great poetic talent. But now that I've warned you that I have no talent whatever, you know that any merit to be found in my tale is due entirely to its truthfulness" (Chernyshevsky, 48). Through undermining the expected devices and conceits of the literary genre in which he is working, Chernyshevsky seeks to place greater emphasis on the content or "truth" of his discourse. It is a strategy mimicking that of Romantic irony, but to an end quite opposed to the Romantic ideology of transcendence: an artistic representation is always inadequate for Chernyshevsky, the proponent of a materialist and utilitarian aesthetics, insofar as it substitutes the concrete and material object represented; so Chernyshevsky undermines his own artistry in order to assert the empirical truth of that which he presents in the novel. The didactic element of the above passage is, if anything, an attempt to undo the legacy of Romantic irony, with its involvement of the reader in the process of the work's creation, and its striving toward infinitely open and transcendent structures. When Chernyshevsky refers to the poetics of his own novel within the novel, it is to short-circuit the aesthetic approach of the well-schooled reader and establish an altogether different interpretive itinerary. Nevertheless, he finds himself carrying out this pedagogic task by means of metapoetic commentary, just like the aesthetes who preceded him and like those, such as Nabokov, yet to come.[5]

The preface ends with kinder words:

> Yet there is among you, dear readers, a particular group of people—by now a fairly sizable group—which I respect. I speak arrogantly to the vast majority of readers, but to them alone, and up to this point I've been speaking only to them. But with the particular group I just mentioned, I would have spoken humbly, even timidly. There is no need to offer them any explanation. I value their opinion, but I know in advance that they're on my side. Good, strong, honest, capable people—you have only just begun to appear among us; already there's a fair number of you and it's growing all the time. If you were my entire audience, there'd be no need for me to write. If you did not yet exist, it would be impossible for me to write. But you're not yet my entire audience, although some of you are numbered among my readers. Therefore, it's still necessary and already possible for me to write. (48–49)

It ends, that is, with kinder words to *some* of his readers. Chernyshevsky's anticipated addressees are split, the preface asserts, into the knowing and the unknowing; and those addressees in the know are invited to snicker and nod their heads as the master instructs his less "perspicacious" charges—

that is, those very readers who are ironically addressed as "perspicacious." Here metapoesis, as a direct authorial address to the reader, establishes a conspiratorial tone, it paves the way for a relationship of familiarity and solidarity between Chernyshevsky and his preferred addressees; and it therefore helps prepare the truly perspicacious reader to detect the manifold Aesopic allusions included between the lines of the work.[6]

Once again, then, Chernyshevsky's communicative strategy harkens back to an era when Russian literary life was organized on the basis of "familiar associations."[7] There, as will be seen in Pushkin's "Little House," metapoetic commentary can create a space for inside jokes and topical polemics, which only the addressee-as-familiar-associate will comprehend and, perhaps, find interesting; it can transmit messages that might indeed prove dangerous to an author's person, or to his work's reception among the broader public, were they more directly stated and widely intelligible. That the Aesopic communication model became quite conventional in Russian literature is itself a convention of literary scholarship, for which the reception history of *What Is to Be Done?* provides notorious and compelling evidence: after Dimitrii Karakozov's attempt on the czar in 1866, investigators retro-interpreted *What Is to Be Done?* so as to conclude that Chernyshevsky knew of this "plot" three years in advance (see Paperno, 30). But a full forty years earlier Petr Viazemsky had already underlined the conventionality of the censor in "The Censor (A Fable)":[8] this overt and epigrammatic denunciation of the censor flaunts the very genre whose specialty was bypassing the censor.

Chernyshevsky makes the traditional Aesopic strategy even more overt, and this is because something is at stake other than the practical issue of conveying private messages on an esoteric plane of meaning. His heavy-handed use of this convention and demeaning references to the "crowd" parody the depiction of the literary communication situation one finds in the metaliterary poetry of Pushkin and others of that earlier period;[9] indeed, his entire approach to the conventional communication situation of the literature of familiar associations is thoroughly parodic. Thus, although the terms delimiting Chernyshevsky's two camps of prospective addressees — the "select" and the "crowd" — derive directly from the earlier tradition, membership into the camps is extended on quite different bases.

Even as Chernyshevsky mocks Romantic notions regarding the poet and crowd, he finds them quite useful, and metapoetic conceits serve an active and positive role in his narrative as well. If metapoesis foregrounds a narrative's addressivity, then for the imprisoned and isolated Chernyshevsky, as well as for his readers, every direct address to the reader, every "you" the narrator utters, can be seen as serving a phatic function; and merely maintaining contact between addresser and a select group of addressees under such conditions was already quite an accomplishment. One might further argue that in eliciting his preferred addressees Chernyshevsky sought (rather successfully) not only to communicate with a preexisting community, but to *create* that community: if one conceives oneself as having been addressed, if one answers the narrator's "you," then one is *ipso facto* a member of this "select" and progressive community.[10]

Even such a short discussion can establish the special interpretive value of attending to the way that *What Is to Be Done?* reflects its own poetics. This is not a result to be taken for granted, given the work's history of reception as an overly tendentious and, from the point of view of form (especially this aspect of its form), deeply flawed novel. We also see how coming to terms with metapoesis in a particular text involves intertextual and contextual considerations. The moments where *What Is to Be Done?* appears most self-involved in fact involve parodic gestures, and cannot be properly understood outside of some sense of the historically variable functions of such self-reflexivity. What is overtly the case in *What Is to Be Done?* also proves true with Gogol, Pushkin, Dostoevsky, Tolstoy, and Chekhov: metapoesis involves a foregrounding of the literary communication situation as such; it marks a site where the author tends to emerge and address a very specific addressee or set of addressees with authorial words.

Let me now proceed to define the term "metapoesis"—chiefly by situating it in regard to a series of related notions—after which I will offer some speculation as to its functions in nineteenth-century Russian literature.

I ▪

The notion of a metapoetic function is derived by analogy with that which linguists have called the metalingual function, as discussed by Roman Jakobson in his seminal article, "Linguistics and Poetics" (see also his shorter "Metalanguage as a Linguistic Problem"). To recapitulate in brief: Jakobson describes six factors involved in any communication situation—

addresser, addressee, context, message, contact, and code — and correlates them with six communicative functions: the emotive, the conative, the referential, the poetic, the phatic, and the metalingual. These functions are hierarchically organized differently in different communication situations. Within the framework of Jakobson's long-familiar, six-function description, the metalingual function is described as the "set" or orientation of speech toward the code ("Linguistics," 21–28). If one considers poetics to be the system of rules and conventions governing the production and reception of literary texts or speech acts, then a metapoetic function would involve utterances about that system, and about the process of creation based upon it, within a literary work.[11]

Jakobson's thirty-year-old theoretical description retains its value as a conceptual framework for systematic approaches to acts of communication, artistic or otherwise; one recent and fruitful application is William Todd's study treating ideologies, institutions, literary traditions, and individual psychological factors comprising the communication situation during the time of Pushkin, Gogol, and Lermontov (*Fiction and Society*). To be sure, over the past few decades followers of Jakobson and others working in the area of poetics, narratology, and speech-act theory have indicated areas where the model could benefit from modification; nevertheless, all refer back to the model laid out in "Linguistics and Poetics," the very simplicity and comprehensiveness of which makes possible any number of productive refinements.[12] Let us consider the most pertinent of them.

First, it has become customary in such revisions to indicate the problematic consequences for literary theorists of Jakobson's linguistic approach to literary art. The opening and closing remarks of "Linguistics and Poetics" do indeed assert, "Since linguistics is the global science of verbal behavior, poetics may be regarded as an integral part of linguistics" (18). And Jakobson's description of the communication situation in the article, instead of serving as the point of departure for a context-oriented understanding of poetic activity, accedes to a search for the "empirical linguistic criterion of the poetic function." This intrinsic, formal feature rendering a verbal message poetic turns out to be parallelism; or, as Jakobson puts it, "*The poetic function projects the principle of equivalence from the axis of selection into the axis of combination*" ("Linguistics," 27; italics in original). Within a given text the poetic function may occupy a different hierarchical position depending upon the situations of its production and reception, but the poetic function itself remains entirely immanent to the text, fixed in its formal, linguistic structures.[13]

It must be emphasized that the notion of a metapoetic function, derived from the six-function model of the communication situation and formulated in reference to the concept of poetics, is not to be confused with, or limited to reflection on, what Jakobson describes as the "poetic function"; nor would such an approach have been acceptable to Jakobson. In the first place, the poetic function as laid out in "Linguistics and Poetics" is chiefly based upon and applicable to the study of verse. Even if Jakobson asserts the relevance of parallelism in prose genres, and at times demonstrates it with fascinating analyses, he also acknowledges that the tools for its study are not the same as those for the study of verse, and that they are in need of a great deal of refinement (Jakobson and Pomorska, 105–9).[14] More to the point here, however, is that in regard to both poetry and prose the literary code entails more than rules regarding the poetic function. It is not meter and rhyme scheme alone that define a particular genre of poetry, Jakobson emphasizes, but also (among other possible features) its distinctive hierarchy of communicative functions:

> [T]he linguistic study of the poetic function must overstep the limits of poetry, and, on the other hand, the linguistic scrutiny of poetry cannot limit itself to the poetic function. The particularities of diverse poetic genres imply a differently ranked participation of the other verbal functions along with the dominant poetic function. Epic poetry, focused on the third person, strongly involves the referential function of language; the lyric, oriented toward the first person, is intimately linked with the emotive function. . . . ("Linguistics and Poetics," 26)

In each of the chapters to follow, therefore, investigating metapoesis will to varying degrees throw us outside the text, beyond immanent structures, to account for other aspects of the communication situation — as was the case with *What Is to Be Done?*

A second area of modification — and one that also speaks to the application of the poetic function to prose genres — was elaborated by the Russian semioticians who so fruitfully pursued Jakobson's ideas. There is a crucial distinction to be made between the linguistic system or code of a natural language and the literary code — in the terminology of Iurii Lotman, a "secondary modeling system" (*Structure*, 9). Essentially the same distinction is also made in Roland Barthes's discussion of "staggered systems" (*Ele-*

ments of Semiology, 89–94), and later in his discussion of connotation (in *S/Z*, 6–11).[15] Analysis of the poetic function in Pushkin's narrative poem, Gogol's drama, and the prose works under study here would thus have to operate on at least two levels: the immanent linguistic, as is the case in several instances of paronomasia treated in the following chapters; and that "secondary" level at which the signifieds of individual words and larger chunks of discourse are in turn treated as contiguous signifiers, which are segmented and juxtaposed to create meaning in accordance with a distinctively *literary* double articulation. In short, there may be just as much projection of the axis of similarity onto the axis of contiguity in prose as in poetry; at issue, rather, is at what semiotic level this takes place — and even here there can probably be no absolute differentiation between prose and poetry.

By the same token, the historical contexts of a literary text's production and reception should not be conflated with the *context* rubric in Jakobson's model. Perhaps it would be less confusing to denote the *referential function* (orientation toward context) as a "modeling" or "construction" function (to borrow terms, respectively, of Iurii Lotman and Tzvetan Todorov), with context in the broader sense understood as the entire multiform and dynamic speech situation.[16]

Even more fundamentally, the objection has been raised that for both language and literature, the code or systemic aspect is always encountered already realized in specific historical and social contexts. It is derived from concrete utterances and literary works — a canon, however personal, and however much in dispute — toward which a speaker or an author will have a responsive attitude. This point has become commonplace in recent years, in part a belated effect of the lessons of Mikhail Bakhtin and Lev Vygotsky.[17] Thus, when Bakhtin speaks of "metalinguistics," he means, rather than discourse referring to code, discourses referring to *other discourse*, "the study of those aspects in the life of the word, not yet shaped into separate and specific disciplines, that exceed — and completely legitimately — the boundaries of linguistics" (*Problems of Dostoevsky's Poetics*, 181).[18] It follows that metapoetic utterances in literary works will not refer in unmediated fashion to an abstract and ideal system or code in relation to which a particular text is produced, but to other utterances, more or less paradigmatic, associated with particular authors or literary periods and saturated with values. As a result, individual-psychological, ideological, and sociological considerations are properly brought into play in a discussion of metapoesis.

This line of argument can lead ultimately to the conclusion that the very notion of code is misleading, even mystifying, and that metapoesis is nothing other than intertextuality or, in a different idiom, dialogue. The spectacular advances in linguistics of the past century involved overcoming this very argument: in his 1942 lectures on the relationship between *langue* and *parole* in Saussure's thought, Jakobson argues against the "excesses of a positivism pushed to its limit" which would consider *langue* "as merely a scholarly abstraction" ("Langue and Parole," 88–89). Theories of poetics have never managed the same degree of success in articulating a literary code as has linguistics, however; this is surely because in literature, unlike in language, the dynamic interaction characterizing both systems between conservative and destabilizing factors—centripetal and centrifugal forces—favors the latter (especially in the novel, as Bakhtin has taught us).[19] Nevertheless, I shall continue to speak of the "code," for even if, in the final analysis, there can be no such thing as a stable literary code, the term is well-suited to describe the abstraction and generalization involved in any processing of such "other" utterances.[20] Moreover, relinquishing the conceptual apparatus and terminology of a poetics means losing all theoretical grounds for distinguishing metapoetic discourse from any other sort, when as a matter of practice both authors and readers do make such a distinction.

To say that centrifugal forces are more prominent in literature than in language is to say that the relationship between literary discourse and its paradigms appears to differ from that of *langue* and *parole* in ordinary speech. The earliest works of the Russian Formalists, with their notions of defamiliarization and automization, imply that literature works *against* any hypothesized code as much as with it. This can be seen in how even a neoclassical work of literature, where the emphasis is on fulfilling models given in advance, relates to its generic models;[21] and it was recently emphasized by the poet Joseph Brodsky in a reproach to systematizing critics:

> Like every other living creature, a writer is a universe unto himself, only more so. There is always more in him that separates him from his colleagues than vice versa. To talk about his pedigree, trying to fit him into this or that tradition of literature is, essentially, to move in a direction exactly opposite to the one in which he himself was moving. In

general, this temptation of seeing a literature as a coherent whole is always stronger when it's viewed very much from the outside. In this sense, perhaps, literary criticism indeed resembles astronomy; one wonders, though, if this resemblance is really flattering. (291)

In fact, as the Russian linguist Karcevskii demonstrated, there are analogous centrifugal forces involved in every articulation of a linguistic sign, literary or not; but in the latter instance such shifts tend to be ignored or suppressed by communicators.[22] Jakobson's own treatments of the Saussurean distinction between *langue* and *parole*, or code and message, emphasize, in contrast to Saussure, their multidimensional and dynamic mutual interaction ("Langue and Parole," "Shifters").

Now this aspect of resistance, denial, or undermining of code is at the same time a reference to code, and could be said to have metapoetic significance; but this would then be true of every work of literature. We are reserving the concept of metapoesis for texts that do not just *do* what we have described, but *depict* it as well, and we are interested in those that do so at some length, as an integral feature of the work. To return to the analogy with linguistics from which we departed: pragmatically speaking, one has to recognize a difference between the linguistic code that allows one to communicate (and to which, in that sense, every act of verbal communication has recourse) and actually *speaking about* the code.[23]

Still, both metapoetic and metalingual discourse may be either overt, as in a language lesson, or covert, as in a conversation between a parent and a child where certain constructions and vocabulary may be used as a way of making a dialogue about diapers or a pacifier *also* a language lesson. Of the works taken up here, Chernyshevsky's preface, Gogol's "Leaving the Theater," and the first part of Pushkin's "Little House" are overtly metapoetic; in the others, metapoetic discourse is advanced indirectly. Now, if discourse that presents itself as referential can covertly function metapoetically—as, for example, the passages regarding Anna's portraits in *Anna Karenina* have often been interpreted—then it is no less the case that overtly metapoetic discourse can (indeed, probably must) serve other communicative functions. Thus, in Gogol's playlet, which presents itself as a metaplay, metapoesis will be seen to serve the emotive and conative functions. In fact, as Jakobson puts it, one could "hardly find verbal messages that would fulfill only one function" ("Linguistics and Poetics," 22). At issue is rather the hierarchical order of functions in a given message, with the predominant function shaping the overall message.

This reveals another interesting aspect of the communication model elaborated in "Linguistics and Poetics" — its dual description of the communication situation. Jakobson first identifies the "factors" involved — addresser, message, addressee, context, code, and contact — and then explains, "Each of these six factors determines a different function of language" — the emotive, poetic, conative, referential, metalingual, and phatic ("Linguistics and Poetics," 22). In theory the duality of *factor* and *function* makes it possible for reference to a given factor to serve a function other than the one it overtly "determines," but this possibility is not taken up in Jakobson's explication of his model. Instead, Jakobson proceeds to demonstrate how particular linguistic signifiers are codified as references to particular factors, which in turn manifest corresponding communicative functions (in a sense, six "master signifieds"). Thus, interjections present "the purely emotive stratum in language" (22); the imperative mood expresses the conative function (23); and equational sentences, the metalingual (25). The verbal message evinces, rather than the monopoly of one function, a hierarchy of many or all; but the individual signs making up the message can be classified by linguistic analysis as referring to particular (or in some instances, duplex) factors. While Jakobson's model allows for a pragmatic and functional approach to understanding the hierarchy of communicative aspects in a given communication situation, then, his own impulse, and his own genius, is to develop as far as possible an immanent linguistic approach to the problem.[24] The notion of function as elaborated by Jakobson remains disengaged from the actual situation of communication; as Linda Waugh points out, it is an "intrinsic quality" of the message itself, linguistically determinable, and must be distinguished from the "usage" to which a message is put (62).

But it is this question of usage that occupies us. We know that an autocratic pedant will use metalingual constructions for emotive and conative purposes — not simply, or even primarily, to "gloss." Utterances explaining the meaning of other utterances do not simultaneously explain their own situational meaning, indeed, could probably never do so. By the same token, it is one thing to categorize passages such as those cited from Chernyshevsky as metapoetic; answering the question of *why*, *to what purpose* does a metapoetic factor emerge in the text, is quite another. To sort this out we can have recourse to other communicative factors: for how else could one answer this question except to view the metapoetic aspect as itself evidencing a hierarchical arrangement of communicative factors? An insecure author foregrounds the metapoetic aspect of his work to forestall the attacks of critics, or an overly secure author indulges in literary pedagogy — in both cases a complex of conative and emotive functions are at work. Or perhaps this extra dimension of self-reflexivity takes part in a general cultural tendency of self-interrogation — here the referential function would be at work through the metapoetic function.

2 ■

Although there certainly has been no dearth of "meta-" terms deployed in contemporary criticism, metapoesis has rarely, to my knowledge, been among them. Its use here reflects more than the desire to remain consonant with the Jakobsonian terminology: other, more frequently encountered terms — such as "metaliterature," "metafiction," "parody," "self-parody," or *mise en abyme* — inadequately describe the phenomena under study. Let us briefly situate the notion of metapoesis in respect to these overlapping, yet different literary concepts.

If one understands metaliterature as literature in some sense about literature, then it is at once clear that metapoesis is included under that rubric, and that the term is impossibly broad. Its compass embraces all utterances regarding any aspect of the literary process, whereas our interest is reference to the code and to the process of the work's making.

The more precise notion of metafiction first entered critical parlance in 1970 in the work of William Gass,[25] and has received many varying (and less elegant) usages since then.[26] To provide a full definition of metafiction one might be expected to first define fiction; but if fiction is to be defined by means of its opposition to truth or reality, Patricia Waugh and others imply that the raison d'être of metafiction may well be the difficulty or even impossibility of this task.[27] Considered in the context of Jakobson's communication scheme, metafiction can be said to focus on the referential function, posing questions about the means and possibility of mimesis. It does so, moreover, as its chief purpose, and not as a consequence of meditations on poetics. This is not to say that metafictions never refer to their own poetics; indeed, they are quite apt to do so. But they do so within a semantic field dominated by the fiction/reality opposition, where poetics is revealed as an artificiality concealed beneath the surface of a discourse which, with deceptive innocence, purports to reflect some or other real world *out there.*[28] For metafiction, in sum, reference to poetics is a way of "undoing" the referential function in literature; or conversely, as Patricia Waugh points out, it can reveal the literariness of our everyday life.[29] Although this aptly describes what takes place in *The Idiot* and *Anna Karenina*, it need not always be the case in narratives I would like to call metapoetic, nor is it true of all the texts taken up in the following chapters.[30]

More difficult is situating metapoesis with respect to parody. All five works treated in this book feature parodic thrusts that must be apprehended if their metapoetic dimensions are to be understood. Indeed, insofar as the parodist tends to make the target text part of the code for the work he has written, it could be argued that parody is always metapoetic.

The reverse, however, is not true: metapoetic discourse need not be parodic, for a discourse can refer to its own poetics without the intermediary step of taking a target external to itself; whereas the most prominent theories of parody view such an outward orientation as fundamental. Thus, in the pioneering discourse typology presented in his *Problems of Dostoevsky's Poetics*, Bakhtin writes that in parody an author

> speaks in someone else's discourse, but in contrast to stylization parody introduces into that discourse a semantic intention that is directly opposed to the original one. The second voice, once having made its home in the other's discourse, clashes hostilely with its primordial host and forces him to serve directly opposing aims. Discourse becomes an arena of battle between two voices. (193)[31]

Although Bakhtin speaks of conflicting voices and values embodied in double-voiced discourse rather than subtexts and processes of codification, an outward orientation remains parody's key feature. Just such a "battle between two voices" is central to the readings of Pushkin, Gogol, and Dostoevsky offered here. But as the chapters dealing with Tolstoy and Chekhov will demonstrate, this need not be the case.

A fine example of the distinction I am drawing here is implicit in a recent reading of Pushkin's *Tales of Belkin* (*Povesti Belkina*), cowritten by David Bethea and Sergei Davydov. The authors' interpretations of "The Shot" ("Vystrel"), "The Station Master" ("Statsionnyi smotritel' "), "The Snowstorm" ("Metel' "), and "The Mistress-Maid" ("Baryshnia krest'ianka") as literary parodies follow a pattern that has become traditional in Pushkin criticism. The agonistic, or to be more precise, dueling metaphors deployed throughout the article suggest a correlative attitude toward the target authors and literary stereotypes on Pushkin's part. Bethea and Davydov also manage to relate the cycle's parodic aspects to the fates of individual characters, and thus to find an edifying principle at work in the tales: those characters who progress past stereotypical poses and mature beyond a position of "frivolity" (*vetrennost'*) come to happy ends (14).

Most illuminating, however, is their interpretation of "The Coffinmaker" ("Grobovshchik"), in Pushkin's cycle the middle tale but reserved for discussion last in the article. A series of convincing correspondences demonstrates that this tale, long considered the most frivolous of the five, is in fact of metapoetic significance. In it Pushkin represents himself as the coffinmaker, and his predecessors as skeletons. The short, apparently nonsensical tale actually serves as an authorial commentary explaining in allegorical (and less agonistic than Davydov and Bethea's own) terms just what the author sees himself doing as he writes this cycle of literary parodies: "By borrowing and reworking the old literary schemes, Pushkin actually repairs them—as coffin parodies—and in so doing makes good on the promise inscribed over his shop ['Plain and colored coffins sold and upholstered; coffins also let out on hire, and old ones repaired']" (16); further, "But Pushkin, a literary coffinmaker, not only buries the dead in his parodies. More important, he gives them new life. As Schultz puns, 'The dead cannot live without coffins' " (18). While the first two and last two tales of the cycle are parodies with more or less identifiable targets, the middle tale, "The Coffinmaker," refers to the creative process behind the cycle as a whole.

Why not enlist the term "self-parody" to describe what Pushkin does in the story? Because "The Coffinmaker" lacks the critical disjunction between its two planes of meaning which, according to both Tynianov and Bakhtin, distinguishes parody. In self-parody we should expect a text representing two distinct planes of authorial consciousness—possibly a former, unselfconscious authorial "I" as "I" used to write, and a present, self-conscious "I" with a critical perspective on how "I" used to write. While metapoesis could involve self-parody, it need not do so as a rule, and the broader term of metapoesis seems more accurate here.

A distinction must also be drawn between metapoesis and theories of literature, treatises on poetics, and so on. Boileau's *Art poetique* (1674), for instance, is certainly about poetics, and it is in verse. It is commonly argued that such treatises, however well crafted, are not literary art because they are not dominated by an aesthetic function, and therefore do not meet the criteria set up at the start of this discussion;[32] the same charge has been made against the work taken up in chapter 1, Gogol's "Leaving the Theater." But such evaluations fail to register how the hierarchy of functions in a text, as conceived by its readers, can change through historical and cultural dislocations.[33] And let us also reiterate the distinction between an outward and an inward orientation of a discourse's reflections on poetics. The works read here may have to refer to other works in order to refer back to their own poetics, and they may become "other" to themselves through the act of critical self-reflection, but we must insist upon the *return*.[34]

Perhaps closest to the notion of metapoesis is the expression *mise en abyme*, coined in 1893 by André Gide and more recently elaborated by Lucien Dällenbach (see Dällenbach).[35] Dällenbach defines the *mise en abyme* as "*any internal mirror that reflects the whole of the narrative*" (36; italics in original); he identifies three types of reflection, which can in turn be applied to either (or some mixture of) the utterance, the enunciation, or the code (Dällenbach, 43). Dällenbach's description of the *mise en abyme* of the code is very close to what I have described as metapoesis. But whereas Jakobson's model leads us to understand metapoetic utterances in the context of a communicative process, here *mise en abyme* is approached as a *formal device*—which in the study verges on having a life of its own—whose theoretically possible hypostases can be elaborated and whose functions in a variety of literary systems are to be described.

In addition, because Dällenbach conforms to certain limits set out in Gide's "charter" definition of the term, and because he resolutely hitches the notion of *mise en abyme* to that of *reflection* in its most literal sense—as by a mirror—Dällenbach also excludes from consideration "reflexive elements that do not concern the spatio-temporal universe of the narrative." This means omitting "any personal intervention by the author within the narrative and also any prologue or invocation of the muse that might announce the forthcoming narrative in the form of a resume" (50). Under such criteria, the opening stanzas of Pushkin's "Little House in Kolomna," which are indeed explicitly metapoetic, do not comprise a *mise en abyme*; nor would the author's introduction to Lermontov's *A Hero of Our Time*; and epigraphs of metapoetic significance, such as the one to *Anna Karenina*, which certainly both inaugurates and reflects one of the novel's central themes, would also be of questionable status, insofar as they too occur outside the narrative.[36] Images and actions reflecting some aspect of the narrative qualify; actual reiterations qualify; but an implied author speaking directly about his narrative does not. Of the works taken up in this book, the painting of Anna in *Anna Karenina* and Chekhov's "The Steppe" would be the most unambiguous examples of what Dällenbach calls the *mise en abyme.*

Finally, the term *mise en abyme* has in recent years acquired a metaphysical significance that need not be attributed to metapoesis. In poststructuralist literary theory especially it is often associated with the infinite regression and groundlessness of meaning.[37] As was mentioned earlier, where *mise en abyme* has been traditionally adduced as proof of the radical disengagement of text from context, metapoesis conceived as a communicative function brings context—that is, the other aspect of the communication situation—back into the interpretive process.

3 ■

What then are the communicative functions of metapoesis in nineteenth-century Russian literature?

The overt function of the metalingual aspect of an utterance, according to Jakobson, is to provide definitions: "Whenever the addresser and/or the addressee need to check up whether they use the same code, speech is focused on the code: it performs a *metalingual* (i.e., glossing) function" ("Linguistics," 25). It follows that the metalingual function plays a great role in the acquisition of language.

An analogous argument is often made regarding metapoesis in nineteenth-century Russian literature. When for instance Lermontov, in his preface to the second edition of *A Hero of Our Time*, remarks upon the difficulty his badly educated readers seem to have understanding irony, he assumes the role of literary pedagogue. Todd contends that in Lermontov's day, when the communication situation of the salon was giving way to new, more commercialized literary institutions with a wider but less educated readership, there grew a need for authors to "play the critic's role within their novels, explaining such elementary concepts as 'irony' (Lermontov), 'beauty' (Gogol'), and 'the novel' (Pushkin) to their readers, they had to make model readers for their works *within* those works. Every novelist does this to some extent, but these early Russian ones do it with unusual persistence" (*Fiction and Society*, 103, italics in original).[38] This argument provides a very attractive way of understanding explicit metapoetic statements in the Russian context; the same phenomenon marks the early English novel (especially Fielding and Sterne). Of the works read here such a pedagogic impulse is most evident in Gogol's "Leaving the Theater" (and in Gogol generally, from before the time the playlet was published—for instance, in the essays in *Arabesques* [1835]—until the end of his life).

But Chernyshevsky's metapoetic digressions, which also explicitly claim a didactic purpose, appear anachronistic in comparison to other major novels written two or more decades after Lermontov's—and this very feature of anachronism hints that something more is going on. And to return to an earlier era, it can hardly be claimed that the explicitly metapoetic, jocular introduction to Pushkin's "Little House in Kolomna"—clearly oriented to those most in the know regarding the contemporary literary scene—is meant to educate the naive reading public. Indeed, many of us require a great deal of teaching if the concepts of irony and beauty are truly "elementary." There is, in sum, quite a difference between the educating that takes place via the metapoetic function in the literary "classroom" and the glossing role of the metalingual function in language acquisition. Explicit metapoetic statements that address the public's reading habits may advance alternative codes by which to read, but they can also constitute aggressive challenges and provocations of complex and ambivalent origin. This seems particularly true of Lermontov, whose "explanations" are likely to raise more questions than they answer; the subtitle of Pushkin's *Eugene Onegin*, "A Novel in Verse" ("Roman v stikhakh"), might best be understood as another such challenge. What would become of the Romantic poet if the "crowd" were a fully competent reader?

As we saw earlier, if Jakobson's elaboration of the metalingual function assumed a direct relationship between form and function, his model does provide for other possibilities. To take overt metapoesis as a lesson in poetics can quite often mean to read naively.

No such hazard attends covert metapoesis, which remains hidden from view for the naive reader—as, until now, has been the case with the narrative and so-called "realistic" portion of "The Little House in Kolomna" and Chekhov's "The Steppe." Why might these authors conceal a metapoetic plane of meaning beneath, let us say, one so referential as a description of the steppe?

The very same social developments that appeared to require a Russian author to educate his reading public by means of overt metapoesis could lead to the opposite procedure — to an esotericism of sorts, to an extension of the same elitism that had prompted Vasilii Zhukovsky to devote the first book of his verse to "the few" (in German, no less: *für wenige*). The changes in readership and means of communication mentioned above created a situation in which an author might resort to metapoesis as a way of preserving a space in the text for an implied reader or interlocutor who is, like himself, a discriminating reader or even litterateur. "The Little House in Kolomna" will be revealed as inscribing just such a privileged — though perhaps not unequivocally esteemed — reader under the surface of a narrative accessible to the most common reader. Even Tolstoy wrote in a draft preface to his first story, "Childhood" (1852), "[T]he distinction between *those who understand* and *those who do not* is for me such a sharp line that I draw it involuntarily among all the people I know"; and he wrote to Nekrasov that his story "Albert" (1857), about an artist, "must not and cannot please the majority, there is no doubt about that."[39] That Tolstoy's later aesthetics are largely defined by the deliberate negation of the "insider" addressee underlines how central and persistent a feature it was of Russian literary life.

If the privileged addressee of metapoesis is a hostile critic, the author may wish to anticipate and defuse eventual criticism, or perhaps reply to criticism already received. This is patently the case in Gogol's "Leaving the Theater," where any pedagogic impulse is at least equaled by motives of self-defense. For Chekhov, a latecomer to the nineteenth-century pantheon producing his first long "serious" work, and the first to be published in a "thick journal," the secondary, secret addressee is more the Russian prose tradition than any living author: this work is to secure his admission to the "club," and in it he displays the requisite esoteric knowledge. Chekhov narrates the tale of a child undergoing a rite of passage, undergoes one himself in the act of writing "The Steppe," and tells that story as well.

It can happen that in a particular literary genre or epoch self-reflexivity is required by the dominant literary code. This was of course the case with Romanticism, and in that context metapoesis is often subsumed under the heading of Romantic irony. Thus Friedrich Schlegel wrote in a well-known fragment from the *Athenaeum* (1798):

> There is a poetry whose One and All is the relationship of the ideal and the real: it should thus be called transcendental poetry according to the analogy of the technical language of philosophy. [. . .] But we should not care for a transcendental philosophy unless it were critical, unless it portrayed the producer along with the product, unless it embraced in its system of transcendental thoughts a characterization of transcendental thinking: in the same way, that poetry which is not infrequently encountered in modern poets should combine those transcendental materials and preliminary exercises for a poetic theory of the creative power with the artistic reflection and beautiful self-mirroring, which is present in Pindar, the lyric fragments of the Greeks, the ancient elegy: and among the moderns, in Goethe: thus this poetry should portray itself with each of its portrayals; everywhere and at the same time, it should be poetry and the poetry of poetry." (Schlegel, 145 [Aphorism 238])[40]

Self-reflection, and especially reference to the code, becomes a necessary part of a Romantic work's consummation; in Romantic irony, the infinitely extendible process of criticism is incorporated into the work itself, as a constant reference to the work's artifices. Criticism becomes, as it is put in one recent discussion of Romantic irony, "an integral and essential part of the artistic process," for a work "requires critical reflection in order to fulfill its artistic function" (Weber, 309).

Yet the very notion of Romantic irony, or metapoesis in the Romantic context, was patently a trans- (and in certain respects even an anti-) literary concept; so that to assert that the Romantics incorporated self-reflexivity into the literary code is to take a formal and mechanistic approach, one failing to account for the theorized metaphysical implications of Romantic irony, its place in the Romantic worldview. Considered in the context of Jakobson's communication-situation model, Romantic irony in this sense manifests the referential function every bit as much as it does the metapoetic.[41] This equivalence between the metapoetic and the metaphysical is evident in the very syntax of the sentence, which is formally metalingual, opening the aphorism cited above: "There is a poetry whose One and All is the relationship of the ideal and the real: it should thus be called transcendental poetry. . . ." Or, as Todorov puts it in his illuminating discussion of Romantic aesthetics, "*Mimesis*, yes, but on the condition that the term be understood in the sense of *poiesis*" (*Theories of the Symbol*, 153).

Romantic irony as such is not at issue in the following chapters;[42] and although the various understandings of irony advanced by Schlegel and his followers could very well be applied to all five works read here, it is not my intention to read from the perspective of Romantic aesthetics. But even such a sketchy presentation of the central features of Romantic irony can help reveal some important aspects of the texts we will be discussing.

The rise of literary realism in Europe and the implicit shift in philosophical orientation and social concerns that propelled it were, generally speaking, not congenial to self-referential literature, be it playful or philosophically profound. If in Romantic irony the metapoetic and referential functions are both mutually implicated and foregrounded, realism by definition involves the pretense of the former function's dismissal and the reification of the latter. It is in this sense that Robert Alter speaks of "an almost complete eclipse of the self-conscious novel during the nineteenth century" (89).[43] But in the Russian context, at least, it is quite misleading to speak in such absolute terms. Thus, although Dmitrii Segal, in his major statement on metapoesis in Russian literature after the Revolution, states that self-reflexivity (or, as he calls it, "autometawriting" [*avtometapisanie*]) is alien to the earlier tradition of the "great Russian novel" (164), he also outlines "*another*" tradition ("diachronic line") in which this feature is prominent; and the texts he discusses—including Pushkin's *Eugene Onegin*, Gogol's *Dead Souls*, and Dostoevsky's *Notes from the Underground*—can hardly be called peripheral. Indeed, self-referentiality is so pervasive in the Russian novel of the nineteenth century that Donald Fanger has adduced it as one of those features making Russian literature distinctively Russian (see "Influence and Tradition" and "Russianness").

The works by Dostoevsky, Tolstoy, and Chekhov discussed in the following chapters arguably demonstrate the persistence of techniques and concerns associated with Romantic irony even after the poetics and ideology of Romanticism had taken a subordinate position in the Russian literary system. But they also suggest that with the rise of realism, the metapoetic tradition becomes esoteric, goes underground.[44] For if we view the five works read here as a diachronic series—though, admittedly, an incomplete one—we see the metapoetic function grow increasingly covert. In Pushkin's "The Little House in Kolomna" this process occurs within the bounds of a single narrative poem: having opened with overtly metapoetic stanzas, the poem suddenly shifts these concerns to a hidden, Aesopic dimension.

And while the poem's second part is covertly metapoetic, it has traditionally been viewed as a step on Pushkin's part toward what would become the realistic tradition of "the great Russian novel."

In this book's short concluding chapter we shall also see that while no consistent set of communicative functions can be attributed to metapoesis on the basis of this sampling, this does not preclude its active role in the constitution and continuation of a tradition.

These points have an obverse side that ought also be kept in mind: the cultural and institutional contexts in which these texts are read, as well as the concerns of their individual readers, are capable of shifting the metapoetic function higher or lower in the hierarchy of functions. The approach taken here has the effect of shifting it higher. The following chapters treat texts gradated from overt to covert in how they refer to their own poetics. With the exception of Gogol's "Leaving the Theater" and Pushkin's "Little House," this corresponds to their chronological order as well, and each author's respective handling of metapoesis is indicative of changing literary norms. But there is a second motivation for presenting the works in this order: to encourage the reader to approach those texts where a metapoetic interpretation may be most subject to question—because metapoesis is most covert—from a perspective more akin to my own. In the end what matters is the degree to which the individual readings of "Leaving the Theater," "The Little House in Kolomna," *The Idiot*, *Anna Karenina*, and "The Steppe" cohere, satisfy, and reveal something new that makes sense about each of these works to my addressees; and in each case, approaching the work as metapoetic is key.

1

Gogol's Metaplay, "Leaving the Theater after the Presentation of a New Comedy"

"Of course, this is a trifle . . .
Since the author's not here, why not tell the truth?
—D. P. Lensky, *Lev Gurych Sinichkin,*
Act II, Scene 2

Gogol's comic masterpiece, *The Government Inspector* (*Revizor*), was first performed on April 19, 1836, and immediately generated vigorous and mixed reactions among critics.[1] Scarcely a month and a half later, racked by anxiety over the public's reaction to his play, Gogol fled St. Petersburg. In the meantime he had written the first version of "Leaving the Theater after the Presentation of a New Comedy" ("Teatral'nyi raz"ezd posle predstavleniia novoi komedii"),[2] a one-act play in which an author is depicted eavesdropping on his exiting audience in order to learn their true reactions to the play.

This version of "Leaving the Theater," completed in the heat of the moment of *The Government Inspector*'s reception, was no more than a rough draft. Not until October of 1842 did he give the work publishable form; but then he assigned the playlet the critical position of the last work to be included in a collection of his works prepared during the summer of the same year. Complaining of the efforts reworking "Leaving the Theater" cost him, Gogol wrote to the friend arranging the collection's publication in St. Petersburg: "So much needed to be redone, that I swear it would have been easier for me to write two new ones. But it's the concluding piece for the whole collection of writings and therefore quite important, and it required some very careful finishing touches" (*Polnoe sobranie sochinenii* [hereafter *Pss*], 12:104). In this edition of Gogol's collected works, "Leaving the Theater" was to be the last word.

In the same letter to his friend N. Ia. Prokopovich, Gogol states that the final version of "Leaving the Theater" is, to his pleasure, much different from the original. Indeed, one suspects that the 1836 version was written in a state of near panic. Its general shape is the same as that which went into Gogol's 1842 collected works—a succession of conversations about the play, framed by two monologues of the author-character, with no interaction between the author and his public. But while in the published version the author-character's words take up less than one-eighth the printed text and are directed toward what the theatergoers have omitted from their discussions, in the earlier version Gogol gave his author-character over half the text, and in the closing monologue the author reacts quite directly to the criticisms that have been leveled against him. There is an element of real fear, even paranoia, in his appeal to the Christian feelings of his public:

> In nobody is there a heartfelt interest [*serdechnoe uchastie*], and there's even some sort of clear wish to incite persecution and victimization, as against someone dangerous for society and the state. Oh, my compatriots, what is it that moves your words—a wish to utter your personal opinion, a desire—instinctive and ill-willed—for the common good, or an involuntary reflex toward saying the first words that come to you, without thinking how they might harm the author? (*Pss* 5:386).

Gogol also flattered the government, probably in the hope of forestalling action against a play and playwright labeled liberal and slanderous of the government in the reviews of conservative critics: "Our magnanimous government has, with its lofty intellect, peered more deeply than you into the purpose of that which has been written" (*Pss* 5:387); he even makes a direct appeal for the czar's protection (*Pss* 5:390).[3] These features are toned down in the final version of "Leaving the Theater," in accordance with Gogol's greater self-confidence and his program, expressed in a footnote on the playlet's first page, of making the author of the play an "ideal figure" (*Pss*, 5:137); in other words, Gogol meant to distance the playlet somewhat from the context of the reception of *The Government Inspector.*

However "ideal" Gogol made "Leaving the Theater," its metasignificance in regard to *The Government Inspector* remains the playlet's chief feature. The words of the spectator-characters distinctly echo both the traumatizing critical commentary on *The Government Inspector* that had appeared in periodicals and certain positive evaluations of the play.[4] As a play which, unlike the other four works taken up in this book, is *overtly* about poetics from start to finish, "Leaving the Theater" renders problematic any boundary drawn between literary art that is metapoetic and literary criticism. The question has to be asked: can "Leaving the Theater" be treated as a play? and if so, what sort of play is it? Finally, how does its metapoetic commentary refer not only to another play, *The Government Inspector*, but to itself as well?

Responding to a letter from S. T. Aksakov, in which the latter conveyed the request of A. N. Verstovsky for permission to stage "Leaving the Theater," Gogol wrote, "[N]aturally, it would be wrong and improper to stage it; and it's completely awkward for the stage" (*Pss* 12:122; Aksakov, 96, 98).[5] In his monograph on Gogol, Vsevolod Setchkarev declares that "Leaving the Theater" "has no artistic value" (181). From the point of view of neoclassical aesthetics, perhaps, "Leaving the Theater" may not be a "play"; but considered in the context of the aesthetics of literary Romanticism, its self-reflexivity and flaunting of generic rules can be understood as Romantic irony.[6] To the present-day reader, accustomed to the works of Beckett and Pirandello, the play's ambiguous status is unlikely to give much pause.

Moreover, neither "Leaving the Theater" nor any of Gogol's other written commentaries on *The Government Inspector* bear final explanatory power in regard to that play. Gogol never seems to have been able to convince even himself, let alone his readers, that he best understood his own words; witness his repeated returns to and reinterpretations of *The Government Inspector.* As Nabokov commented, Gogol's "intentions" tended to be formed *after* the creative act, and were notoriously changeable.[7] Debreczeny finds that Gogol took four distinct positions on the meaning of *The Government Inspector* over the decade and a half between the play's conception and the playwright's death.[8] The history of these changes is a narrative which, rather than explaining Gogol's artistic productions, compounds the enigmas.[9]

A certain duality of approach seems the best path to follow here—one that neither ignores the playlet's status of reaction to and commentary on the reception of *The Government Inspector*, nor forgets that this metaplay is a play in its own right which, like *The Government Inspector*, must be interpreted. In the past certain shortcuts have often been taken in the interpretive process. In particular, readers of the playlet have been quick to identify certain characters as representing Gogol's own views, without taking into account the extent to which there is a dramatic interaction between the various voices and positions, and the nature of the author-character's reactions to these viewpoints. In the literature on Gogol, one can even find statements by characters (especially the author-character) cited as the direct word of Gogol.[10] A more prudent approach would be to show where viewpoints similar to those expressed in "Leaving the Theater" are presented elsewhere in Gogol's works,[11] while discussing the treatment of these viewpoints in the context of "Leaving the Theater."

V. Sh. Krivonos, in an extended discussion of "Leaving the Theater," lends support to the position taken above with the complaint: "In the literature on Gogol we do not find an analysis of 'Leaving the Theater' as an artistic whole" (103). His own analysis goes far toward remedying this situation, especially in its situation of the playlet's dialogic form in respect to the Socratic tradition, and in its treatment of the theme of laughter. Yet, Krivonos's study maintains a suspiciously eulogistic perspective on Gogol. For instance, he suggests that Gogol had a fully worked-out theory of laughter, which is quite rationally presented in "Leaving the Theater." Furthermore, appearing as it does in the author-character's monologue at the end of this last piece in Gogol's 1842 *Sochineniia*, laughter is to be understood as the "positive hero" and unifying idea of the whole collected works (Krivonos, 142). There is something too sane and calculating about Krivonos's Gogol, and one wonders whether such an unequivocally affirmative view of laughter might not be simplistic.[12]

Nevertheless, our approach to the play resembles that of Krivonos. First we will also discuss the formal organization and generic characteristics of "Leaving the Theater." Rather than repeating the points many others have made about the work's relation to a tradition of plays about plays, on which Gogol surely relied,[13] we discuss the work in the context of the dominant one-act dramatic genre of the day: *vaudeville* (*vodevil'*).[14] After a few remarks on the complementary relationship of "Leaving the Theater" to *The Government Inspector*, we will then take up that which the play is most overtly about: the reception of another play, and its author's reactions — that is, the relationship between the author and his public.

I "Leaving the Theater" and the *Vaudeville*

S. S. Danilov, writing of the Russian theatrical repertoire of the 1830s and 1840s, says:

> Moreover, in the final analysis the character of the Russian dramatic theater of that period was essentially defined by two chief repertorial lines, as Gogol himself noted: "What sort of things get played on our stage?" is the question he puts in the article "The Petersburg Stage in 1835/36 [*Peterburgskaia stsena v 1835/36*]"; he answers laconically: "Melodrama and *vaudeville*." (109–10)

Gogol's antipathy to the *vaudeville* has often been remarked, and can be observed particularly well in the second section of "The Petersburg Stage in 1835/36," which was written, incidentally, in the months before the first production of *The Government Inspector*: "For five years already melodramas and *vaudeville*s have taken over the theatres of the whole world. What apishness!" (*Pss* 8:181). In the original draft of this section, Gogol called *vaudeville*s "the illegitimate children of the mind of our century, total deviations [from] nature, which have introduced a multitude of trifling absurdities" (*Pss* 8:552). He objected to the light, banal laughter of the *vaudeville* and to the essential foreignness of both genres: "But where is *our* life? where are we with all our contemporary passions and peculiarities?" (*Pss* 8:182). Gogol's reaction to the dominance of these genres is not just intellectual: "I'm angry at melodramas and *vaudeville*s" (*Pss* 8:186). Danilov points out analogous references to *vaudeville* in "Leaving the Theater" (112–14). Yet, as Vasilii Gippius points out, Gogol was not inhibited when it came to borrowing from the *vaudeville*'s repertoire of techniques ("Problematika," 82).

The popularity of the *vaudeville* and the melodrama in the early 1830s is best appreciated against the background of a feeling, pervasive among serious litterateurs during these years, that Russian drama had reached a dead end (Gippius, "Problematika," 154). According to Iurii Mann, this was a situation Gogol had taken into account and sought to alter with *The Government Inspector*; he writes, "In the struggle to renew comedy Gogol had a broad, theoretically grounded program . . ." (*Komediia*, 70).

Many of the new comedy's innovations and subversions of the typical features of melodrama are elucidated in "Leaving the Theater" by the Second Lover of the Arts (*Pss* 5:142–43), whose views Mann finds closest to Gogol's own (*Komediia*, 70). If we consider some of the typical features of the *vaudeville* genre, against which Gogol rails in his "Petersburg Notes," then the same process of subversion and innovation can be seen at work in "Leaving the Theater." This is not to assert that the *vaudeville* was foremost on Gogol's mind as he wrote "Leaving the Theater"; it should be enough to show the usefulness of considering "Leaving the Theater" in the context of the enormously popular and, in Gogol's expressed opinion, pernicious short comedic form.

*Vaudeville*s were short comedies of situation, with loosely outlined characters, designed primarily to "amuse and entertain" (Gottlieb, 24).[15] It was customary for a *vaudeville* to be performed after the main theatrical feature, as is the case depicted in "Leaving the Theater." At a time when most main theatrical productions were of plays dating from the eighteenth century, and new material was subject to "Asiatic censorship" (Gogol's complaint), quickly written and quickly forgotten *vaudeville*s answered the public's craving for new material. While there were first-rate authors who wrote *vaudeville*s (Khmelnitsky, Pisarev), the great majority were dilettantes from actors' circles. Writes Varneke, "[I]t is difficult to conceive of any other type of plays better suited to the abilities of society dilettantes. They managed to acquire the reputation of playwrights with the least effort" (192).

The *vaudeville* was a genre capable of assimilating elements of both tragedy and comedy, the joke as well as social commentary, music, lyrics, dance, melodramatic and exotic settings and events, and extended monologues. Needless to say, the genre did not subscribe to any set of neoclassical conventions; according to Gottlieb, "[T]he *vaudeville* created its own 'rules' and conventions, and was not bound by the classical 'unities' or other requirements" (Gottlieb, 22). The *vaudeville* could also be quite topical, though allusions to contemporary people and events were not necessarily incorporated into the play's actual structure, but instead relegated to peripheral and easily censored *kuplety*, verses set to music. Moreover, everything that took place in a *vaudeville* became shaded with insignificance. As Danilov puts it, "The 'triviality' [*malovazhnost'*] of the *vaudeville* was its own sort of world-view, it was, so to speak, a 'philosophy of triviality.' The Russian theatre compelled its viewer to view contemporary reality through a prism of 'triviality,' thereby deliberately leading him away from social problems" (113). It could be argued that this pernicious (especially so from the perspective of orthodox Soviet scholarship) feature of the *vaudeville* was all the more significant because of the audience it attracted: *vaudeville* appealed to a broader and lower-class population of theatergoers than did more serious fare, and was in turn more varied and "democratic" in the settings and classes of characters it portrayed (Karlinsky, *Russian Drama*, 269–70).

This eclecticism makes it difficult to establish the sort of stable poetics of the *vaudeville* that would let us ascertain instances of its parodic treatment. There is one aspect of the *vaudeville*'s topicality inviting special attention, however. It was very common for a *vaudeville* to take as its object another play, author, or aspect of literary culture. Such attacks (and defenses) had constituted a large part of the history of the Russian theater over the previous several decades. Russia's first prose comedy, *Tresotinius* by Aleksandr Sumarokov, "inaugurated the custom of presenting onstage a vicious caricature of some contemporary adversary" by lampooning Trediakovsky (Karlinsky, *Russian Drama*, 94–95). Moving closer to Gogol's time, Shakhovskoy's one-act comedy, "The New Sterne" ("Novyi Stern"), staged in 1805, poked fun at the typical themes and linguistic innovations of Sentimentalism and the followers of Karamzin; his 1815 *The Lipetsk Spa* (*Urok koketam, ili Lipetskie vody*) continued the polemics with rough treatment of Zhukovsky, the result of which was to aid in polarizing Russian literary life into the two parties of the "Archaists" and "Innovators." Mikhail Zagoskin wrote and staged his three-act *Comedy versus Comedy* (*Komediia protiv komedii*) to defend *Lipetsk Spa* while the latter was still in its first run on the stage.[16] From the 1830s on, Russian theatrical parody was to be found chiefly in *vaudeville*s (Poliakov, 17).

This generic feature of the *vaudeville* can perhaps be traced back to its carnivalesque origins:

> Very much a form of "low comedy", the vaudeville was initially performed in the little theatres of the Paris fairs. These *pièces en vaudevilles*, as they were called, had to be staged as dumb-shows (owing to the monopoly of the Comedie Francaise) and regularly parodied the plays and productions of the legitimate theatre, with musical choruses inserted on well-known themes. (Gottlieb, 22)[17]

In Gogol's "Notes of a Madman" ("Zapiski sumashedshego"), the narrator and hero Poprishchin refers to a *vaudeville* that touches both the theme of literature and that of the lowly civil servant:

> Went to the theatre. . . . There was also some sort of *vaudeville* with entertaining rhymes about copyists, especially about one collegiate assessor, which were so freely written, that I wondered how the censor could have passed them. . . . There was also a very

entertaining song [*kuplet*] about journalists: that they love to rail against everything, and that the author asks for protection from the public. (*Pss* 3:198)

The *vaudeville* Karlinsky calls "the masterpiece of this genre" (*Russian Drama*, 275)—D. P. Lensky's "Lev Gurych Sinichkin, or the Provincial Debutante" ("Lev Gurych Sinichkin, ili provintsial'naia debiutantka," 1839)—is just such a metatheatrical, depicting quarreling actresses, authors, directors, and patrons (*Russkii vodevil'*, 161–230).

This feature of the *vaudeville* provides a point of departure for discussing "Leaving the Theater" as anti-*vaudeville*. In it, rather than parodying a particular play, playwright, or reviewer, Gogol takes the contemporary theatergoing public—and, by extension, the reading public[18]—as his object. By portraying a fictional audience engaged in critical practice, Gogol places the real readers or viewers of "Leaving the Theater" in a position to criticize the critics, and he also forces them to examine their own literary responses. As a result, the meaning of "Leaving the Theater" becomes somewhat abstract, less bound by the context comprised by the historical event of the reception of *The Government Inspector*; although very specific allusions to published evaluations of *The Government Inspector* are included in "Leaving the Theater," recognizing these allusions is by no means essential to interpretating the playlet as a whole. More importantly, by the time "Leaving the Theater" was published, in 1842, these specific polemical thrusts were less likely to be perceived by the majority of Gogol's readers, though they would have been by his literary intimates and enemies. The typical metaliterary *vaudeville* provided the spectacle of one author, attached no doubt to a particular literary clique, mocking the person or work of another author, representing some other clique, for the entertainment of a wide and dimly understanding public; in "Leaving the Theater," Gogol depicts this dimly understanding public for the entertainment of fellow litterateurs, and to produce in the wider public the shock of recognition and a greater understanding of its own responses.

The letter in which Gogol states that "Leaving the Theater" was not meant to be performed has been cited here. It is certainly hard to imagine the playlet competing with the broad appeal that *vaudeville*, as a hybrid, comedic form, was able to command. Yet the performative aspect of "Leaving the Theater" remains relevant (as it does indeed to Gogol's prose); one can sense this in the piece's dialogic form, in the designations Gogol uses for characters (most of which are like stage directions regarding the character's dress and bearing), and in the speech characteristics of the characters, all of which underline the importance of the *tone* in which statements are made. "Leaving the Theater" was quite successful when read aloud to Gogol's partisans by Aksakov, and was reported by the latter to the author as one of the most appreciated works in the 1842 collected works (Aksakov, 97).

Even the positioning of "Leaving the Theater" in Gogol's collected works is quite reminiscent of that of the typical *vaudeville*: "Leaving the Theater" was printed as the last work in Gogol's *Sochineniia*; it might be recalled that *vaudeville* were customarily performed *after* the main dramatic feature, and while the main feature was often a long-familiar play, the audience could expect something new in the *vaudeville.* It is relevant that Gogol planned to have the metaplay he wrote later, "The Denouement of *The Government Inspector* (Razviazka *Revizora*)," performed immediately after *The Government Inspector*—that is, once again, in the place normally taken by *vaudeville*s. (In Russian theater the principle of accompanying the main production with something light extends to earlier times: neoclassical prose comedies, beginning with Sumarokov's *Tresotinius*, were written to provide the traditional short comedic curtain-raisers preceding the presentation of tragedies [see Karlinsky, *Russian Drama*, 94]). Moreover, the production of "The Denouement of *The Government Inspector*" was to be done in benefit performances for the actors Shchepkin (in Moscow) and Sosnitsky (in Petersburg), and it was customary for authors (as well as friendly pseudo-authors) to write *vaudeville*s expressly for the purpose of benefiting actor-friends.

One is even tempted to speculate that Aleksei Verstovsky's request for permission to stage "Leaving the Theater" reflects his recognition of certain *vaudeville*an possibilities; for in addition to being the de facto head of the Moscow theaters (Aksakov, 266), Verstovsky was a leading composer of music for the *vaudeville* (Varneke, 192).

If the genre of the *vaudeville* is indeed a legitimate frame of reference for the reading of "Leaving the Theater," then we must ask in what way the dramatic structure of the playlet engages the conventions of the *vaudeville.* To be sure, the personality and ideas of the author emerge as more important than any plotted situation, and this is not what one would expect from a *vaudeville.* Yet, the opening of "Leaving the Theater" could very well have led to *vaudeville*an developments. The stock-in-trade comic device of eavesdropping and the specific situation of an author attending incognito the performance of his play and spying on the audience's reactions comprise a fine *zaviazka* (tying of the dramatic knot) involving authorial vanity.[19] One could argue that "Leaving the Theater" engages the conventional expectations of readers familiar with the one-act *vaudeville*, only to leave them unrealized. If this were true, it would be proper to speculate, on the basis of our understanding of the poetics of the genre, that *vaudeville*an treatment of the situation would add some sort of love intrigue to the playlet and provide the spectacle of a humorous deflation of the comic's authorial vanity. There might be song and dance as well.

"Leaving the Theater" flaunts the same lack of a love intrigue as does *The Government Inspector.* In one of the most frequently cited passages from the playlet, the Second Lover of the Arts proclaims that the love intrigue is no longer suited to contemporary reality, where the acquisition of rank and capital have become prime motivators (*Pss* 5:142). Commentators on *The Government Inspector* have noted that the dramatic convention of the love intrigue is not merely absent in the play, but parodied in Khlestakov's simultaneous courtship of the mayor's wife and daughter (Gippius, *Gogol*, 87–88). There is a touch of this treatment in "Leaving the Theater," as well, in the interest accorded the author's personality by two young married women (with the exception of one short line by the High-Society Lady [*Svetskaia dama*], the only female characters in "Leaving the Theater"). "I don't know why, but I wouldn't want for him to be an egoist," says one (*Pss* 5:159). This odd comment reveals an emotional investment in the author-character, some vague and undeclared yet positive sentiment, and a wish not to have this sentiment proven ill-conceived; it indicates, however subtly, the activity of fantasy and desire. The object of this desire, however, is the author as the woman imagines him to be, not the "real" author who is listening to her words, and absolutely nothing comes of it. We might speculate that the closeness of the author-character to Gogol, both in Gogol's own mind and in the anticipated views of his reader, made more overt play with the possibilities of a love intrigue (as in *The Government Inspector* and *Dead Souls*) taboo.[20]

Interest in the person of the author is by no means restricted to the two women in the playlet. Yet, the dramatic tensions inherent in the author's initial separation from his audience are quite consciously left unresolved. Although the author's initial plans require that he stay hidden from his audience, it is remarkable that he does not come out of hiding to justify himself and clear up misunderstandings in his audience; nor is he exposed in his espionage and subjected to his audience's direct recriminations (some rather severe punishments are suggested by members of the audience, and a confrontation would certainly allow the introduction of some *vaudeville*an touches). No confrontation takes place, and in the end audience-characters are left with a variety of muddled perspectives on the author. Each time a group of conversants leaves the stage, then, a quantum of the dramatic energy that usually intensifies in anticipation of a play's denouement is left unexploited. One might contrast this aspect of "Leaving the Theater" with the events set into motion by the conversation between the "Lady Agreeable in All Respects" (*Dama priiatnaia vo vsekh otnosheniiakh*) and the "Agreeable Lady" (*Priiatnaia dama*) in chapter 9 of the first part of *Dead Souls*, which ends with Chichikov's flight (*Pss* 6:170ff).

The debate among audience-characters as to the new comedy's value also provides a degree of dramatic possibility. Thus, in the same segment where the two Lovers of the Arts discuss the absence of a traditional *zaviazka* (tying of the knot) in the new comedy, one says: "We've gotten *tied up* in an argument about comedy (*Spor* zaviazalsia *u nas o komedii*"; *Pss* 5:144; added emphasis mine). Nevertheless, it is hard to find dramatic structure or, for that matter, progression of an expository or analytical kind in Gogol's deployment of various points of view. Commentators have been quick to identify certain members of the audience — especially the Second Lover of the Arts and the Very Modestly Dressed Man — as the bearers of Gogol's own word, and the correspondences are indeed quite evident. All, however, have failed to notice that the exchanges in which these characters make their statements are completed within the first third of "Leaving the Theater." If the humble civil servant is the bearer of Gogol's socially relevant, didactic message, one wonders why the fictive author makes only passing reference in his closing monologue to the words of this servant; and why does the segment of "Leaving the Theater" containing the civil servant's words comprise less than four-and-a-half pages out of thirty-five and appear in the first third of the play, that is, in a rather unmarked position? The other character in the play whose opinions are most often associated with Gogol's — the Second Lover of the Arts — speaks even less, and in an equally unmarked position (his segment covers three pages, extending over the fourth through the sixth pages of the play). Gogol's handling of the characters who are supposed to represent him is thus quite peculiar, for the play's overall shape actually marginalizes their voices. The more obvious rhetorical strategy would be to give those whose opinions Gogol wishes to validate the last words.

In fact, quite the opposite happens. The serious discussants of the play's merits and problems are depicted as planning to continue their conversations elsewhere. For these members of the audience, what they have said about the new comedy is only the point of departure for a fuller discussion of the play. Readers who use "Leaving the Theater" as an interpretive key to *The Government Inspector* would do well to remember this point. Those members of the audience whose illogical, reductive, gut reactions to the play are chiefly negative, on the other hand, say what they have to say in a few words and leave. There is no room for development of their ideas.

The judgments of the audience have a curious effect on the author. While in the 1836 version of "Leaving the Theater" the author does respond, point by point, to the criticisms he has overheard, this is not the case in the final version; rather than taking up the critical remarks as such, he comments on what he feels to have been missing in them. "It's strange," he laments, "I'm sorry that nobody noticed the honest character who was in my play. Yes, there was one honest, noble character acting throughout the play. This honest, noble character was—*laughter*" (*Pss* 5:169); whereupon follows the theory of laughter which, drawing a great deal of attention from students of Gogol, is more often cited than interpreted.

The comic's reproach is not entirely justified, however. While none of the audience formulates the matter quite as he does, several remark that the play is funny and that they laughed a great deal. In this respect the *zaviazka* comprised by the initial situation of the author spying on his audience is doubly negated: it has only the slightest effect on the playlet's culmination, the author's final bombastic rhetorical effusion (the principle structural device of which is anaphora).

The one comment that does provoke the author's vigorous response comes from one of the last audience-characters to speak: he calls the new comedy—indeed, all literary works—"just tales" (*pobasenki*), and he denies all value to literature. His words, the most extreme in the whole play, sound ridiculous; the character is further undercut by his distinctive designation as one of "a group of people of God knows what sort of characteristics, but of noble looks and well dressed" (*Pss* 5:167). And yet, this is the comment to which the author responds in his eruption, repeating the word "*pobasenki*" no less than sixteen times.

This monologue, with its exclamation and question marks, is a solitary event, perhaps triggered by what has preceded, but not conditioned by and not really *answering* it. The comic claims that he is not speaking in defense of his own works, the faults of which he can readily see, but in response to the slander perpetrated against the most perfect masterpieces of authors such as Shakespeare (*Pss* 5:170); yet, the bombastic tone of his speech, inflated by righteous indignation, reflects a swelling of the authorial ego as well. This of course is precisely the opposite of what the poetics of the *vaudeville* would have led us to expect (remember, we suggested that a comic deflation would have been quite fitting).

In his initial monologue, the author had declared himself to be immune to such a turn, saying he had grown "cold" to his audience's applause (*Pss* 5:137). Gogol of course made such claims as well. In a letter to the censor Nikitenko (October 1842) he makes one of his habitual pleas for criticism of his own work, and then writes: "I have one virtue which one rarely encounters on earth, and which nobody wants to acknowledge in me. This is the absence of authorial pride and irritability" (*Pss* 12:112). The more he made such claims, however, the more his acquaintances came to believe the opposite.

As an ending to this discussion of "Leaving the Theater" and the poetics of *vaudeville*, we cite the last words of the comic's closing monologue:

> And who knows, perhaps afterwards it will be recognized by all that, by force of those very laws according to which the proud and strong person appears insignificant and weak in misfortune while the weak grows like a giant amidst troubles, by force of those very same laws, he who often pours heartfelt, deep tears, it seems, laughs more than anyone else on earth!.. (*Pss* 5:171)

Here the author-character expresses, in heightened, emotionally intense rhetoric, nothing other than the law of comic reversal on which the denouement of the *vaudeville* is typically based. One can also recognize the variant of a proverb in his words: "He laughs, who laughs last" (*Smeëtsia tot, kto smeëtsia poslednii*). Proverbs, it should be recalled, quite often served as the basis for titles, punch lines, or central ideas of *vaudeville*s.[21] This is arguably no less the case in "Leaving the Theater," where the author-figure does not enter into dialogue with his critics, and where no character is given the role of arguing in the author's stead; rather, the author's word is held in reserve to trump all those that proceded it—precisely in accordance with the logic of the proverb, "He laughs, who laughs last."[22] But Gogol's anti-*vaudeville*, instead of ending in laughter, ends in a passionate encomium to laughter.[23]

2 "Leaving the Theater" and *The Government Inspector*

As we said above, "Leaving the Theater" has most often been interpreted as a belated "explanation" of *The Government Inspector*, one of a series of such explanations offered by Gogol. Having proposed a framework for discussing the playlet on its own terms, let us briefly take up the relationship of "Leaving the Theater" to Gogol's full-length comedy.[24]

In discussing the shadow-like *vaudevillean* dramatic structure of "Leaving the Theater," we emphasized the nonresultativeness of each distinguishing feature. The case was perhaps somewhat exaggerated, however: an answer to the enigma of the comic's personality *is* given, for example, and debate as to the value of his new comedy *is* resolved. In the author-character's monologues, these questions are shifted to the other side of the stagelights and answered for the "real" audience of "Leaving the Theater." The missed dramatic opportunities in the body of the playlet serve to effect something outside its bounds, within its readers.

In this sense, "Leaving the Theater" picks up where *The Government Inspector* left off. The most remarkable structural feature of that play is its final scene, in which all the characters—stunned by the announcement that the real government inspector has arrived—freeze in various poses for ninety seconds. This occurs just after the reading of Khlestakov's letter and the mayor's violation of the "fourth wall" in his address to the audience beyond the stagelights: "[I]t's not enough that you're made into a laughing-stock—some pen-pusher, a scribbler, will put you in a comedy. That's what hurts: he won't spare rank or title, and they'll all laugh and clap. What are you laughing at? You're laughing at yourselves!.. Oh, you!.." (*Pss* 4:94). As Judith Robey has pointed out,[25] the epigraph of *The Government Inspector* implies that the drama serves as a mirror, and the mayor's address to the audience, combined with the freeze scene, draws the audience into the play's moral and ethical sphere of action. In short, the actors freeze in order to make the audience squirm.

This rupture of the artistic frame of *The Government Inspector* makes "Leaving the Theater" a natural sequel to the play. The audience's dispersal in "Leaving the Theater" is but the next episode in *The Government Inspector*, and the image of the audience dispersing chaotically presents a direct antithesis to that of the actors frozen on stage at the end of *The Government Inspector*. This "whirlpool" (*vodovorot*) motion may not be quite the result Gogol had wished to effect in his audience as he planned *The Government Inspector*, but as an image of frenetic action it does provide a semantic counterbalance to the motif of freezing on the spot with which *The Government Inspector* ends.[26]

The freeze scene in *The Government Inspector* results from the news that a real government inspector has come to the town and demands the local officials' presence. The comic's position in "Leaving the Theater" can perhaps be more fully understood if it is compared to that of the *The Government Inspector* in Gogol's comedy: his investigation of the reception of his own word is analogous to that of a government inspector probing the conduct of those who have been entrusted with the czar's power at a local level, that is, away from the center of power. Both situations are created by the awareness that people will lie in the presence of authority, and that authority (and its representatives) must use disguise and surprise in order to learn what is *really* going on. Written reports in particular, whether of government officials or of literary critics, are not to be relied upon.

Drawing such a parallel only serves to underscore the comic's lack of authority to fix the meanings of his own words once they have been put into circulation, however. He is powerless to set things right, his presence cannot provoke a "thunderbolt" effect like that of the true government inspector in *The Government Inspector*; this appears to have been a source of great anxiety for Gogol, especially as reviews of *The Government Inspector* began to appear in print. In "Leaving the Theater" the author resigns himself to avoiding any response to his audience other than that mediated by its encompassment in artistic form.

3 The Communication Situation

As a play about a play, "Leaving the Theater" is remarkable in its attempt to depict the full range of communicative factors involved in literary reception, as represented in Jakobson's scheme (discussed in the introduction).[27] In applying the communication situation scheme to "Leaving the Theater," one would have to speak of two situations: the one depicted in "Leaving the Theater" (the members of the audience speaking to one another and being overheard by the author-character), and the one comprised of Gogol, "Leaving the Theater," and the latter's readers. Complications grow geometrically if one considers that, as a metaplay, "Leaving the Theater" recapitulates, as it were, each aspect of the communication situation in the referential function, since the context or referent of the playlet is, overtly, the communication situation of a play. Add to this the fact that in a real communication siutation each aspect described statically in the scheme functions in dynamic relationship with the others, and a rigorous, point-by-point application of the model to "Leaving the Theater" becomes impossible. Here we would like to say a few words focusing on the addresser and the addressee components, first as represented within the textual bounds of "Leaving the Theater," and then as comprised of Gogol and his reader.

The overarching action of the playlet hinges on the emotions of the author-character, who both reports the way he feels and iconically reflects those feelings in his heightened rhetoric. In the opening monologue he is dissatisfied and depressed; in the final monologue, from the anger he expresses at the notion that literary art is "*pobasenki*" ("just tales"), the comic evolves to feeling inspired: "Forward, and with courage! [*bodrei zhe v put'*]" (*Pss* 5:170). One might call "Leaving the Theater" a play of ideas, and weigh carefully the arguments and evaluations put forward by the members of the audience,[28] but in viewing the playlet as one whole action what matters most is how these statements make the comic feel. And Gogol represents his comic as a person whose entire emotional life is wrapped up in his literary endeavors. Thus, the comic's emotions are depicted in "Leaving the Theater" as reactions to his audience's reactions to his play, rather than as preexisting feelings that the author puts into literary form (as, say, one often conceives of the emotive function at work in lyric poetry).

Indeed, the comic's very sense of self seems, at the start of the play, to be contingent upon the audience's reaction. His unique identity as a comic makes it necessary to know the genuine reactions of his audience:

> No, it's not applause I would wish for now; I would now wish to be suddenly transported to the boxes, to the galleries, to the orchestra seats, to the upper balcony, to penetrate everywhere, to hear everyone's opinions and impressions while they are still fresh and

> virginal, while they have not yet been submitted to the talk and judgments of experts and journalists, while each is under the influence of his own judgment. I need this: I am a comic. All other works and genres are subject to the judgment of a few, only the comic is subject to the judgment of all. . . . (*Pss* 5:138)

The author expresses a wish to hear even negative evaluations of his work. This craving for an immediate and honest reaction from his audience is the key component of the fictive author's attitude toward his message, at least at the start of "Leaving the Theater." It corresponds to the sense of isolation, even loneliness, which is depicted as the comic's lot: eavesdropping is the closest he can come to genuine contact with his audience. Here are called to mind Gogol's own persistent pleas, while living abroad, for honest reports of reactions to his works.[29]

At the same time, it could be argued that there is a more purely literary reason for the comic author's special relationship with his public. From the time of Aristotle and the ancients on, comedy had been that genre which most incorporated the mores and realia of contemporary life, and it was chiefly in comedy that all spheres of society could be represented. The author of comedies must therefore expect audiences to respond to a comedy's material from a position of authority: each viewer can consider that the play is about something of which he or she has some knowledge. (This, of course, is no guarantee that the viewers' remarks are going to be intelligent or truthful.) Throughout his literary career Gogol asked family and friends to send him detailed information about life where they were. In the chapter from *Selected Passages* (*Vybrannye mesta*), "What a Governor's Wife Is" ("Chto takoe gubernatorsha"), taken from an 1846 letter to A. O. Smirnova (editors' notes, *Pss* 8:795), Gogol requests that he be sent all information about *everyone* in various walks of life in the town: "For my sake you should begin anew the examination of your provincial city" (*Pss* 8:311).

By the end of "Leaving the Theater" the author's attitude has changed. His final words are a declaration of emotional independence from the judgments of his audience. Indeed, in oblique terms he asserts that he is right and they are wrong: "Forward, and with courage! And don't let your soul be troubled by the judgments. . . . The world is like a whirlpool [*vodovorot*]: opinions and rumors are propelled in it eternally, but time grinds everything down. The false flies off like husks, what remains are immobile truths" (*Pss*

5:171). In the context of "Leaving the Theater," the theater foyer is a microcosm of "the world" (*mir*), and there is no more apt image for the whirl and centrifugal movement of the audience-characters and their evaluations just witnessed by the author than that suggested by a "whirlpool." And now, at the end, *he* has remained on stage, standing in one place — as opposed to the audience which is "flying away" from the theatre in various directions[30] — uttering the truth, or even *being* the truth. The comic author's final response to his audience is rather different from what might have been anticipated during the opening monologue; rather than taking the critical words into account and perhaps incorporating them into his poetics, the author follows a line of reasoning that frees him of anxieties over the audience's reaction.

Moreover, instead of pursuing a "horizontal" dialogue of any sort with his audience, the comic author has, by the end of the playlet, assumed the position of an author contemplating potential characters:

> What a motley heap of gossip! Happy is the comic who was born amidst a nation where society has not yet fused into one immobile mass, where it has not invested itself in a unitary crust of ancient prejudice which imprisons the thoughts of all into one and the same form and measure, where each person has his opinion, where each is himself the creator of his own character. (*Pss* 5:168)

Here the audience is approached not as a judge of the new comedy so much as material for comedy; they are both judges and the judged. As a character in "Leaving the Theater," the comic author is put on a higher level of being than are the members of his audience.

This is reinforced by the author's peculiar position vis-à-vis his audience. He is spying on them, listening to their words without engaging in any reciprocal communication — not even when he witnesses the circulation of ridiculous rumors regarding his person. In short, the comic author sees *everything* that happens in "Leaving the Theater." Gogol portrays an unequal, one-way relationship between an audience and an author with an "all-seeing eye" (see Stilman). It is worth a short digression to compare this situation with the portrayal of author and audience and the results of their contact in the metapoetry of Pushkin and Lermontov.[31] The latter two depict unsympathetic crowds, while Gogol's is more mixed. More significant is the difference in the sources of authority these authors claim for their words: Pushkin and Lermontov depict author-figures who have been "touched" somehow from above, and whose authority — no matter whether the depicted crowd accepts that authority — is grounded in their contact with the muses, from their exalted inspiration. Gogol's author, on the other hand, begins by standing with or even below his audience, but through his study of the audience rises to a position above it (even as he claims to be accepting their judgment); his authority derives not from his special receptiveness to the muses, but from his "all-seeing" perspective in regard to his audience-characters — a perspective which he has worked to achieve. The author's starting point *in* the crowd is a position inherent in his identity as a writer of comedies; indeed, there is no tradition of viewing the comic author as analogous to inspired poets.[32] The struggle to achieve a higher position, on the other hand, is best understood as something specific to Gogol, and is also a chief component in some of the more disturbing aspects of his biography. We might recall *vaudeville* as a good example of a genre where the comic author does not even consider rising above his crowd.

This comic author's all-embracing vision is, of course, the counterpart of the audience's blindness. The author asserts that there is one thing his entire audience failed to see: the honorable character of laughter. (Here he responds to the objection, voiced by the High-Society Lady, that the comedy is without even one attractive character [*Pss* 5:153].) Critics have literalized this metaphor and claimed, for instance, that laughter plays the same role in *The Government Inspector* as the character Chatsky in Griboedov's *Woe from Wit* (*Gore ot uma*) and good government in eighteenth-century Russian comedy (Vishnevskaia, 206ff). But it seems important to register the fundamental difference between a character in a play and the spontaneous reaction of the play's audience, especially when that reaction is observed by a character in the play and redirected toward the audience, as happens in the mayor's frame-breaking outburst. To say that laughter is the hero of a play is to say that, in a sense, the conative function is in a dominant position in the play's hierarchy of communicative functions. The conative function, in turn, can be seen as a test of the author's authority.

A number of audience reactions to the play are depicted in "Leaving the Theater." The most notable, perhaps, could be characterized by that image we have already summoned so many times, the "whirlpool of opinions": people talk to one another, the play becomes a kind of currency of exchange. But this takes place after the new comedy has ended; during it there was laughter. Laughter tends to be an involuntary action, with sources in the unconscious, and a playwright can make the audience laugh so long as it is seated and viewing the playwright's work. But no such control can be exerted once the play is over. The fictive author's lament that laughter had gone unnoticed is thus equivalent to complaining that the audience did not acknowledge the effect the author had on it.

At the same time, it is important to remember that the comic is pursuing a particular kind of laughter:

> Not that laughter which is born of a temporary irritation, a morbid disposition of character; nor as well that light laughter which serves for the idle amusement and entertainment of people, but that laughter, all of which flies forth from man's radiant [*svetloi*] nature, flies forth from it because it contains at bottom an eternally gushing spring; and this spring deepens its object, compels to appear vividly that which would have crept by without that penetrating power, of which the triviality and emptiness of life would not fright man so. (*Pss* 5:169)

The right kind of laughter here becomes a metonymy for the inner state of the viewer: "No, only a deeply kind soul can laugh with kind, radiant laughter" (*Pss* 5:170). It is not that Gogol expects to reach only those viewers who are already "deeply kind souls," but that he wishes to place his audience, separated from its normal everyday existence for a few hours and viewing the play as a collectivity, into the position of the honest, good person, by provoking a certain type of laughter in them.

According to Donald Fanger, "Leaving the Theater" represents a new phase in Gogol's relationship with his reader (*Creation*, 198). The image of Gogol as one in possession of higher knowledge, and the didacticism that will come to the fore in his work within a few years—most notably in the 1847 *Selected Passages from Correspondence with Friends* (*Vybrannye mesta iz perepiski s druz'iami*, *Pss* 8:213–418; see especially letter 14, on the theater, 267–77)—can be considered in the context of the pursuit of an "effect" in the audience. In rather crude terms, perhaps, the differences noted earlier between the 1836 version of "Leaving the Theater" and the one finally published in 1842 could be described as reflecting Gogol's transition from paranoiac to prophet and lawgiver. No great qualitative shift in Gogol's psyche needs to be postulated for the intervening years—just the feeding of his authorial ego, which we know to have taken place.

Still, the function of "Leaving the Theater" appears less to be didactic as such than to lay the groundwork for didacticism.[33] In simplest terms, as a didact Gogol's claim to authority rests on the question of his knowing something that others do not, while at the same time convincing others that what he knows is important and true. This question of *what the author knows* does come up toward the end of "Leaving the Theater" (that is, in a highly marked structural position), in the discussion of the "group of people of God knows what sort of characteristics, but of noble looks and well dressed." One remarks: "But all the same, he must know something; otherwise it's impossible to write" (*Pss* 5:167). While concentration on the addresser end of things might lead one to view a metaliterary play like "Leaving the Theater" as the manifestation of a wish to defend oneself from criticism, the play serves a more active, conative function as well: it asserts its author's higher consciousness. Thus, in his closing monologue the fictive author no longer views the opinions of the public as necessary to him; they do not, after all, embody a perspective on his work inaccessible to him without their help: "No, I see my defects, and I see what deserves reproaches" (*Pss* 5:168). It is rather his vision that gathers in what others do not see, his word that ought to be heard as authoritative.

2

The Aesopic Content of Pushkin's "The Little House in Kolomna"

Pushkin's "The Little House in Kolomna" ("Domik v Kolomne") is in many ways a curious poem: it opens with a series of stanzas in which the poetic persona declares his intentions, yet the resulting composition demands interpretation all the more. The relationship of the poem's larger, narrative portion to this explicitly metapoetic introduction is especially problematic, and readers have tended to discount one or the other. Those who concentrate on formal aspects (Briusov, Tynianov ["Arkhaisty i Pushkin"]) focus their attention on the first part, while psychologically oriented critics (Gershenzon, Ermakov) emphasize the entertaining anecdote making up the poem's second segment. What has been lacking is a perspective that gives equal weight to both parts and perceives how they function together; by demonstrating how the poem's metapoetic aspect is carried through the poem's longer and lighter portion, this chapter achieves such a perspective. Whereas metapoesis was explicit in Gogol's "Leaving the Theater," in "Little House" metapoetic commentary shifts to an allegorical plane of discourse after the Parasha tale begins, and continues under a coherent and "realistic" surface.

1 The Two Parts of "Little House"

As first published in the literary almanac *Novosel'e* in 1833, "The Little House in Kolomna" is forty stanzas (319 lines) long.[1] The poem's metapoetical introduction takes up the first eight stanzas. Here the narrator speaks as a poetic persona: he identifies himself as a poet and discusses such literary matters as his relationship to certain poetic traditions and genres, the poets associated with these traditions, contemporary literary life, and the relationship between poet and critic. This part of the poem is a witty literary polemic couched in classical allusions and references to both the contemporary literary scene and that of seventeenth- and eighteenth-century France.

The main thrust of the opening verses might be paraphrased as follows: All hell has broken loose in the world of literature, because the heritage of Classicism is exhausted. Poets have taken their lyre to the marketplace; there has been a Fall; poets are attacking poets in an undignified fashion, and any one poet who attempts to remain above the fracas can expect the others to unite against him. This poetic persona plans nonetheless to stand alone and unveil the true faces of the others.

As Valerii Briusov pointed out, these verses are accessible to a limited group of people; their addressees are insiders, litterateurs (89). Not all insiders are friendly, however, and the poetic persona clearly intends to insult, hurt, or verbally annihilate certain literary enemies. At the same time, this sort of message presumes addressees who will witness the act of offending, agree with the poetic persona, and be entertained by the entire spectacle.

Because the poetic persona in this part of the poem identifies himself as a poet, critics have tended — simplistically, perhaps — to consider him Pushkin's literary stand-in or self-portrait. We will return to this point later.

The next two stanzas (IX, X) begin the verse tale about a widow and her daughter Parasha, a husband- and fatherless, low-bourgeoisie family living in the Kolomna district of Petersburg. The poetic persona states that he knew these women, but his recollection of them and the place where they once lived gives rise to a feeling of sadness which, in an elegiac moment, grows so great as to displace the women as the poem's subject matter (stanzas XI, XII).

Stanza XIII takes up the description of Parasha. Recalling the maiden's fondness for folk songs leads to further metapoetic comments: "To doleful strains the Russian maiden uses / Who is a grieving singer, like our Muses" ("Поёт уныло Русская девица / Как Музы наши, грустная певица" [XIV]); the following stanza discusses the sadness lurking beneath the surface in every member of the "family" of poets.

The next three stanzas return to the characterization of Parasha and her mother. But the poem's metapoetical tendencies surface again in a brief parenthetical remark made in stanza XVIII. As Parasha, longing for romance, remains awake on summer nights and gazes through her bedroom window at the moon, we read: "(No novel can do without it / Such is the rule)" ("[Без зтого не одного романа / не обойдётся: так заведено!]").

Stanza XX informs us that it is the custom of Parasha and her mother to attend church every Sunday. The poem's poetic persona attends the same church, but not for reasons of piety; he finds the Orthodox liturgy aesthetically pleasing. The next four stanzas (XXI–XXIV) tell of a certain countess who also frequents the church in Kolomna. There are hints of a tragic story behind this character, whom literary historians have associated with a live, historical figure;[2] and it appears that the poetic persona once paid her court without success. These digressive stanzas allude to a story that will not be told, then bring the poem back to Parasha and her mother by declaring that "simple Parasha" is a hundred times more blessed than this proud woman.

Stanzas XXV and XXVI describe Parasha's appearance and relate her habit of sitting at a window and watching members of the horse guards ride by. Only with stanza XXVII is the action proper of the tale begun; and from the episode narrated there, in which the household cook is taken ill and dies, the tale proceeds uninterrupted to its shocking denouement and nonending (that is, resolutionless) ending.

The last two stanzas of the poem are, like the poem's introductory stanzas, metapoetical: they present a dialogue between author and reader in which the reader objects to the tale's discontinuities, its joking nature, and its failure to provide moral instruction. The poetic persona answers with a nonsensical mock-moral.

In contrast to the poem's first part, the verse tale rounding off "Little House" appears to make no special demands on its reader. Its humor is accessible to all, not just literary readers, and it seems to have been designed above all else to entertain. How the story is told involves a corresponding shift. Although the poetic persona who relates the verse tale is the same as that of the metapoetic introduction, what was a lyric "I," speaking of his own problems and emotions is an I-You discourse, has become a poet-narrator who tells a story about other people. The role of this poet-narrator in the narrative he relates is ambiguous. How did he come to know Parasha and Parasha's story? Why does he experience such an intense emotional reaction when walking by the spot where the widow's little house once stood? The figure of the poet-narrator in this part of the poem is also much more distant from the author than is the poetic persona of the first part; one is not so tempted to identify the storyteller as Pushkin.

Perhaps the most significant difference between the two parts of "Little House," however, is that in the Parasha tale literary matters no longer function in any apparent way as positive, thematic material. Without doubt, the tale serves a metapoetic and polemical function, since it deliberately violates certain norms posited by literary critics of the day (more on this in a moment). There also remain plenty of interventions by the chatty narrator, and one could argue that a very perceptible ironic tone, aided by the playful juxtaposition of words from high and low stylistic planes, carries through the metapoetic theme initiated in the poem's first part.[3] But in the Parasha tale, making war on critics is no longer the poem's subject matter. Such a shifting of the metapoetic aspect from the level of theme to that of style is in line with our notion of the Parasha tale as a defiant act. In sum, rather than being *about*, now the poem *is*.

The situation becomes more complicated if one considers that the original, manuscript version of "Little House," which circulated for a couple of years before the poem was published, included an epigraph and fourteen additional stanzas. All were placed before stanza IX of the published version, and all belong to that group of stanzas we have called metapoetical. Most critics seem to feel that the poem profits from the absence of these stanzas (see Harkins, "Little House," 64); some suggest that the omitted verses were so context oriented and polemical that their inclusion in the poem would have grown damaging over time. Indeed, the two-and-a-half-year interval separating the poem's composition and its publication may have made the subject matter of the omitted verses anachronistic, or at least in poor taste, since in the meantime some of Pushkin's targets had suffered at the censors' hands (Goffman, 31–32; "Varianty," 596). Since Pushkin originally planned to publish this poem anonymously, he may also have considered it unwise to print some of the more pointed stanzas once he decided to attach his name ("Varianty," 598). The opposite motivation is proposed by S. A. Fomichev, on the other hand; he believes that the critical stanzas were omitted because they were too soft ("K tvorcheskoi istorii," 56–57).

Our reading of the poem relies heavily on these omitted stanzas—a strategy that, it is hoped, will be justified by the results obtained. For references to the text we have adopted the following convention: Stanzas occurring in both versions of the poem are given two numbers. Capitalized Roman numerals refer to the place of a particular stanza in the work's edited, published version; lowercase Roman numerals refer to the stanza as found in the original version of the poem. If a stanza is referred to only with lowercase Roman numerals, then it is one of the omitted stanzas.[4]

2 The Literary Polemic

Discussions of the literary-polemical aspect of "Little House" generally concentrate on formal features. The poem's mixture of "high" form and "low" content negates certain rules which had been posited by the "young archaists," as Tynianov calls them ("Arkhaisty i Pushkin"). This group of writers was battling to maintain the neoclassical, prescriptive correspondence between language level and subject matter in strictly differentiated high, middle, and low genres. For our purposes the most significant representative of archaist trends is the poet and critic Pavel Katenin. "Little House in Kolomna" must be read in the context of Katenin's pronouncements on the epic genre.

In an 1822 "Letter to the Publisher" of the journal *Syn otechestva*, Katenin proposed a Russian version of the Italian *ottava rima* as the verse form most suitable for the epopee, a genre treating elevated subject matter. Katenin's *ottava rima* was an eight-verse stanza made up of iambic pentameter lines, with a caesura after the second foot. Instead of using triple rhymes and having the first lines of stanzas alternate between masculine and feminine endings, as did the Italians (in the scheme: aBaBaBcc DeDeDeFF, which Katenin considered too difficult in the Russian language), the following scheme was proposed: aBaBccDD eFeFggHH, and so on. As an example, Katenin translated five verses from Tasso's *Gerusalemme liberata* (Katenin, *Razmyshleniia*, 188–91; see also Tynianov, "Arkhaisty i Pushkin," 120–25).

The polemic surrounding the *ottava rima* was still alive at the time Pushkin wrote "Little House in Kolomna" and is an important part of the poem's background. Pushkin's poem in *ottava rima* diverges from the program of Katenin in three significant respects: First, it employs this verse form to create a frivolous, risqué tale rather than a work of the epic romance genre. To Katenin, who insisted on the neoclassical, coded correlation of verse form and content, such a move would certainly be distressing.[5] Second, Katenin's prescription that a caesura be maintained after the fourth syllable or second foot is recalled only to be mocked. In the following line (from stanza VI), "I like a caesura at the second foot [Люблю цезуру на второй стопе]," Pushkin states that he loves the caesura, yet *breaks* the caesura with the very word "caesura." Finally, Pushkin's poem is written in *ottava rima* with triple rhymes, that is, in the very rhyme scheme Katenin deemed too difficult for the Russian language; Russian, Katenin had said, is "too poor in that respect" (*Razmyshleniia*, 189).

The first stanza of "Little House" makes it clear that Pushkin had Katenin's *ottava rima* in mind:

The iambic quadruped has had full scope;
I'm sick of it. It should be relegated
To youngsters as a toy. My cherished hope
To write in octaves has now germinated
For quite some time: and really, I could cope
With threefold rhyme; to work, with breath unbated
Rhymes, after all, have lived with me like kin;
Two'll volunteer, the third will be dragged in.

Четырстопнвій ямб мне надоел:
Им пишет всякой. Мальчикам в забаву
Пора б его оставить. Я хотел
Давным давно приняться за октаву
А в самом деле: я бы совладел
С тройным созвучием. Пущусь на славу!
Ведь рифмы запросто со мной живут;
Две придут сами, третью приведут.

I mean to write in *ottava rima*, says Pushkin, but I mean to use triple rhymes; that is, to supersede Katenin. This aspect of the Katenin connection has been amply discussed by Tynianov and others. The dialogue between Katenin and Pushkin involves much more than a squabble over form, however.[6]

In 1828 Katenin sent Pushkin a 300-line poem, "Staraia byl'," along with a 75-line poem dedicating the latter to Pushkin. Pushkin arranged for Katenin's "Staraia byl' " ("A True Story of Old") to be published alongside his own "Otvet Kateninu" ("Answer to Katenin"), but—to Katenin's annoyance—without the dedicatory "A. S. Pushkinu" ("To A. S. Pushkin"). "Staraia byl' " is a narrative poem, set in the time of the Kievan Prince Vladimir, which tells of a competition between two poets. One bard is a Russian *voevoda* (army commander), the other, a young Greek castrato. The Greek, a "faithful slave" of the prince, sings first and wins hands down; for on the advice of Vladimir the Russian concedes without singing, saying:

"I sang of heroes bold in battles
Long since buried in graves;
I sang of love and joyous days—
Now the sweetest sleep forever;
But to sing of great czars and princes
I lack the wisdom and strength."

"Певал я о витязах смелых в боях—
Давно их зарыли в могилы;
Певал о любви и радостных днях—
Теперь не разбудишь всемилы;
А петь о великих царях и князах
Ума не достанет, ни силы."

The Greek is awarded a *bogatyr*'s (epic hero's) horse and valuable armor; because the Russian served Vladimir's late father, he receives the consolation prize of a chalice. Some of the warrior's old friends arrange a traditional "bread and salt" dinner for him (Katenin, *Izbrannye proizvedeniia*, 175–83).

Iurii Tynianov's allegorical interpretation of "Staraia byl' " has become canonical. The poem secretly refers to contemporary Russian reality: Prince Vladimir represents Czar Nicholas I; the Russian *voevoda* stands for Katenin, who had indeed served the preceding czar well in the War of 1812; the Greek castrato is none other than Pushkin. In both verse form and thematics, "Staraia byl' " makes unmistakable allusions to certain of Pushkin's works, namely "Stansy" ("Stanzas," 1826) and "Pesn' o veshchem Olege" ("Tale of the Prophet Oleg," 1822). "Staraia byl' " at once concedes to Pushkin the title of premier Russian poet and accuses him of selling out to the czar.

"Pesn' o veshchem Olege" had asserted the poet's independence—always of first importance to Katenin[7]—but the more recent "Stansy," written to flatter the czar in the hope of winning his support for reforms, aroused in Pushkin's friends (among whom Katenin counted himself) the fear that he was cuddling up to the czar.

Katenin's literary stand-in, by contrast, proves his own courage: at the banquet with which "Staraia byl' " ends, the Russian bard uses the cup given him by the prince to drink a toast "to the memory of their days of youth / And to the honorable memory of the brave one" ("в память их юности дней / И Храброго в память честную"). Here Katenin alludes to the Decembrist revolt and, in particular, to the Decembrist poet Ryleev, who was hanged by Nicholas. Such an allusion certainly proves Katenin's courage.

The dedicatory poem helps unlock this hidden meaning, which is likely why Pushkin declined to publish it with "Staraia byl'." Katenin tells Pushkin that the prizes won by the Greek have perished (the horse collapsed and the armor was taken by French Crusaders when they plundered Constantinople); but the cup now rests in Pushkin's hands. With allusions to the epics of Tasso and Ariosto, Katenin invites Pushkin to try out some of *his* drink in the cup, while warning him that this drink may be enchanted, and that only those born of Apollo may drink it. The last lines are:

> Having poured, I offer you the cup
> Drink up, it will set your soul a-boil,
> and our quiet chat
> Will resound in your Byronic singing.
>
> Налив, тебе подам я чашу,
> Ты выпешь, духом закипишь,
> И тихую беседу нашу
> Бейронским пеньем огласишь.
> (Katenin, *Izbrannye proizvedeniia*, 185–87)

Tynianov interprets this request to "echo our conversation with Byronic singing" as an invitation to write revolutionary poetry ("Arkhaisty i Pushkin," 160–77; also Kharlap, 223–24).

Four or five months after sending Pushkin the poem, Katenin complained in a letter to N. I. Bakhtin that Pushkin had made no answer; he worried that

Pushkin might have been offended. While Katenin insisted that he wrote "Staraia byl' " and "A. S. Pushkinu" "out of the good wish to please and honor him [Pushkin]," he also wrote rather equivocally: "Of course, it's not my fault, the kitten knows who's lard it's eaten" ("Конечно, не моя вина, знает кошка, чьё сало съела"; Sept. 7, 1828; *Razmyshleniia*, 285).

In "Otvet Kateninu," the short poem Pushkin published with "Staraia byl'," the drink from the cup is declined. "I am in the service too," writes Pushkin, and "now it is time for me to go home, to peace" (*Pss* 1:521). Pushkin also wrote a letter to Katenin in which he promised to "follow his footsteps to glory at some later time"; ever since then, critics have wondered when and where this event took place.

M. Kharlap takes Tynianov's reading of this exchange one step further and suggests that Pushkin's full reply came in "Little House in Kolomna." There Pushkin pretends to accept the program outlined before by Katenin—and "refutes it by reducing it to the absurd." Pushkin writes in *ottava rima*, that is, he drinks the brew of Katenin; but the poem he writes treats a low, trivial, and domestic topic rather than one worthy of the epic form. Even the suggestion that Pushkin "echo our quiet conversation with Byronic singing" is mockingly reflected in the poem's formal recollection of Byron's joking poems (such as "Beppo," which was written in *ottava rima*), rather than the works of Byron containing revolutionary sentiment (229).[8]

If this interpretation of "Little House" is valid, it is nonetheless insufficient: the greater part of the poem—the Parasha tale—is still considered meaningful only because it is trivial.[9] After examining the narrative portion of "Little House" more closely, it will become apparent that the tale bears a meaning irreducible to the negation of certain norms posited by Katenin. As a result, our understanding of the exchange which took place between the two poets will also have to be altered. This meaning—which is allegorical—stands out sharply when the Parasha tale is viewed against the double background of its generic relationship to the fabliau genre and to the subtext of "Staraia byl'."

3 The Parasha Tale as Fabliau

Boris Tomashevsky has written that the Parasha tale was probably modeled on a verse tale from Jean de la Fontaine's *Contes et Nouvelles* (*Stories and*

Novellas). In "La Gageure des trois commeres," three ladies compete in "pulling the wool over the eyes" of their husbands, and one of the adulterous women manages her affair as does Parasha. The *Contes et Nouvelles* are a seventeenth-century manifestation of that tradition of humorous, bawdy tales traceable back to the medieval French fabliau, with stops at Boccaccio, Ariosto, and Rabelais. La Fontaine, situated squarely within this tradition, had an enormous influence on Pushkin. As a child Pushkin wrote (in French) imitations of La Fontaine's fables, and, according to Tomashevsky, the *Contes et Nouvelles* remained among Pushkin's favorite reading. While Pushkin came to regard the fables of Krylov more highly than those of La Fontaine, the *Contes* were, according to him, "unsurpassable" (Tomashevskii, 121, 248, 255).[10]

Pushkin also had several collections of fabliaux in his library (Modzalevskii). He mentions having studied them along with other medieval French literary forms, and he even tried his hand at translating Old French verse into Modern French (see Tomashevskii, Stenbock-Fermor). Moreover, in letters and articles Pushkin writes that Romantic literature has its origins in this medieval tradition. If indeed the Parasha story reflects the structural demands of the fabliau, then Pushkin's negation of the poetic norms discussed above must be seen as the assertion of something positive — not just the negation of the rules of the archaists. After discussing the fabliau-like features of "Little House," I hope to show that Pushkin's "fabliau" can be related to the preceding metapoetic portion because it represents, in addition to a tale that is a literary act with metapoetic significance, an acting out or dramatization of a competition between poets echoing the one in "Staraia byl' "; that is, Pushkin exploits the allegorical possibility that inheres in the genre of the fabliau as its "fable" aspect.

Fabliaux are medieval French verse tales designed to entertain. " 'Les fabliaux sont des contes a rire en vers' " is the much-quoted, general definition of the genre given by Bedier (Johnston and Owen, v). There are about 150 of these tales extant today; they date from the twelfth or thirteenth centuries; most of them are about 250 lines long, and all but one are composed of octosyllabic couplets (Eichman, 2). They are fast-moving and economical, with sharp turns at their endings.

The laughter that the fabliaux provoked "was full and often bawdy" (Johnston and Owen, viii), and while these tales lampoon a wide spectrum of human weaknesses, vices, and sins, "most important from the numerical point of view are the bawdy or scatological ones" (Johnston and Owen, ix). Three-fourths of the fabliaux on record are openly erotic, and nearly half of them deal with the theme of the adulterous triangle (Eichman, 6). Women in these tales are typically crafty, deceitful, and sexually aggressive. Parties guilty of adultery often perform right under the nose of a cuckolded husband, who is somehow made to doubt that what he is perceiving corresponds to reality; disguises are often employed to this end.

The sexual act is sometimes a means of revenge in the fabliau: a mistreated wife will take a lover and make a fool of her husband, or an ill-received traveler will wreak sexual havoc in the household where he has been insulted. Priests are often at the butt of the fabliau's humor, and one index of the low regard afforded them by writers of fabliaux is their lack of success as seducers (Eichman, 7).

It was common practice to end a fabliau with a moral, a "compact lesson appended to the tale by the author" (Johnston and Owen, xvii). Some fabliaux presented their morals in all seriousness; this creates a rather odd effect if one considers the moral against the background of a tale that is quite graphic in its portrayal of various human vices and free in its use of obscenities. More often than not, however, the moral presented by a fabliau would be mocking or parodic. These mock-morals are probably symptomatic of a demand, felt by fabliau writers, that literary art provide moral instruction.[11]

In connection with the fabliau's tendency to provide a moral, mockingly or otherwise, Johnston and Owen discuss the genetic relationship between the fabliau and the Aesopic fable. Fabliaux, they suggest, might be seen as fables in which the animals—usually the fable's chief characters—are replaced by humans (Johnston and Owen, xviii). While the origins of the fabliau remain unclear, most scholars do seem to feel that they are closely related to the fable or animal tale (Harrison, 4). At the same time, the fabliaux are generically associated with the high literature of their time: many are mock romances assuming knowledge of the chivalric code in order to make fun of it.

Fabliaux were written by individual authors, but because their transmission involved being copied by creative or unreliable scribes and being memorized and related orally by jongleurs prone to improvisation, a fabliau was likely to become less literary over time. R. Harrison writes that "many versions trace out a descending arc that begins in literature and ultimately disappears in folklore" (6). The fabliau did not "disappear," however, but in many ways became the predecessor of the modern novel: fabliaux stand behind stories told in Chaucer's *Canterbury Tales* and Boccaccio's *Il Decamerone.*

Here, before we take up the question of the relationship between Pushkin's "Little House" and the fabliau, is the plot summary of one typical fabliau, titled "De la Saineresse," or "The Lady-Leech" (from *Cuckolds*, 105–9). A bourgeois boasts that no woman could deceive him; this does not sit well with his wife, who decides to prove his boast a lie. One day when the husband and wife are sitting together in their house, a "quite good looking," "noble" rogue dressed as a woman arrives with instruments for cupping and bleeding and says that the lady of the house has called for him. The bourgeois's wife tells her husband that she has gout and needs to be bled; she and the transvestite midwife go upstairs, lock the door, and then:

> The rogue grabbed hold of her and rocked
> Her body backwards, stretched her flat
> And screwed her three times.
> After that, when they'd had all the fun they wished,
> Screwed, embraced, and hugged and kissed,
> They rose and went downstairs again.

The husband sees to the medical girl's payment; the noble rogue leaves, but because "She did not feel the game was won / Till she had told him all she'd done," the wife launches into a description of her treatment which turns out to be a very thinly disguised—and very detailed—depiction of the sexual act. The fabliau ends with a moral: No man should boast as did the bourgeois, since

> This country doesn't have, however,
> A man so wise, a man so clever,
> Despite his prying, spying, snooping,
> Who can avoid a woman's duping.

I think most of the features of the fabliau outlined above should be apparent in this example. How are they reflected in the Parasha tale?

We have already said—along with most readers of "Little House"—that Pushkin's tale about Parasha and the cook seems designed primarily to arouse laughter and entertain, as are fabliaux. The Parasha tale, which is of fabliau length, is also no less streamlined than the typical fabliau. The only digression from the tale comes near its start, when the poet-narrator speaks of the countess who used to visit the same church as did he and Parasha (XXI–XXIV, xxxv–xxxviii); since these stanzas introduce the countess explicitly in order to compare her with Parasha, one need not really call them digressive. It may even be that a wish on Pushkin's part to conform to this generic rule of the fabliau explains why the metapoetic stanzas and the narrative stanzas were kept more or less separate. In Byron's "Beppo," by contrast, digressive stanzas, while making up most of the poem's first part, are generously mixed in with narrative stanzas throughout the poem.

The tale Pushkin provides in "Little House" certainly merits the adjective "bawdy," for in it a young maiden smuggles a man into her home for carnal reasons. A certain difference between Pushkin's tale and the fabliau must be noted, though: Pushkin's tale is not nearly so explicit about sexuality as are the fabliaux, nor is it so free with vulgar language. In fact, some early critics of the poem even failed to realize that an unstated love intrigue lay behind the poem's surprise ending.[12] Pushkin of course had to contend with a puritanical state censorship apparatus (unlike the tellers of fabliaux, though La Fontaine was sharply criticized for his *Contes et Nouvelles* and disavowed them as an old man). Moreover, collections of fabliaux like those Pushkin had in his library, printed in France in the late eighteenth or early nineteenth centuries, were likely to suppress, edit, or paraphrase in order not to offend the higher sensibilities of a more modern, moral age.[13] The key point here, however, is that Pushkin plotted something more than a frivolous, bawdy tale when he wrote "Little House"; while his Parasha tale may have stretched the bounds of "good taste" in serious literature, Pushkin's intent was not to brazenly offend such taste.

There is no situation of adultery in Pushkin's Parasha tale, since Parasha is not married. But Parasha does dupe her mother with the help of a disguise. One can speak of a metaphoric cuckolding if one considers that the compromising of Parasha's virtue is a violation of the mother's sexual authority over her daughter, just as the activities of an adulterous wife contest her husband's control of her sexuality. Moreover, something akin to a love triangle can be found here if one takes into account the relationship of the poet-narrator to both Parasha and the countess (we will return to this later).

The final stanza of "Little House" presents a mock-moral, and so conforms to yet another generic feature of the fabliau. We need not speculate as to whether this mock-moral is a response to demand, of the sort felt by fabliau writers, that literary art provide moral instruction — Pushkin dramatizes this demand, making the final two stanzas of his poem a dialogue between poet-narrator and reader: "Have you at least some moral admonition [Да нет ли хоть у вас нравоученья]?"

If the fabliau can be seen as a genre parodying the highest genres of the time, this is no less true of "Little House." Pushkin took the verse form designated by Katenin for the epopee and used it to compose a frivolous tale.

We have already said that Pushkin was very familiar with the fabliau, and that he was occupied with translations from Old French during the 1830s. In various critical articles Pushkin suggests that Romantic literature originates with genres like the fabliau. In an 1825 draft entitled "O poezii klassicheskoi i romanticheskoi" ("On Classical and Romantic Poetry"), for instance, Pushkin defines Romantic poetry as all those forms unknown to the ancients or those ancient forms that have undergone alteration. He credits the troubadours of medieval France with giving birth to Romantic poetry. Of central importance for Pushkin is their experimentation with rhyme, and the establishment of the ballad, rondeau, and sonnet. La Fontaine's tales are mentioned as monuments of "pure Romantic poetry" (*Pss* 5:265–67).[14]

Pushkin's Parasha tale thus returns to the very origins of Romantic literature. Interesting in this regard is the emphasis Pushkin gave rhyme as the distinctive feature of budding Romantic literature in medieval France; "Little House" employs a very complex rhyme scheme, and one that must have been difficult to sustain over the course of such a long work.

Finally, "Little House" was written during a time when Pushkin was evolving an entirely new aesthetic: he was now working in artistic prose. Pushkin was aware of the fabliau's genetic relationship to the novel and may have employed the fabliau as a step toward that genre. For many critics, especially Soviet ones, "Little House" also constitutes an important step toward a poetics of realism (Goffman, 72–73). Our explorations will proceed in a different direction, however.

4 The Parasha Tale as Fable

Pushkin doubtless had the genre of the fabliau in mind as he wrote "Little House." Yet nowhere in the poem is there mention of the fabliau — not even in the metapoetic stanzas. Pushkin does, however, refer to the genre of the fable (or, rather, to Aesop, whose name the genre commonly bears); we recall that the fabliau is generally considered to be derived from fable. What is more, beyond any such genetic relationship between the two genres, fable and fabliau find a factual, existential contiguity precisely in regard to the figure of La Fontaine, whom we know above all for his masterful treatment of the Aesopic fable.

Aesop appears at a structurally crucial point in "Little House": in the two stanzas preceding the start of the Parasha tale and comprising a transition from the metapoetical part of the poem to its narrative, fabliau-like segment. These stanzas (xxi, xxii) belong to the group of stanzas omitted when the poem was published.

> But probably they haven't noticed us
> Me, together with my octaves.
> But our time has come. You see I have prepared
> A story — and here I am, joking pretentiously
> And making you wait for nothing.
> My tongue is my enemy; it knows no limits,
> It's gotten used to bantering about everything!..
> A Phrygian slave, having bought a tongue at market
>
> Boiled it... (At Mr. Kop's
> They smoke them). Aesop then
> Served it... Again! Why have I woven
> Aesop with his boiled tongue
> Into my verses? There's no need to talk
> About what all of Europe has read.
> A reckless rhymster, I've barely managed
> To get out of this difficult octave.

> А верятно, не заметят нас,
> Меня, с октавами моими купно.
> Однако ж нам пора. Ведь я рассказ
> Готовил— а шучу довольно крупно
> И ждать напрасно заставляю вас.
> Язык мой враг мой; всё ему доступно,
> Он обо всём болтать себе привык!..
> Фригийский раб, на рынке взяв язык,

Сварил его... (у господина Копа
Коптят его). Езоп потом
Принёс на стол... Опять! Зачем Езопа
Я вплёл с его варёным языком
В мои стихи? что вся прочла Европа,
Нет нужды вновь беседовать о том.
Насилу-то рифмач я безрассудный
Отделался от сей октавы трудной.

The poetic persona has prepared a story, and it is time to begin; but the story he wishes to tell gets off to a false start. Instead of the tale about Parasha, he begins a story about a "Phrygian slave" who once bought and cooked some tongues.

Here Pushkin is alluding to an episode in "The Life of Aesop," a framing story that traditionally accompanies collections of Aesop's fables.[15] When Aesop's master, the philosopher Xanthus, orders him to prepare a meal with "the best, the finest thing imaginable," Aesop presents a meal made up entirely of pork tongues; what more appropriate dinner could one offer a professional talker? Xanthus, ill from eating these spicy tongues, then orders Aesop to cook "the most worthless, the most inferior thing there is"; Aesop again cooks pork tongues. Through a crafty use of language, Aesop manages to insult his master, to serve him an odious meal and yet compel him to eat that meal. More precisely, Aesop interprets his master's words in such a way as to give them meanings opposite to those intended by his master, and he then validates his interpretations through semantic quibblings which his master, a philosopher, must acknowledge as legitimate; and Aesop speaks in allegories: he utters transvestite words — words which mean something other than that which they show on their surface — so that he can seem compliant even as he insults his master.

It is for just such episodes that Aesop is the paradigm of a speaker who exploits the ambiguities inherent in language and the corollary possibility of conveying indirect, secondary meanings, to say things that would otherwise be dangerous to say. Thus a victory over enemies of greater power can be gained for the politically disadvantaged — if only in language, or symbolically. This corresponds to the explanation of the genre given by Phaedrus: "Now I will explain briefly why the type of thing called fable was invented. The slave, being liable to punishment for any offence, since he dared not say outright what he wished to say, projected his personal sentiments into fables and eluded censure under the guise of jesting with made-up stories" (cited from Needler, xii).

It is important to see that Aesopic communication, in providing two different messages with one text, presumes two different addressees or readers as well: a naive or dumb, but dangerous, reader and a smart one. The former, who receives only the surface message, is not just spoken to but also duped; and the latter, who receives another, hidden message, in spite of any censorship, is not just spoken to but also entertained by the spectacle of the duping. This is of course a crude model of Aesopic communication. The exchange between Aesop and Xanthus discussed above represents a playful variation of this model in which the speaker intends a singular meaning, but the addressee extracts a second meaning from the words — a meaning which the speaker cannot refute, even though it is to his disadvantage. The addressee appropriates the message from its source and sends it back, accented in such a way that the original speaker now becomes the smart listener. The original speaker is separated in time from the self who was the utterance's source, and if good-natured, he laughs at himself.

It can also happen that the two addressees are combined into one: the duped addressee perceives the insult delivered below the surface of the speaker's message, but the speaker maintains that he meant no more than the literal meaning of his words, all the while delighting in the addressee's chagrin. In such cases Aesopic language involves a single addressee, referential duplicity, and metalingual dishonesty. All speech addressed to the paranoiac will be perceived as this sort, and he will imagine that he is a spectacle of entertainment for some second, preferred addressee.

We are describing a communication situation that is depicted as an entertaining spectacle by the message of another communication situation. These messages are materially the same, but the second, smart reader has a wider perspective on the context or speech situation, and he interprets the message through reference to that context. The dumb reader, by contrast, relies more on the coded, lexical meaning of the message.[16] Such a simultaneous addressing of an insider and an outsider parallels the communication situation found in the first part of "Little House."

One can easily see how Aesopic communication relates to "Staraia byl'," for Tynianov has made us all smart readers. We can hear the message Katenin sent to Pushkin, and we enjoy the spectacle of the czar and his censors being made into fools.[17] But what has this to do with "The Little House in Kolomna"? That is the very question asked by the poem's poetic persona (xxii, 3–6). An answer: the digressive allusion to Aesop suggests that a certain analogy be drawn between the poem's poetic persona and Aesop. Pushkin's position vis-à-vis certain readers is juxtaposed with Aesop's before his master; and that which follows these stanzas, we might infer, will be Aesopic. The tale about Parasha may thus relate to the preceding, metapoetical portion of the poem in an allegorical manner.

If we are to see Aesop as a transitional link between the two parts of "Little House," we must nevertheless acknowledge him to be a missing link, since Pushkin eliminated these stanzas from the poem's published version. According to M. L. Goffman, the stanzas cost Pushkin a disproportionate amount of effort,[18] yet were stricken out quite early in the process of the poem's composition (64). This does not preclude the possibility that, sometime before publication, literary intimates saw these two stanzas (along with the rest of the poem, as did Gogol; see below). Perhaps those whom Pushkin wished to understand the allegorical meaning of the Parasha tale had the information necessary to do so; or perhaps the allusions to Aesop made this meaning too obvious.

On what basis can we draw an analogy between the poem's poetic persona and Aesop?[19]

Aesop is referred to in "Little House" as poet, slave, and cook. The analogy between Aesop and the poetic persona depends upon a certain parallelism between the poetic persona's statements about himself and what he says about Aesop. An implicit play on the word "to prepare" (*gotovit'*) and an explicit play on the word "tongue" (*iazyk*) are involved here. "You see, I've prepared a story" (*ved' ia rasskaz / gotovil*), says the poetic persona (my italics). The verb "*gotovit'*," "to prepare," used in reference to a story, functions as a synonym of "to write" or "to compose." But its selection here is significant because this verb can also be used to mean "to cook" or "to prepare dinner." The polysemousness of the word "*iazyk*" (tongue) is exploited in these stanzas as well. There is a shift in meaning from "*moi iazyk*" as a metonymic substitution for "my words, what I say," to "*iazyk*" as the physical tongue of a pig which is cooked and served for dinner. Note that the shifts of meaning here (from "*gotovit'*" as "to compose or write" to "*gotovit'*" as "*svarit'*," "to cook," and from "*iazyk*" as words to "*iazyk*" as a physical tongue) are concretizations: the meanings of the words in question shift from something abstract to something concrete. We suggest that the tale which follows is an allegory in which the poet-as-cook metaphor underlying the first part of the poem has been concretized, giving us a real, live cook — Mavra.

Here is another stanza (xviii) in which the poet-as-cook metaphor is apparent:

Then God help me run away... For some reason
I don't want to sign my name here;
Now and then I really mix it up with this verse,
All the same, it's not the first time,
But when before? that I won't tell.
I'm marching on the critics, not whistling,
Like a bogatyr of old; but how do I attack...
What? I bow and invite them to dinner.

Тогда давай бог ноги... Почему-то
Здесь имя подписать я не хочу;
Порой я стих повертываю круто,
Всё ж, видно, не впервой я им верчу,
А как давно? того и не скажу-то.
На критиков я еду, не свищу,
Как древний богатырь— а как наеду...
Что ж? поклонюсь и приглашу к обеду.

After constructing an elaborate military metaphor to characterize the polemical aspect of his literary project, the poetic persona informs us that he means to attack his critics by bowing and inviting them to dinner. If the writing of this poem equals attacking one's critics, and attacking one's critics is inviting them to supper, then writing a poem must be seen as the equivalent of providing supper. Note that the words "*naedu*" (I will attack) and "*obedu*" (dinner) are rhymed in the couplet ending the stanza; the expression "*Ia stikh povertyvaiu kruto*" finds itself similarly juxtaposed in the minds of readers with the idiomatic expressions, "*kruto zamesit' testo*" and "*kruto zavarit' kashu.*"[20] This stanza thus sets up a metaphoric relationship between cooking and writing that is central to the poem's unity.

The metaphorical association between cooking and writing extends to the character of Mavra, the transvestite cook whom Parasha sneaks into her mother's home. Mavra bows deeply when he is introduced to the widow, repeating the gesture promised by the poet-narrator in stanza xviii. On the allegorical plane of the bawdy tale forming the second part of "Little House," this cook can be seen as a counterpart to the poetic persona; that is, he is a concretization of the poet/cook metaphor.

The importance we are giving to the figure of the cook seems more legitimate if one considers that the poem's original version apparently bore the title "Kukharka" ("The [female] Cook"); or so Gogol, having read "Little House" in manuscript form, refers to the poem in a letter to A. Danilevsky (Briusov, 90; Gogol, *Pss* 5:214). But the poet/cook metaphor is not the only link between Mavra and the poetic persona; there are also the common motifs of anonymity, disguise, and military life.

In stanza xviii, cited above, the poetic persona states that he does not wish to sign his name to the poem he is writing. This associates the narrator with Mavra, whose true identity remains unknown. What is more, publishing anonymously is explicitly linked with the motif of taking to one's feet: "*Togda davai Bog nogi...*" Mavra does indeed run away from the widow's home at the poem's end in order to keep his identity a secret.

Motifs of disguise and trickery also link the cook and the poetic persona. Mavra disguises himself to fool Parasha's mother while fooling around with Parasha; and in stanza xx the poetic persona wonders if he might not be able to say what he wishes with the aid of a mask:

> Oh, if no-one in the merry crowd
> Could recognize me under a light mask
> When a stern critic would smack another
> In my place with his ruler!
> Then I'd stir all the journals
> with a surprise denouement!
> But enough, will I have such a holiday?
> There's too few of us. A prankster can't hide.

> Ах, если бы меня под лёгкой маской
> Никто в толпе забавной не узнал!
> Когда бы за меня своей указкой
> Другого строгой критик пощекал
> Уж то-то б неожиданной развязкой

Я все журналы после взволновал!
Но полно, будет ли такой мне праздник?
Нас мало. Не укроется проказник.

Under the cover of a mask, the poetic persona might manage to carry out a vengeful prank while directing the wrath of critics toward someone other than himself; the whole business would have a surprise ending. The metaphoric substitution of the cook, Mavra, under the mask of a comic, nonsensical tale may be just what Pushkin had in mind here. The tale about Parasha certainly presents a prank with a surprise ending, a "*neozhidannaia razviazka.*"

The extended metaphor likening the writing of "Little House" to a military campaign, elaborated from the third stanza onward, sets up another parallel between the poem's poetic persona and Mavra. We can assume that the transvestite cook is a member of the Horse Guard. Stanza XXV (xxxix) speaks of how the guardsmen paraded past Parasha's home, lured there by the sight of this maiden sitting at the window. The following stanza begins: "Among these swains did any one more keenly / Engage her heart, or are we to report / Unbiased coolness? We shall see [Меж ними кто был сердцу ближе, / Или рзвно для всех она была? / Душею холодна? увидим ниже]." Since the narrator has promised that the tale to come will answer this question about Parasha, we can infer that Mavra was the guardsman closest to her heart.

Finally, as Ermakov pointed out in his psychobiographical treatment of the poem, and as Pushkin's contemporaries would have been quick to infer, the signature of Pushkin may in fact be found in name of the cook: given that Pushkin's African heritage often emerged in his poetic persona, "This descendent of the Moors could indeed have called himself 'Mavrusha' — Mavra" (from the Russian *mavr*, "Moor" ; Ermakov, 26).

As the figurative link between Mavra and the poetic persona grows clear, two echoes from "Staraia byl' " can already be heard. First, in Katenin's poem the poetic persona offers his smart addressee, whom he is criticizing, something special to *drink*, and this drink is metaphorically associated with poetry; in "Little House" the poetic persona offers his critics something to *eat*, and this meal is also metaphorically associated with poetry. Second, the Russian bard of "Staraia byl' " was, like Katenin, a military man; in "An

Answer to Katenin," Pushkin claimed this status for himself as well, and we have seen that the poet/cook figure Pushkin develops is also a military man.

We definitely agree that "Little House in Kolomna" responds to Katenin's "Staraia byl' "; but we are going to have to interpret the allegorical meaning of the Parasha tale and ascertain its relation to the poem's metapoetical opening before understanding this response. We might start by attending to relationships between characters in the tale, especially those involving the poet-narrator/cook. There are certain moments during the tale when the poet-narrator reacts to his own story in an emotionally heightened way, and this provides insight into such relationships.

In stanzas XI–XII (xxv–xxvi) the poet-narrator expresses anger toward the three-storied structure that has replaced the home of Parasha and her mother:

I grew quite sorrowful: I looked askance
At that tall house, and if a conflagration
Had then engulfed it wholesale by some chance,
My spiteful eye with venomous elation
Would fair have gloated on it. Some weird trance
At times envelops our imagination;
Much nonsense clouds our reason as we wend
Our aimless way alone, or with a friend.

Blessed he who curbs his words, contains his stable
Of swarming fancies in an iron grip,
He who has learnt to silence or disable
The hissing snake that lurks behind the lip;
While he who blabs will soon incur the label
Of miscreant... As for myself, I sip
My Lethe; grief is bad, says my physician:
So I will drop this — with your kind permission!

Мне стало грустно: на высокий дом
Глядел я косо. Если в эту пору
Пожар его бы охватил кругом
То моему б озлоблоенному взору
Приятно было пламя. Странным сном
Бывает сердце полно; много вздору

Приходит нам на ум, когда бредём
Один или с товарищем вдвоём

Тогда блажен, кто крепко словом правит
И держит мысль на привёзи свою,
Кто в сердце усыпляет или давит
Мгновенно прошипевшую змею;
Но кто болтлив, того молва прославит
Вмиг извергом... я воды Леты пью.
Мне доктором запрещена унылость:
Оставим зто— сделайте мне милость!

In the first stanza the poet-narrator expresses a desire to burn down the three-storied building, that is, to carry out an act of aggression. When in the following stanza he speaks of the need to restrain himself, however, the aggressive impulses he seeks to suppress have to do with words rather than arson and murder. This shift calls to mind that feature of Aesopic speech noted earlier: the channeling of dangerous, aggressive impulses into superficially innocent verbal acts. More importantly, this outbreak marks for us the address of the poetic persona's bitterest feelings: this is, both geographically and figuratively speaking, the place of a dumb but dangerous reader, an addressee to whom one dare not say what one wishes; here lives the one who must be duped.

Another moment of insight into the poet-narrator's emotional life occurs when he tells of his relations with the countess (stanzas XXI–XXIV [xxxv–xxxviii]). He observes her at church (XXIII):

Here was a goddess of the frigid creed
Of vanity, you would have joined in saying:
Through her outward hauteur, though, I could read
A different story: long-felt sorrow preying,
Complaint subdued... And it was these, I plead,
That touched my soul and kept my glances straying...
But this the countess could not know about;
She booked me as a conquest, I don't doubt.

Она казалась хладный идеал
Тщеславия. Его б вы в ней узнали;

Но сквозь надменность эту я читал
Иную повесть: долгия печали,
Смиренье жалоб... В них-то я вникал,
Невольный взор они-то привлекали...
Но это знать графиня не могла,
И верно, в список жертв меня внесла.

The poet-narrator has an insight into the countess's situation which might, given the chance, reverse the polarity of their relationship. His attitude toward her is more one of understanding and pity than love-struck admiration. She cannot conceive of such a perspective, however, and it annoys the poet-narrator that he has been unjustly included in her list of conquests.

Yet, the very act of writing and publishing such verses is one way of informing the countess of that which "the countess could not know about" ; so that this little four-stanza story about the countess indicates both one source of the poet-narrator's agitation and the addressee of his verses pertaining to that agitation. Just as the verses of the poem's first part serve in a literary battle, these verses serve in a sexual battle. But the narrator's purpose is less to expose or insult the countess than to find a way through her armor of haughtiness and communicate with her. Thus, he shows a certain compassion toward her: he tells her that he knows the truth about her, but this truth is kept below the surface of his speech, where only she can hear it. Note that this special communication situation is described as the reading of a tale with a hidden meaning: "Through her outward hauteur, though, I could read / A different story" (XXIII). The addressee of these verses is the poetic persona's smart reader. The countess figure is meant to understand this ambivalent, seductive yet aggressive, and vengeful message.

Parasha is deeply involved in the relationship between the poet-narrator and the countess. The stanzas pertaining to the countess end with a comparison: "A hundredfold more fortunate was she, / My reader, the young friend I sought to usher / Into your heart, my simple, kind Parasha [Блаженнее стократ ея была, / Читатель, новая знакомка ваша, / Простая, добрая моя Параша]." The tale that follows reveals Parasha to be a crafty, sexually aggressive female in the tradition of the fabliau, and it explains why this simple girl should be happier than the countess: she is uninhibited by the bonds and restrictions accompanying the countess's high position and assumed role.

The countess betrays an interest in Parasha: in the final three lines of stanza XXI and the first half of stanza XXII the poet-narrator is gazing at the countess who, in turn, is gazing at Parasha. The countess is apparently struck by the piousness of Parasha, but the girl repays her with indifference — just as the countess ignores the poet-narrator:

And her [the countess's] proximity distracted greatly
This sinful wretch. Parasha, our poor miss,
Looked poorer still against a foil like this.

At times the countess from her grand position
Gave her a casual look. But she would pray,
And in untroubled stillness and submission
Seemed unaware of it in any way.

Бывало, грешен! всё гляжу направо,
Всё на неё [на графиню]. Параша перед ней
Казалось, бедная, ещё бедней.

Порой Графиня на неё небрежно
Бросала важный взор свой. Но она
Молилась Богу тихо и прилежно
И не казалась им развлечена.

If we accept the proposition that these gazes demonstrate the desire of each character for recognition — or even love — from the one who is gazed upon, it follows that the situation presented by these stanzas is a peculiar sort of love triangle. I suggest that the triangular relationship between the poet-narrator, the countess, and Parasha mirrors the relationship between the poetic persona of the poem's first part, certain of his addressees (the insiders), and the muse or, by extension, poetry itself.

It is easy to see how the relationship between Pushkin, his fellow poets or critics, and poetry might be seen as a love triangle. Pushkin and his critics are, in a sense, vying for the favors of the muse. Much of their battle concerns the proper definition of that muse, and of what poetry ought to be and ought to do.[21]

One wonders what would annoy a writer more: being harshly treated in a critic's review, or the thought that a critic of talents inferior to one's own dismisses one's work with the absolute certainty that he knows what is wrong with this work, and that his opinion is of great significance to the author. This second circumstance is rather like the situation described in stanza XXIII (xxxvii), cited above. It seems that his rejection by the countess does not annoy the poet-narrator of "Little House" so much as the woman's self-centeredness, the way in which she considers him conquered and yet has no sense of his deep understanding of her and that which has passed between them.

It follows, then, that on the poem's allegorical plane the countess corresponds to the critic against whom the polemics of the poem's first part were directed: Katenin. The noisiness and self-centeredness of the countess make her like the critics Pushkin speaks of; she is also described as "*surovaia*" (severe, strict), while the critic whom the poetic persona wishes to humiliate in stanza xx receives the synonymous adjective "*strogoi*," and Boileau—apostle of neoclassicism and France's foremost critic and literary lawgiver during the time of La Fontaine—is called "*stepennyi*" (staid, sedate).

Parasha—like Tatyana in *Eugene Onegin*—can be associated with the poet's muse, or with poetry itself. Stanzas XIV (xxviii) and XV (xxix) tout Parasha's musical talents:

> She sang "There mourns the purple dove," recited
> "Shall I go forth," she played on the guitar,
> Nor was that older repertory slighted
> Which in drear autumn by the samovar,
> Or when in winter dusk the stove is lighted,
> Or walking in a vernal glade afar,
> To doleful strains the Russian maiden uses,
> Who is a grieving singer, like our Muses.
>
> Both plain and metaphorical, our tune,
> From poet laureate to mere domestic,
> Is in a doleful key. A wailing croon
> Is Russia's song. Well-known characteristic:
> What starts with merry toasts turns all too soon
> To passing-bells. The chords of both majestic
> And rustic Muses draw from grief their glow;
> One likes the plaintive cadence even so.

> Играть умела также на гитаре,
> И пела: "*Стонет сизый голубок*"
> И "*выду ль я*" и то— что уж постаре;

Всё, что у печки в зимний вечерок
Иль скучной осенью при самоваре
Или весною, обходя лесок,
Поёт уныло русская девица;
Как музы наши, грустная певица.

Фигурно иль буквально: всей семьей,
От ямщика до первого поэта,
Мы все поём уныло. Грустный вой
Песнь русская. Известная примета!
Начав за здравие, за упокой
Сведём как раз. Печалию согрета
Гармония и наших муз и дев.
Но нравится их жалобный напев.

Note that in the final couplet of the first stanza "*russkaia devitsa*" (Russian maiden) is explicitly compared with "our Muses"; in the penultimate line of the following stanza, muses and maidens are again equated. In both instances, the poet-narrator may be speaking of Russian maidens in general, but Parasha is the Russian maiden in question. Thus, on the poem's allegorical plane, Parasha may be seen as figuratively representing—in a purposefully ironic tenor—the poetic muse, or poetry itself.

The poetic persona of "Little House" and his critic are literary men in competition for the same object of desire: Poetry, or Parasha. This situation of a competition between poets mirrors that found in "Staraia byl'."[22] Note the first-person plural possessive pronoun modifying "muse" in both the lines pointed out above; the addressee of these verses is someone who, like Pushkin, lays claim to the muse. But the poetic persona-as-cook and the critic-as-countess have entirely different visions of just what this object of desire is. The countess sees a pious, high-minded Parasha; we can cite as analogous Katenin's view that the verse form used in "Little House" is proper only for the epopee, a "high" genre in the neoclassical canon. For the poetic persona of "Little House" the muse is neither pious nor holy; in "Little House in Kolomna" he calls her "*rezvushka*" (spunky, frisky one; IX, xxiii, 2).[23]

The sexual metaphor elaborated here echoes Katenin's opposition between a virile Russian warrior and a Greek eunuch. This metaphor had been employed by Pushkin in reference to Katenin long before the "Staraia byl' " exchange, however. In an 1820 letter to Viazemsky, Pushkin characterized the difference between Katenin's relation to poetry and his own in terms strikingly similar to those we have found in "Little House in Kolomna"; he wrote:

> [Katenin] . . . was born late — he belongs to the eighteenth century, not by virtue of ideas (of which he has none), but because of his character: the same author's pettiness and pride, the same literary intrigues and gossip. For the most part we've all gotten used to viewing poetry like a well-known flirt, on whom we now and then drop in to lie a bit and play the rake, without the slightest heartfelt affection, and entirely without respect for her dangerous charms. Katenin, by contrast, comes to her powdered and in fancy shoes, and sits beside her all day with platonic love, reverence, and pomposity (April 20, 1820; cited from Oksman, 625 [see *Pss* 6:19–20]).

The characterization of Katenin as belonging to the eighteenth century is also relevant to "Little House," a text rich in allusions to the Russian literary scene of the preceding era.

In the metapoetic introduction of "Little House" the poetic persona wishes he could disguise himself and play a trick on his "severe critic (*strogoi kritik*)." The Parasha tale carries out just such a trick. The poetic persona has gotten the better of his critic; and he has done so in the terms of the fabliau, through translating their competitive relationship as litterateurs into a sexual context. The poetic persona has also made use of Aesopic language to tell his victim what he has done, thereby completing his triumph. The fabliau "Lady-Leech" ended with a similar incident, and in "The Life of Aesop," too, Aesop cuckolds his master, then tells him about it (*Aesop*, 67–68).[24]

5 Poets and Czar

There remain large gaps in our understanding of the poem. What, for example, is the widow's place in the allegorical configuration developed here? Also, in "To A. S. Pushkin" ("A. S. Pushkinu") Katenin had challenged Pushkin to *echo* the *silent* or *quiet* conversation ("*tikhaia beseda*") of "Staraia byl'." That which remained hidden in Katenin's poem, remember, was its insult to the czar and toast to the Decembrists. Meeting the task set by Katenin would have involved something truly dangerous for Pushkin;

but where is such political content to be found in "Little House"? And how can it be the promised full response to "Staraia byl' " if there is no such content?

As a farcical reflection of, or extended pun on, "Staraia byl'," "Little House in Kolomna" can be expected to reflect as well the allegorical content of "Staraia byl' " (a depiction of the relation between Pushkin, the czar, Katenin and poetry). The place of action in Katenin's poem is the court of Prince Vladimir, which in turn metaphorically takes the place of the court of Czar Nicholas I; and since "Little House in Kolomna" reflects "Staraia byl'," we can suspect that the little house is a metaphoric substitution for the Winter Palace of Nicholas I (which, incidentally, is three-storied). In this set of correspondences, the weak-eyed widow would stand in a position parallel to that of the czar himself.

The relationship between the prince and the widow is one of identity in opposition; the widow is proven as stingy as the prince of "Staraia byl' " is generous. Moreover, it is precisely the stinginess of the widow and the generosity of the prince that make them vulnerable to the insults they suffer: the Decembrists are toasted with the very gift the czar figure had given the Russian bard, and Mavra gets his/her job as cook because he is willing to work "for nothing." There is also a subtle parallel between the details provided about the dress of the prince and the widow: the prince emerges to attend the holiday festivities "wearing his crown and with sceptor in his right hand [*V ventse i so skiptrom v desnitse*]," while the widow "wore mobcap and specs [*nasila shepchik i ochki*]." Two articles of clothing are described in both instances: headwear is mentioned first, with the mobcap serving as a debased, ironic reflection of the prince's crown; the prince's sceptor — a symbol of the long reach of royal power — also finds such reflection in the spectacles of Parasha's mother, whose powers of perception and control (or *censorship*) of her daughter were indeed weak. Both carry out their acts of choosing (a bard, a cook) at a holiday.

Now we see that the place of the critic, of the countess, is that of the smart reader; this makes sense, for in spite of their difficult relations, Pushkin always showed a great deal of respect for Katenin. Indeed, in the same year when Pushkin finally got around to publishing "Little House in Kolomna," some four years after receiving "Staraia byl'," he also published an article on the works of Katenin, "Sochineniia i pervody v stikhakh Pavla Katenina" (*Pss* 5:76–78),[25] in which he called Katenin Russia's only true literary critic "in the tradition of the Schlegels." This article may be read as serving the same function as did the dedicatory poem Katenin sent along with his "Staraia byl'." It praises Katenin without condescension or hypocrisy, and it speaks of "Staraia byl'," "where there is so much ingenuousness and true poetry." To characterize the exchange we have been describing as a violent polemic would be wrong; it is more a competition between friends, even if the friendship is difficult and unequal: a pat on the back, a kick in the rear.[26] Finally, by designing "Little House" as a parody of Katenin's "kicking" poem, Pushkin not only met the challenge but far outstripped it. He also managed to evade the element of compulsion — the slavishness — involved with meeting such a challenge in the first place.

The czar — who, after all, was officially Pushkin's personal censor — is the weak-eyed but powerful reader assumed by this fable, and it is against him and his censorship apparatus that its vengeful wit is directed. It seems that Pushkin did not "reduce Katenin's program to absurdity"; he took the challenge of "Staraia byl' " quite seriously, and he found a way to meet it. Just as Katenin proved himself by insulting the czar and recalling the Decembrists in print, so Pushkin juxtaposes the czar with a poor, witless, stingy old woman, who is so to speak cuckolded. The stanzas in which the poetic persona vents his anger at the three-story building and speaks of the need to suppress memories can be read as an allusion to the Decembrists. It is true that the poetic persona negates this recollection, declaring "As for myself, I sip / My Lethe; grief is bad, says my physician"; but negation inevitably calls forth that which must be stricken out, and so constitutes a condition under which such a significant and politically dangerous allusion might appear, making it an excellent Aesopian device (as well as psychological defense mechanism [see Freud, "Negation"]). Moreover, this situation may be seen as a negative analogue to that of Evgeny in "The Bronze Horseman" ("Mednyi vsadnik"): there the unhappy hero does give way to despair, and, on a walk like that of the poetic persona of "Little House," does *not* hold his tongue as he casts a sidewards glance at the symbol of the cause of his loss (the equestrian statue of Peter the Great); the result is madness and death.[27]

These similarities between "Staraia byl' " and "Little House in Kolomna" underline an essential difference, as is always the case in parody: while Pushkin's poem is light-hearted and ironic, there is a deadly seriousness to Katenin's work. "To A. S. Pushkin" ("A. S. Pushkinu") had alluded to the heroes of epic romances, the highest genre according to neoclassical poetics, to which Katenin then subscribed; Pushkin's response was cast in the terms of the fabliau, a low genre that exists in a parodic relationship with the epic romance and chivalry in general, and which Pushkin saw as a forerunner of Romanticism. Pushkin's poem about a transvestite is itself a *travesty*, a mock epic.

Nevertheless, we can hardly claim to have disrobed "The Little House in Kolomna" and revealed what it really is. The poem's original version bore an epigraph taken from Ovid: "*Modo vir, modo foemina*" ("Now as a man, now as a woman"). On the one hand, these words foreshadow and underline the punch line of the anecdote aspect of the poem; but the motif of transvestism has far greater significance, occurring as it does in a poem that demonstrates two different ways of saying the same thing: the militant way of the man, or master, who says directly what he means to say; and the way of the woman, or slave, who must dress what he means to say as a joke, "projecting his sentiments into the fable" in order to escape punishment. Pushkin and Katenin each emasculate the other when they figure themselves into poetry (Pushkin becomes a Greek castrato, Katenin a countess); "You are without a phallus," each tells the other, "you cannot relate to the muse as I can." Yet, each takes up the woman's and the slave's way of speaking, for each writes a fable. Moreover, "Little House," like any work of art, is as much the garment it has thrown over itself to disguise the truth as it is that truth. The tale from which this epigraph is taken points to the impossibility of conceiving the poem as a simple truth hidden under a deceptive surface, for these words appear in the preface to the story of Hermaphrodite (Ovid, IV, 280).

Indeed, one grows unsure where "Staraia byl' " ends and "Little House in Kolomna" begins; nor does it seem possible to determine finally which of the two poet-figures in the allegory presented by "Little House" stands for Pushkin, and which for Katenin. Exposing the dialogic nature of "Little House in Kolomna" creates a wholeness every bit as enigmatic as Hermaphrodite's. Consider the following instances of the poetic persona's double-voicedness:

In the poem's very first line, "The iambic quadruped has had full scope; / I'm sick of it [*Chetyrestopnyi iamb mne nadoel*]," the poetic persona—whom we have until now identified with Pushkin—utters a condemnation of iambic tetrameter of the sort that Katenin was wont to make; moreover, this condemnation is written in iambic pentamer, a meter Katenin considered his own.

The same year in which Pushkin composed the lines, "I'm marching on the critics, not whistling [*Na kritikov edy, ne svishchu*]," Katenin's most substantial effort as a literary critic — "Razmyshleniia i razbory" — was appearing in a journal coedited by Pushkin (*Literaturnaia gazeta*); of this work Katenin had declared, "I am, so to speak, conducting a war, or want to, and in war one should never miss an opportunity."[28]

The start of Katenin's career as a writer about aesthetics and theory of literature was marked by scandals over the use of pseudonyms — just the sort of "pranks" threatened by the poetic persona of "Little House" in the metapoetic introduction. One of these instances involved an article on Pushkin's "Ruslan i Liudmila," which was signed with a pseudonym Katenin had been using. The article was widely — and wrongly — attributed to Katenin. In his memoirs ("Vospominaniia o Pushkine"), Katenin writes: "After a few days Pushkin ran into me in the theatre and said: 'Your criticism stings a bit, but it's so smart and good-natured that it's not only impossible to get angry, but even....' I interrupted: 'What made you think the article was written by me?' " (*Razmyshleniia*, 209; see also Frizman, 19–20).

Katenin considered himself to be Pushkin's equal, and he viewed the success and celebration of Pushkin and his own decline into obscurity with a resentment not unlike that of the poetic persona as he observes the countess in the church (Tynianov, "Arkhaisty i Pushkin," 171; Rozanov, 110).

Katenin served as an officer in the ultra-elite Preobrazhensky Regiment, the officers of which were known for their tall stature, beards, and mustaches (Simpson, 20–21). This leads one to consider associating Katenin with Mavra on the basis of the shaving motif — certainly more so than Pushkin.[29]

Finally, in the article about Katenin mentioned above, Pushkin speaks sympathetically of Katenin's troubles with his critics while in effect acting as such a critic; so that the poetic persona of "The Little House in Kolomna," who is suffering at the pens of his critics, is a figure as close to Katenin as he is to Pushkin. One might even speculate that Pushkin originally wanted to publish "Little House" anonymously not so much to protect himself as to make the voice of the poem blend all the more with a voice the reader would associate with Katenin's — to play a trick.[30]

Taking note of such ambiguities may make a neat allegorical scheme appear to disintegrate into heterogeneous associations; but, I would suggest, the particular combination of polemic, parody, and fable found in "Little House," along with its gaming aspect — a kind of one-upsmanship in the arena of genre — come together to create a semantic field in which ambigu-

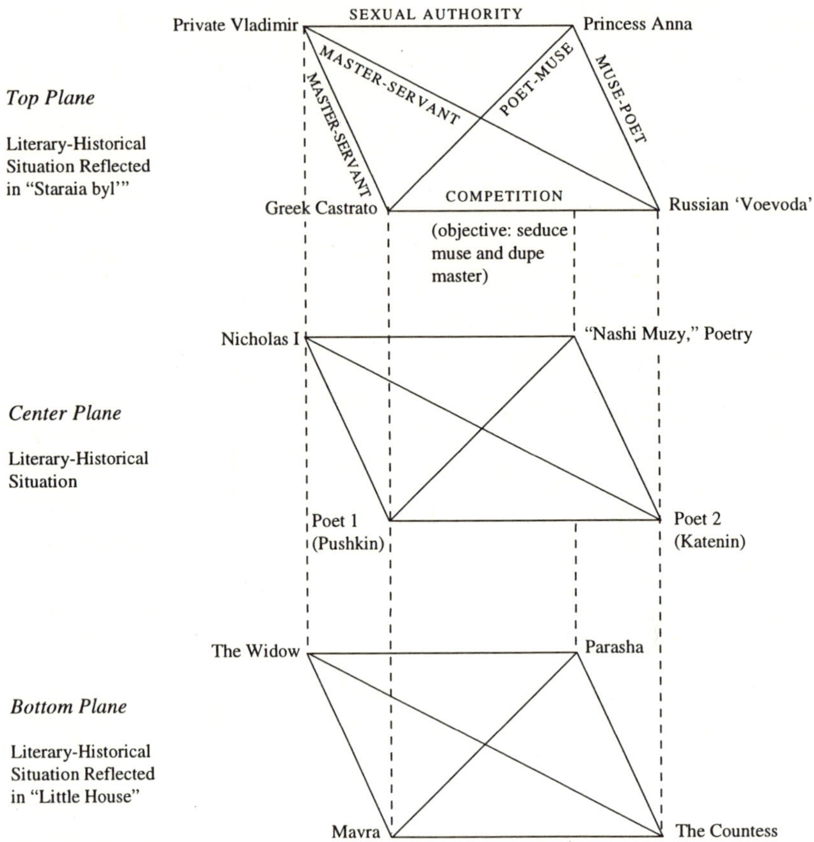

Figure 1. The three planes of competition between poets in "The Little House in Kolomna."

ity is unavoidable. Figure 1 attempts to represent in diagram form the relationship between poems, poets, poetry, and the czar which I have laid out here. Note that this scheme is three-storied.

It is true that allegorical interpretation leaves much space for the imagination of the interpreter. One should recall, then, the extent to which Pushkin and his contemporaries, especially members of Arzamas, practiced this sort of literary gamesmanship, and how seriously they took it.[31] How fitting also to Pushkin's personality that he should superimpose the fabliau motif of cuckoldry onto Katenin's situation of a competition between poets: think only of the infamous Don Juan list left by Pushkin, and the circumstances of his death.

3

Genre and Incarnation in Dostoevsky's *The Idiot*

"What, shall we suffer an ass to play the philosopher to us?"

—Apuleius, *The Golden Ass*, Book IV

Self-consciousness pervades every aspect of Dostoevsky's writings; that it touches upon the novelist's own poetics, including him among Russian authors of the nineteenth century for whom thoughts about the poetics of one's narrative become themes in the finished work, is no surprise. Indeed, polemical richness and play with the literary conventions of his own and previous days have been viewed as central to Dostoevsky since the beginning of his career (see Tynianov, "Dostoevskii i Gogol' "). Among the four late novels commonly considered Dostoevsky's greatest—*Crime and Punishment* (1865–66), *The Idiot* (1869), *The Devils* (1871), and *The Brothers Karamazov* (1880)—this is particularly true of *The Idiot*, a work which, over the past decade, has perhaps attracted more than its fair share of attention from Dostoevsky scholars.

The novel has many explicitly metapoetic moments. In particular, there are digressions in its latter part where the narrator despairs of telling his story fully, thereby thematizing the very narration of *The Idiot.* One such instance, a discourse on character in the novel, is given the prominent position of opening part 4 (383ff).[1] This theme of storytelling is also pursued, though less directly, through the proliferation of characters who tell stories, that is, by the function of inserted narratives in *The Idiot.* These fairly obvious instances of metapoesis have been given full attention in recent years.[2]

This chapter instead takes up the ways this concern about poetics is expressed, more extensively, below the surface of *The Idiot*, in a distinctive convolution of problems of poetics with problems of ethics. Authoring becomes a metaphor or model for the way Dostoevsky's hero approaches the others around him. Considered from the point of view of poetics, Dostoevsky presents Myshkin in the active role of an author who errs fundamentally in his choice of genre: he attempts to create a Petersburg tale on the model of that which he accomplished in Switzerland. This malpractice, as well as its connection with the figure of Rousseau, has been noted by Dostoevsky scholars for quite some time, whether or not they have stated it in these terms.[3]

Scholars have also remarked a certain connection between Myshkin and the typical Dostoevskian dreamer.[4] This character type responds to live human beings with aesthetic rather than ethical activity—he spins dreams but cannot respond to a live, bodied other. Dostoevsky is most concerned with the ethical consequences of authoring, and in this sense *The Idiot* can be read as a meditation on the practice and pitfalls of taking the attitude of an author toward others. The novel presents a full range of possibilities for the nature and composition of such an attitude, while in Myshkin two extreme possibilities compete. The first is associated with one of the novel's central themes, that of Christ and the enigma of incarnation; the second, once again, with Jean-Jacques Rousseau.

This view of the novel owes much to Mikhail Bakhtin, in particular to his early philosophical work "Author and Hero in Aesthetic Activity." If my basic lines of inquiry have been followed before, I think I can promise fresh discoveries regarding the manner in which they are intertwined and connected to the novel's subthemes—discoveries enabled by the thought of the early, and less known, Bakhtin. Key among them is a rich parallel between the problematic relationship of an abstract generic model to a concrete literary text, which is written and apprehended in very specific and always changing spatial and temporal contexts, and the enigma—central to the novel's thematics—of the ideal man, the only wholly positive instance of which in life and literature, as Dostoevsky wrote to his niece, was Christ (*Pss* 27[2]:251).

It is true that the theme of authoring is not underlined in Dostoevsky's notebooks to the novel. Yet, recalling the difficult creative history of *The Idiot* provokes speculation that the shift of concerns displayed by the novel's fictional narrator somehow reflects a process undergone by Dostoevsky as well: the more problems this novel gave him—and it is notorious in that respect—the more the problems of authoring managed to enter the novel at the thematic level.

I Myshkin as Author

Narration as a theme and Myshkin as a narrator are introduced early in *The Idiot.* The epileptic prince has arrived in Petersburg, after a lengthy period of rehabilitation in a clinic in Switzerland, with no money or letters of introduction, and hardly a change of clothes. He calls on General Epanchin because the general's wife—alone, it would appear, in all of Russia—shares Myshkin's family name and may be a relation. What follows is a series of tests, the passing of which gains the prince entry to the Epanchin family and proves his special capacity for storytelling.

But the novel goes beyond representing a certain oral and aural activity. Each of the stories Myshkin relates calls attention to some of the formal problems and limitations inherent in this activity; they foreground the generic aspect—the how of seeing, writing, and reading. The stories have a generic specificity and a pragmatic function that both he and his listeners acknowledge: he has come to teach, he is a philosopher who will transform his experiences into educational parables. "It may be that you are right," the prince admits to Aglaya as he tells of his recuperation in Switzerland. "I may really be a philosopher, and who knows, maybe I actually intend to teach..." (51). But in casting these experiences into stories he underlines the limits beyond which individual, contingent experience can be codified into repeatable paradigms. The specific direction in which Myshkin pushes those limits is highly significant. In his striking presentations of the internal perspective of a man condemned to death during the final moments of life, for instance, Myshkin reproduces and thereby raises to the level of the typical a perspective belonging to that most singular and contingent moment in an individual's life, a moment that in reality can never be communicated to another.

Myshkin's calligraphic talent further marks him as a literary sort, if only in a reduced, synecdochic way. When General Epanchin gives him pen and paper to assess his clerical skills, the prince offers "the personal signature of the High Monk Pafnuty, from a reproduction of the fourteenth century" (29). Myshkin has reproduced a type of written discourse which by definition represents a unique individual: after all, a person's signature is a metonymic substitution for the person himself. Myshkin approaches Pafnuty's signature with an eye for both its generic and its distinctive, personal features; he reproduces this writing style not as an abstract calligraphic form, but as one saturated with personality. Myshkin himself reflects: "They signed their names excellently, all our old High Monks and Metropolitans, and at times with such taste, with such effort" (29). His short catalogue of other writing styles organized by nationality (a hint of the chauvinism that will burst forth toward the novel's end) follows similar principles.[5]

For the general, of course, these subtleties are irrelevant; he is not the least bit interested in *what* Myshkin has written, nor does he consider significant the association between the sort of man Pafnuty was, the content of his written speech, and the graphic form of that speech. All he cares about is the purely formal *how.* The same is less true of the general's wife, however. When she demands: "I want to know how you tell stories" (47), her test of Myshkin's narrative competence will be more comprehensive, and she and her daughters will react to Myshkin's tales in a fuller, more complex manner.

Myshkin tells a series of five tales to the Epanchin women during this examination. The first relates his arrival in Switzerland as an idiot (48–49); the second describes his walks through the mountains, hallucinations of a "calling," and dreams of entering a new life (50–51); the third tells of an acquaintance who, at the last moment, had been given a reprieve from a death sentence (51–53); the fourth presents Myshkin's imaginative reconstruction of the internal perspective of a man sentenced to death during the very last moments of life, based on a painting he has seen in Basel (55–56);[6] and the last, and longest, is the story of Myshkin's relationship with the consumptive fallen woman, Marie. Each of these stories will be touched upon here, with the greatest attention going to the first and the last.

The prince's status as one who has lived abroad interests the Epanchin women a great deal. The middle daughter, Adelaida, is a painter in search of a subject to paint, and nothing in her immediate environment attracts her. (That this dull environment is the very milieu Dostoevsky is depicting in *The Idiot* reflects upon Adelaida's own artistic understanding and means.) Adelaida expresses her problem by reciting a line from Lermontov's 1840 metaliterary poem, "The Journalist, Reader, and Writer" ("*Zhurnalist, chitatel' i pisatel'*"), "The East and the South have long been described...," and she requests of the prince, "Find me a topic for a painting." It is not just that the prince, having been abroad, has seen new things, novel topics for a painting: "You see, abroad the Prince has learned how to look," she declares (50). The prince's education in Switzerland is thus associated with the acquisition of a different perspective on the world, a way of seeing anew that which has grown too familiar for the amateur artist, Adelaida.[7]

The novel's action represents the testing and shattering of this world-view, chiefly through the juxtaposition of two stories: that of Myshkin's rehabilitation in Switzerland and his relations with the peasant girl, Marie, and the broader narrative sequence comprised of Myshkin's relations with Nastasya Filippovna. The Switzerland story is associated with the life and writings of Rousseau.[8] It becomes a generic model for Myshkin, and his unhappy place in the novel as a whole can be understood as that of an *author* attempting to shape a Petersburg story on the model of the Switzerland story.

In his capacity as a character who approaches fellow characters as though he were their author, Myshkin is far from unique in the novel. At the moment he returns to Petersburg, several members of the milieu in which Myshkin finds himself have been incubating their own plots, and each of them is hoping to shape Totsky's former concubine, Nastasya Filippovna, into the heroine necessary for that plot; so it has been with Nastasya Filippovna from the time Totsky began "educating"—that is, creating—her: "God, what could have been made of such a character, and so beautiful! But in spite of all my efforts, even education, it has all perished! A rough diamond—I said that several times..." (149), he will remark after the name-day party scandal.

Now Gania Ivolgin is planning a social and economic triumph in the spirit, perhaps, of a Balzac novel: if he were to marry Nastasya Filippovna and free Totsky to marry as well, he would put his hands on a great deal of money. General Epanchin hopes to attach to Gania's his own subplot, rather pathetic and fanciful for a man his age, according to which Nastasya Filippovna would become his mistress at virtually the same time she becomes Gania's wife; Rogozhin is counterplotting; and so on. All these narrative threads precede the time of the novel and are to have a simultaneous *razviazka*, or denouement, during Nastasya Filippovna's name-day party, when *everything will be decided.* A number of characters are plotting their own private twists to the ending of Nastasya Filippovna's story, and, accordingly, the evening is saturated with an air of suspense; but there is common agreement that the matter is certain to be finally decided, a resolution will be chosen for this fallen woman's story. When a vigorous ring of the bell announces Rogozhin's arrival late in the evening, we read: " 'A-a-a! Here's the *denouement* [*razviazka*]! Finally! It's half past eleven!' exclaimed Nastasya Filippovna. 'Please sit down, ladies and gentlemen, this is the *denouement*' " (131; italics mine). None of the possible outcomes are attractive to Nastasya Filippovna, and her motives are wavering and ambiguous: is she finally to receive just compensation (money, the social respectability of marriage) for the wrongs she has suffered; is she concretizing the guilt and self-reproaches suffered these past five years through a deliberate, arrogant public step into harlotry; or is she sacrificing herself for the good of her community?[9]

Perhaps the best way of describing what is to happen is to say that Nastasya Filippovna is wavering between exercising her tremendous power as a *resistant hero*[10] and submitting to the plot concocted by Totsky and General Epanchin, a plot in which she, a tainted woman, will sacrifice herself for the happiness of the pure and deserving Aleksandra Epanchin and the stability of high society.[11] Here should be noted the unavoidable association between Nastasya Filippovna's family name—*Barashkova*—and the nonecclesiastical Russian for that sacrificial animal, the ram, "*baran*," or even closer, the diminutive "*barashek*" (lamb). Nastasya's sacrificial marriage to Gania Ivolgin will free Totsky to marry the eldest Epanchin girl, and Nastasya's bridegroom will be her executioner; thus, she speaks of Gania at the name-day party: " 'No, now I believe that his sort would *slit* a throat for money! These days such a thirst has seized them all, they go to pieces over money, they've become real fools. Find a child—he's already trying to be a pawnbroker. But this one would wrap a razor in silk, take a position quietly behind a friend, and slit his throat *like a ram* . . .' " (137, my italics). At this point, however, Nastasya Filippovna has already cast Gania aside in favor of a more potent headsman—Rogozhin.

Myshkin's advice that Nastasya Filippovna not marry Gania and, later in the evening, his own proposal to Nastasya Filippovna upset everything: he turns what should be a story's *razviazka* (denouement) into a new *zaviazka* (complication) through the introduction of a new story-possibility—redemption and resurrection. Nastasya Filippovna says as much after the prince has made his proposal: "It means I'm actually a princess! [. . .] An unexpected denouement... I... expected differently..." (140), and "It is only now that my real life will begin!" (141). To the extent that Nastasya and other characters orient themselves toward Myshkin and take on the shape that figures into his story, he becomes their author. But of course his story attracts grafters with their own subplots and twists, and his inheritance provides another, contradictory reason for characters to orient themselves toward him.

For Nastasya Filippovna, Myshkin is a dreamt-of author:

> Didn't I used to dream about you myself? You're right in that, I long ago dreamt of it, back at his place in the country, where I lived five years all alone; I'd think, and sometimes fantasize, and imagine someone like you, as good, honorable, fine and maybe a little bit dumb, who'd suddenly come and say: "You're not guilty, Nastasya Filippovna, and I worship you!" (144)

If the story-possibility of sacrifice is linked with Nastasya Filippovna's family name (*Barashkova*), then, according to Al'tman, one can associate her proper name with this second story-possibility of redemption: "Nastas'ia" or "Anastasiia" is derived from the Greek for "the one who is arising" — metaphorically, "the one who is being resurrected" — and is thus related to a whole series of episodes involving the motif of resurrection (70).[12]

All the above comments regarding Myshkin as an author beg the question of what sort of story he wishes to write. His model, I have suggested, is given in the cycle of stories he tells when examined by Madame Epanchin. Especially evident are the correspondences between the overarching narrative of *The Idiot* and the last and longest of the five tales he narrates to the Epanchin women, the story of Marie; let us discuss each of these tales, beginning with the last.

While the paradigmatic relationship between the story of Marie and the novel as a whole (a "Petersburg" story) has struck a number of critics,[13] few of the correspondences between these two stories have been elucidated. Both are stories of fallen women, and both end with the deaths of their heroines. Myshkin's feelings toward both Marie and Nastasya Filippovna are characterized as pity rather than love, yet he plays the role of lover toward both.

The eyes of these women draw special attention: when Myshkin first meets Nastasya Filippovna, at the Ivolgin apartment, he tells her that he feels he has seen her eyes before; she too feels that she has seen Myshkin somewhere before (89–90). Eyes, of course, are traditionally viewed as a portal into the human soul; while all others see her external shape and her behavior, her phenomenal beauty and pride, Myshkin sees what is going on inside: suffering and a desire for redemption.[14] In Romano Guardini's excellent discussion of the novel's Christological implications, this moment reveals the existence of another "domain" for the novel's action, "where Myshkin and Nastasya 'have already seen each other.' " Further: "This domain where an 'eternal' meeting has unfolded may enlighten us as to the meaning of the Platonic 'Idea.' Certainly, in the novel we are meant to see that within the actual historical meeting, something eternal has unveiled itself" (369). If we recall what Myshkin has told the Epanchin women of Marie's eyes, that which is "eternal" in Nastasya Filippovna is but a repetition of the sufferings and desire for redemption of Marie. Myshkin's dim recollections are meant to refer back to the Swiss girl.

This association of a fallen woman from Petersburg high society with the poor peasant woman in Switzerland is presented as belonging to the plane of the prince's consciousness; moreover, both women recall the figure of Mary Magdalene from the Gospels (Bethea, 83). But many of the details associating the two women belong quite clearly to a consciousness beyond the bounds of Myshkin's, one able to view the novel from the outside as a completed whole—that of the novel's author. They reveal the hand of the maker, and they mark this juxtaposition as a key structural feature of the novel.

For instance, Marie's clothes were in tatters; her situation was so poor that she was forced to go about in bare feet. One of the several striking details that depict the slain Nastasya Filippovna at the novel's end is her bare feet protruding from under the cover. When Marie died, the children Myshkin had gathered around him decorated her coffin with flowers, and placed a wreath at its head (63); Rogozhin proposes to Myshkin that they cover Nastasya Filippovna with flowers (505).

Myshkin's gifts to Marie—especially the diamond stick pin he sells to raise money for her—are echoed in the diamond earrings and packet of money Rogozhin offers Nastasya Filippovna.

The children who had been persecuting Marie and whom Myshkin brought to forgive and love her are associated with the adults of Petersburg high society in the Petersburg story—not only in Myshkin's mind, but through Dostoevsky's use of talking names: Myshkin repeatedly refers to the Swiss children as "*ptichki*" (little birds). Among those members of Myshkin's Petersburg milieu most important for the plot of *The Idiot*, family names with roots associated with the names of birds predominate (*Ptitsyn*, *Ivolgin*, and *Lebedev*).[15] While "the splendid creative gap between the notes and the actual novel" (Miller, *Dostoevsky and "The Idiot,"* 7) makes it difficult to rely on Dostoevsky's notebooks for evidence to back up such theses,[16] it should be noted that the one name that appears fairly early in Dostoevsky's notes and also in the final product is that of Ptitsyn; the rest of these names sprang into Dostoevsky's plans only toward the end, and more or less simultaneously with the theme of Myshkin's relations with children (Dostoevsky, *Notebooks*, 66, 159ff.).[17] At one point in the notebooks Dostoevsky planned to make Myshkin "czar" of a children's club in Petersburg, but he apparently gave up this idea because it was too direct a repetition of the situation in the tale of Marie ("Primechaniia," *Pss* 9:364).

All of these correspondences hint at a meaningful connection between the story of Marie and the novel as a whole. On the one hand Dostoevsky the author prefigures what is to come; more importantly, however, Myshkin-as-author transforms the story of Marie into a generic model that he will apply to the situation in Petersburg. This project of realizing an abstract form in an uncongenial concrete situation — Myshkin's "test-tube" idea — is paralleled in the novel's theme of corporality, through the presentation of the "wholly positive" or ideal man (Myshkin) as an *ill* man.

2 Myshkin as Ass

How does the notion of incarnation link Dostoevsky's metapoetic treatment of Myshkin as an author-figure with his novel's deeper Christological plane of meaning? My point of departure for discussing this aspect of the novel's symbolics might surprise at first — we'll approach the Christological from its rear, so to speak — but the results prove quite revealing. If Myshkin is figuratively associated with an author and with Christ, he is also, oddly enough, associated with a donkey.

In the Switzerland story, the beginning of the idiot's rehabilitation and transformation into an educated adult is heralded by the braying of an ass. The episode, striking enough in itself, is further accented through the reactions of the Epanchin women. It is also a significant moment from the point of view of plot: the braying of the Swiss donkey ushers Myshkin into consciousness, while in the novel's denouement we see Myshkin go mad again, so that the donkey episode is marked as one of the endpoints of that trajectory of Myshkin's active life in the world of the novel. And this image of the donkey, extremely rich in other intratextual and extratextual associations, is a dense, nodal moment in the novel's thematics, and therefore an excellent point of departure for a discussion of incarnation in *The Idiot.*

Myshkin relates to the Epanchin women how this primitive, perhaps even primordial communication act, heard upon his entry into Switzerland, penetrated the fog in his head and set the stage for his coming to consciousness.

> I remember: I was unbearably sad; I even wanted to cry; everything bewildered and upset me: what had a terrible effect on me was that it was all *alien*; that much I could understand. This foreignness was killing me. It was in Basel that I completely awoke from this darkness, I remember; on entering Switzerland the braying of an ass at the marketplace woke me up. The ass made a great impression on me and for some reason pleased me intensely, and at the same time suddenly everything seemed to clear up in my head. (48)

The prince continues: "From that time I have been terribly fond of asses. . . . I became convinced that this is the most useful animal, hard-working, strong, patient, cheap, long-suffering; and via this ass I suddenly began to like all Switzerland, such that my former sadness passed entirely" (48). Not only does this common beast of burden awaken Myshkin from a state of complete idiocy and alienation; it also serves as a natural symbolization of the values he holds dearly.

The donkey motif is echoed also in the episode where Myshkin's life takes its sharp downward turn, during the scandal with the Chinese urn. Just before Myshkin recounts his entry into Switzerland and his awakening by the braying ass, the society matron Princess Belokonskaya is first mentioned. In fact, when Madame Epanchin orders the prince to tell a story, it is so that she can then report to Belokonskaya: "I want to know how you tell stories. I want to be completely certain, and when I see the Princess Belokonskaya, the old woman, I'll tell her all about you" (47). The introduction here of the figure of the princess feels flimsy and contrived from the point of view of plot, but can perhaps be understood as a way of establishing, on the basis of contiguity, a link between her figure and the story about the ass. Such an association is already implicit in the name Dostoevsky has chosen for this woman: "*Belokonskaia*," literally translated as "white steed." The princess is thus marked as a relative and semantic opposite to the ass. Just as the ass's braying marked the beginning of Myshkin's recovery, the princess's comments will signal Myshkin's return to madness; for she is presented as having ultimate authority for the social milieu described in the novel, and Myshkin must gain her approval in order to marry Aglaya Epanchin. Although she never becomes a fully embodied character in the novel—she is just a talking name attached to the notion of high-society matriarchy—it is she who passes final judgment on Myshkin when he smashes the Chinese vase and suffers an epileptic fit in her presence: "Well, there's good and bad in him, but if you want to know my opinion, more of the bad. You can see for yourself what kind of person he is—a sick person!" (459).[18]

Belokonskaya is also drawn into a semantic relationship with Prince Myshkin as the only *princess* who is an even remotely significant character in the novel. What is more, Myshkin, as will be shown, is very clearly associated with the figure of the donkey; so that Prince Myshkin is to Princess Belokonskaya as a donkey is to a white steed.

"Ass" (*osël*) and "idiot" (*idiot*) are codified as synonyms in Russian (although in the context of *The Idiot* each term takes on a wider field of meaning): donkeys are traditionally associated with dull-wittedness—perhaps because of their stubbornness, perhaps because of the abuse they can endure. Myshkin's pronounced affection for donkeys leads to his further identification with the creatures, in both his own and others' eyes. Madam Epanchin defends his strange orientation to her girls, who find Myshkin's tale laughable: "On the contrary, there's nothing strange here, any one of us could fall in love with an ass.... It already happened in mythology" (48). The statement proves to be prophetic: one of the girls, Aglaya, *will* fall in love with an ass, Myshkin. Moreover, in the subsequent exchange, Myshkin himself states that he "stands for the ass"—apparently meaning that he reaffirms his warm feelings for this animal and wishes to defend it—while Madame Epanchin draws attention to the association of Myshkin with the ass, if only to deny that this was her intention:

> "I still stand for the ass: the ass is a kind and useful person [*A ia vsë-taki stoiu za osla: osël dobryi i poleznyi chelovek*]."

"And are you kind, Prince? I'm asking out of curiosity," asked the general's wife. They all began laughing again.

"Again that cursed ass has turned up; I wasn't even thinking about him," cried out the general's wife. "Prince, please believe me, I didn't mean to make any..."

"Allusion? Oh, I believe you, without doubt!" (49)

The allusion has been made, however, as the laughter and Myshkin's response make clear. Moreover, Myshkin has himself laid the groundwork for a metaphoric association between himself and an ass, by calling the ass a "useful *person*" (my italics). This metaphor, Myshkin as ass, proves to be no less central to the novel's meaning than the much-discussed connections between Myshkin and the figures of Don Quixote and Christ (see below).

If for Myshkin the ass is most significant in its capacity to stand for the values of hard work and humility, within the novel as a whole this metaphor adds a much more complex and ambivalent meaning. To begin with, Myshkin is not the only character in *The Idiot* associated with the ass. At Nastasya Filippovna's name-day party Ferdyshchenko tells General Epanchin: "Don't worry, Your Excellency, I know my place: if I said that we're the Lion and the Ass from Krylov's fable, then I am of course taking the role of Ass for myself, while Your Excellency is the Lion . . ." (117). There is no humility here, however: the codified opposition of lion (powerful ruler and lawmaker, center of official discourse) to ass (lowest of the low, but impudent purveyor of unofficial discourse) sets up a situation of carnivalesque overturning of authority. In Krylov's fable, the lion, aged and no longer able to defend itself, is anticipating a kick from an ass — an insult to which death would be preferable;[19] at the name-day party, Ferdyshchenko insults his social superiors without any apparent retribution: it is expected of him, it is his role. *The Idiot* sets up an implicit comparison between Ferdyshchenko and Myshkin on the basis of this ass motif. Myshkin as ass is humble and seeks to serve, yet the result of his actions is to upset Petersburg society catastrophically; Ferdyshchenko as ass is an impudent buffoon, and yet there is a place for him in high society, his insults add salt to Petersburg life without being consequential. His kind of upsetting can be repeated, indeed, appears to be part of the natural life of this society.

The ass motif also leads to intertextual allusions. That Madame Epanchin's remark about falling in love with an ass refers to Aglaya becomes apparent only as the novel proceeds, in retrospect. But her reference to mythology invokes *The Golden Ass* of Apuleius,[20] and this raises the question of what meaning the Apuleian subtext might bring to *The Idiot.*

In Chapter 10 of *The Golden Ass*, while Lucius (in the form of an ass) is earning a good living for both himself and his master by performing tricks, a young, attractive, and biped society matron falls in love with him and purchases a night of erotic pleasure. This transaction is most agreeable to Lucius, but when his master decides to incorporate the new feat in a public spectacle — to be enacted with a murderess already condemned to death — Lucius runs away. It is at this point that Lucius, in response to prayer, is returned to human shape, whereupon he devotes himself to the religious cult of the Goddess Isis.

Madame Epanchin's allusion to this rather pornographic episode in *The Golden Ass* is surprising, since no noble lady of her time would have read the work, let alone discussed it with her daughters; her source must have been some expurgated paraphrase of the ancient work.[21] But if Mme. Epanchin does not know what she is talking about, Dostoevsky and his readers most likely do, and *The Golden Ass*, in its scandalous, unexpurgated form should be taken as a subtext to *The Idiot.* Madame Epanchin, with her habit of stating frankly whatever comes into her mind, of speaking and acting whimsically and in contradiction to herself, earns for herself a range of possible utterances that makes her perfect for this task of uttering the author's word under cover of her own.

At the level of generic models, *The Golden Ass* is exemplary of the kind of parodical undermining of established, serious genres of discourse we associate with Dostoevsky (Bakhtin, *Problems*, esp. chap. 3). As a lowly and ignoble animal, a stupid animal, the ass is tailor-made for carnivalizing roles (this is the thrust of the buffoon Ferdyshchenko's own identification with the ass). The theme of love in *The Golden Ass* encompasses both an extreme carnality, involving harlots, procuresses, and bestiality, and more sublime versions: the legend of Cupid and Psyche, and worship of the Goddess Isis. Dostoevsky's notebooks suggest that one of the organizing thematic principles of *The Idiot* is the desire to show "*Three* kinds of love in the novel: 1) Passionate and spontaneous love — Rogozhin. 2) Love out of vanity — Gania. 3) Christian love — the Prince" (*Pss* 9:363; *Notebooks*, 220).[22]

The Idiot stages a provocative association between this Classical, pagan subtext and the novel's much-discussed Christological dimension; as is well known, Dostoevsky referred to Myshkin as "Prince Christ" in his manuscripts ("Primechaniia," *Pss* 9:365). The accompaniment of Myshkin's entry into Switzerland by the braying of an ass, and his entry into Petersburg society with the *story* of an ass, recall Christ's entry into Jerusalem on an ass (John 12:14–15; Matthew 21:1–7). This moment, the salvation of the daughter of Zion (Jerusalem) and the wedding of the daughter of Zion with her King, is traditionally interpreted as the fulfilment of the prophecy found in the Old Testament book of Zechariah (9:9). For Nastasya Filippovna, remember, Myshkin's offer of marriage, and through it a salvation of sorts, is the fulfilment of something long ago dreamt-of, like the arrival of Christ (144; cited above). Gania tells Myshkin he plans to become "King of the Jews" through the capital he will gain by marrying Nastasya Filippovna (105), and while his model is presumably Rothschild rather than Christ, his expectations take on added irony when viewed in this context.[23] When Myshkin breaks the vase, that too is no accident but the *fulfilling of a prophecy*: "But we must mention a certain odd sensation which struck him at that very moment and stood out clearly among the crowd of all the other dim and strange feelings: neither the shame, nor the embarrassment, nor the fear, nor the suddenness of it struck him as much as the sense of a prophecy come true!" (451).

The ass is also involved in biblical motifs of animal sacrifice. In Exodus 13, after the Jews have left Egypt, certain commandments regarding animal — and human — sacrifices are made: "Thou shalt set apart unto the Lord all that openeth the womb; every firstling that is a male, which thou hast coming of a beast, shall be the Lord's. And every firstling of an ass thou shalt redeem with a lamb; and if thou wilt not redeem it, then thou shalt break its neck." This passage sets up an economy of sacrifice that is echoed by Nastasya Filippovna's situation in *The Idiot.* By the novel's end, for Myshkin (ass) to marry Aglaya and have happiness, it will be necessary for Nastasya Filippovna (sheep) to sacrifice herself by staying with Rogozhin. After Myshkin receives a slap from Gania which had been directed toward Varia — that is, after he sacrifices himself for her — he is called a sheep: " 'He'll be sorry!' shouted Rogozhin, 'you'll be ashamed of yourself, Gania, for insulting such a... sheep! (he couldn't find another word)' " (99). The narrator's explanation of Rogozhin's diction even underlines the epithet. Rogozhin will himself later raise a knife against Myshkin, but fail to carry out the murder attempt; one cannot help wondering whether Myshkin's death would have made Nastasya Filippovna's unnecessary. (It should be recalled that both the ass and the sheep are animals associated with Christ.)

When Myshkin and Aglaya, with real dread, anticipate what could go wrong at the evening party, Myshkin's choice of words is especially suggestive: " 'Listen, Aglaya,' said the Prince, 'I think you're very afraid for me, afraid that tomorrow I might flunk [*srezat'sia*]... in that society?' " (435). Aglaya objects to the use of the word "*srezat'sia*," ". . . a schoolboy's word, a rotten word! I suppose that tomorrow you intend to use such words." Her objection underlines Myshkin's choice of this word, here apparently meaning "to flunk," but through its root understandable as a kind of *cutting*; as such, Myshkin links his impending disaster at the party with the motifs of violence, murder by knife, and sacrifice deployed throughout the novel. At the same time, the schoolboy's rhetoric here recalls the frame of reference invoked by Mme. Epanchin when she tested the Prince's storytelling abilities: "You've sure passed the exam!" she cries out when he has finished (65).

At least one more extratextual association is called forth by Myshkin's affection for the ass, and also by the last words he utters before being stricken by a fit at the Epanchin salon: "Oh, it's just that I can't express it—but how many beautiful things there are at every step, things that even the most lost man finds beautiful? Look at a child, look at God's sunrise, look at the grass, how it grows, look into eyes that are looking at you and love you..." (459). These words are reminiscent of "The Canticle of the Sun" of Saint Francis of Assisi, "God's Fool," who referred to his body as "brother *ass.*" V. E. Vetlovskaia has shown that the figure of St. Francis was one of Dostoevsky's models for the character of Father Zosima in *The Brothers Karamazov.*[24] There is reason to suspect the same is true of Myshkin in *The Idiot.* It must of course be acknowledged that, to the extent a character is oriented toward the image of Christ and saintliness, he will inevitably display certain expected characteristics.[25] Still, it is striking that virtually all the features of St. Francis that Vetlovskaia discerned in Zosima can be found in Myshkin, together with others not mentioned by Vetlovskaia.

St. Francis was remarkable for his insistence that he and his followers live in poverty, and that they serve as itinerant preachers. While Myshkin does return to St. Petersburg in order to lay claim to an inheritance, he arrives with very little money, inadequate clothing, and no concern regarding shelter and food. He jokes with the Epanchin women about being a philosopher and having come to Petersburg to teach, while Madame Epanchin declares to him she believes that God has sent him to her from Switzerland (70). The prince takes twenty rubles from General Epanchin with the humility of a holy man accepting an offering, that is, with none of the ambivalence and resentment of a typical hypersensitive Dostoevskian hero or, for that matter, of Dostoevsky himself (30).

St. Francis was from childhood on a fanatic in his regard for the chivalric life, and after his conversion used chivalric metaphors to describe his religious quest: "Francis likened his followers to the knights of Charlemagne and Roland. [. . .] Francis, like any knight, pledged his love and fidelity to a chosen lady: Lady Poverty" (Cunningham, 60). A chivalric frame of reference, most often associated with *Don Quixote*, is invoked by Aglaya's free reading of Pushkin's "The Poor Knight" ("Bednyi rytsar' "), in which Myshkin is cast as a *poor knight.*[26] The Prince's impulse to defend Nastasya Filippovna deserves to be called Quixotean.

St. Francis was also distinguished by a special capacity for feeling the suffering of others. While he extended his love and empathy to animals and inanimate objects, above all he was blessed to participate in the sufferings of Christ. The holy stigmata which St. Francis experienced near the end of his days were the apotheosis of this gift. In *The Idiot* no character feels more acutely the sufferings of others than does Myshkin;[27] moreover, his obsession with the thoughts and feelings of people who are about to be executed begins a train of associations that ultimately leads to Christ in the Garden of Gethsemane, awaiting his arrest and crucifixion.

When one thinks of St. Francis, one recalls among others those frescoes and episodes from *Little Flowers* depicting him as a friend and preacher to wild beasts, and especially birds. It is in the spirit of St. Francis for Myshkin to call the children gathered around him in Switzerland "little birds."

St. Francis opposed precisely those aspects of Roman Catholicism against which Myshkin rails before shattering the Chinese vase — its pursuit of temporal power, progressive institutionalizaton, and intellectualization. He exhorted his friars to be "*idiota et subditus omnibus* (unlettered and subject to all)" (Cunningham, 16). This very positive association with the term "idiot" is especially noteworthy, since in *The Idiot* Dostoevsky creates an analogous, nonnegative (or at least ambiguous) context for the word's interpretation.[28]

Perhaps it is not so much the question of a Franciscan subtext to *The Idiot* as one of values shared by St. Francis and Dostoevsky's "*polozhitel'no prekrasnyi chelovek*" (positively beautiful person).[29] Unlike the case of *The Brothers Karamazov*, here there is no overt signal of an allusion to St. Francis. But even if St. Francis was not a conscious source for the figure of Myshkin, the Russian prince makes more sense when placed side by side with the saint, precisely in regard to the theme of corporality. For St. Francis's response to being in this world was a joyful asceticism, one which did not deny the body.[30]

At this point it is necessary to reflect on the common threads running through the various manifestations of the ass motif touched on above. According to Olga Freidenberg, the meanings of the ass in Judeo-Christian and pagan mythological contexts derive from common ancient cultic beliefs.[31] Her central point, especially relevant to the figure of Myshkin, is that "the image of salvation is inseparably connected with the image of fertility, especially that of the sexual act; saviors are gods of marriage and agriculture" (496). Myshkin's eventual failure as a savior has often been related to his failure as a man, his inability to couple in a fruitful marriage: "I can't marry anyone, I'm ill," he tells Gania (82), and earlier in the novel he states to Rogozhin that he does not know women at all (14).[32]

At a mythopoetic level, then, the ass motif in *The Idiot* represents the fulfilment of a prophecy of salvation, the conjunction of two temporalities spanned by a wish and a promise. This salvation takes the form of a god's arrival in corporeal form, a sexual coupling and fertilization, a marriage, and a rebirth. The St. Francis complex may seem incompatible with this generalization, but its key feature is that it represents a spirituality which, ascetic to be sure, has managed to accept corporality with a smile, a joke: "Brother Ass." This is no trivial feat; it means overcoming that terrible, faith-threatening paradox presented in the Holbein painting of Christ, a copy of which hangs in Rogozhin's home, and which is at the center of the novel's thematics.[33]

Freidenberg's archetypical scenario can be seen as underlying the two stories of coupling and salvation comprising the surface structure of *The Idiot*—Myshkin and Marie, Myshkin and Nastasya Filippovna. In each, however, it is idealized or, better, disembodied in the process of its transformation and surfacing in the conscious actions of Myshkin. His epilepsy bears witness to a failure in incarnation, and his impulses in his relations with Marie and Nastasya Filippovna are curiously asexual: he is no fertilizing god. This defect is of little account in his relationship with the dying Marie, where, since there can be no question of consummation, it is enough to briefly play the role of lover. But the same strategy will not work with Nastasya Filippovna, who sees through him. What we are arguing here reverses the common interpretation of Myshkin's flaws holding that Dostoevsky made Myshkin ill so that this Christlike character would be believable as a man.[34] Christ *was* a fully bodied man, and it is the defect in Myshkin's own corporality that bars him from following the pattern of the Savior.

3 Author and Hero in Aesthetic Activity

The themes of authoring and incarnation so central to *The Idiot* find a fascinating theoretical treatment in the early philosophical fragment of Mikhail Bakhtin, "Author and Hero in Aesthetic Activity." This work of Bakhtin provides a helpful context for discussing the way these themes are woven together in *The Idiot*; more accurately, it was only while under the influence of Bakhtin's work that this dimension of Dostoevsky's novel grew visible to me.

According to Bakhtin, an author must by definition take a position outside his hero, one from which the exterior visages of body and soul can be given values as wholes. The creative process reveals itself in the aesthetic object in the tension between the hero's self-experience—his "I-for-myself"—and the hero as portrayed from the outside by an author, with the key formal moments being those where the author's excess of seeing, his transgredience to the hero's consciousness, is manifest. Against this ideal norm for the relationship between author and hero, Bakhtin discusses, with characteristic broad sweep, the value of the human body in history, which has altered depending upon whether the "idea of man" is founded either in *self*-experience or in the experience of the *other* human being" ("Author," 52; *Estetika*, 48).[35]

The scheme is as follows: in classical antiquity, says Bakhtin, this "idea" was anchored in the values of the other; it was the exterior visage of one's body and soul, perceived and evaluated in the consciousness of others, that mattered most, that was indeed one's self. "Everything corporeal was consecrated by the category of the *other*, and was experienced as something immediately valuable and significant; inner axiological self-determination was subordinated to being determined externally through the other and for the other: the *I-for-myself* was dissolved in the *I-for-the-other*" ("Author," 53; *Estetika*, 49). In stages marked by the appearances of the cult of Dionysus, Epicurianism, Stoicism, and finally Neoplatonism, an opposite extreme, "the highest point in the denial of the body—as my body" was achieved ("Author," 54; *Estetika*, 50). Bakhtin calls Neoplatonism "the purest and the most consistently prosecuted axiological comprehension of man and the world on the basis of pure *self*-experience: the universe, God, other people—all are no more than *I-for-myself.* Their own judgment about themselves is the most competent and the final judgment" ("Author," 55; *Estetika*, 50).

Relevant here are the changes that Bakhtin sees as having taken place in Christianity as it evolved through the centuries following Christ. Two trends are adduced: in one Neoplatonic tendencies predominate, meaning that "the other is first and foremost *I-for-myself*, and the flesh is in itself an evil—both in myself and in the other"; in the second, "Both principles of axiological relationship [values grounded in the self, and values grounded in the other] find expression in oneself as well as the relationship to the other" ("Author," 57; *Estetika*, 52). For Bakhtin, whose major point is that in art the representation of humans is special precisely in that it achieves a consummating perspective, one accepting a being's givenness in total, the second tendency was preferable, and he associates it with the Christianity of St. Francis of Assisi.[36]

Within the second trend, the paradox of the embodied, mortal god—a theme pushed to its extreme in *The Idiot* in the treatment of the painting by Holbein—is no longer faith-threatening. Recall that Ippolit, while wondering how witnesses of the crucified Christ could have possibly believed in his resurrection, notes that the early church maintained ". . . that Christ suffered not figuratively, but in reality, and that even his body was entirely and completely subjected on the cross to the laws of nature" (339). Dostoevsky's student Bakhtin answers: "Even God had to incarnate himself in order to bestow mercy, to suffer, and to *forgive*—had to descend, as it were, from the abstract standpoint of justice" ("Author," 129; *Estetika*, 113). The complex of associations that Freidenberg finds underlying the image of Christ's entry into Jerusalem on an ass can also be situated within this second tendency.

By the time of the Renaissance, however, the "I-for-myself" tendency had come to dominate Christianity. "The naive acceptance of the body characteristic of Antiquity could not be restored after all the inward experience accumulated in the Middle Ages; one could not help but read and understand St. Augustine along with the Classical authors . . ." ("Author," 58; *Estetika*, 53). Finally, argues Bakhtin, "In the following two centuries the position of authoritative 'outsidedness' with respect to the body was definitely lost. In the Enlightenment [i.e., in Rousseau] the body degenerates at the end into an organism as the sum total of the needs of 'natural man' " ("Author," 58; *Estetika*, 53).

To return to *The Idiot*: Bakhtin's outline of this historical process also aptly limns the transformation of the deep mythic structure surrounding the ass image as it surfaces and is realized in the figure of Myshkin.[37]

Myshkin has no "authoritative 'outsidedness' with respect to the body." To him physical beauty is an enigma and a challenge, and he passes over it straight into the soul of the other.[38] Thus, on his first meeting with the Epanchin women, when he shows them the photograph of Nastasya Filippovna, Myshkin responds not to the woman's beauty, but to the suffering he reads in her eyes, portal to the inner self (69).

The initial situation of *The Idiot* presents Nastasya Filippovna as an object to be bartered for and exchanged among Totsky, Gania Ivolgin, General Epanchin, and Rogozhin. The arrangements they propose to her are all a sort of death, in which she would become an "I-for-an-other" whose values are hedonistic and socially pragmatic (there is little conflict between these values in high society as depicted by Dostoevsky). This is yet another sense in which all Nastasya's past and present suitors (and especially Rogozhin, the carouser and man of the flesh who comes to the name-day party with his packet of rubles) can be opposed to Myshkin.[39] Myshkin appears at the name-day party and addresses her *as she feels about herself*, not as an object of others: "You're not Rogozhin's woman!" (136). This is why Bakhtin calls Myshkin "the carrier of the *penetrative word*, that is, a word actively and confidently interfering in the interior dialogue of the other person, helping that person to find his own voice" (*Problems*, 242).

On the other hand, when Aglaya asks Myshkin to say something about her inner nature (as he has about her sisters), the prince responds:

> "I cannot say anything now; I'll tell you later."
>
> "Why? Is it noticeable?"

"Oh yes, it's noticeable; you are an exceptional beauty, Aglaya Ivanovna. You are so beautiful that it's frightening to look at you."

"Is that all? But what about her virtues?" insisted the general's wife.

"It's difficult to judge beauty; I am not yet ready for that. Beauty is an enigma." (66)

Myshkin cannot come to terms with beauty insofar as it is a value assigned only to the outer body.

Two other of Myshkin's most distinctive characteristics indicate a lopsided emphasis on the "I-for-myself." One is Myshkin's *iurodstvo*, his association (evidence in Dostoevsky's notebooks, where Myshkin is called "*iurodivyi*") with the characteristics of the holy fool.[40] For Bakhtin, "Being ashamed of rhythm and of form is the root of "*playing a fool* [*iurodstvo*]" ("Author," 184; *Estetika*, 105–6). To understand what is meant here, one needs to recall that in his discussion of author and hero in aesthetic activity Bakhtin attributes "formal rhythm" to the plane of the *author's* perspective ("Author," 216; "Avtor," 11); that is, form and rhythm together manifest a point of view outside and above the work, a point of view able to consummate the work (and the hero in it) as a whole. Bakhtin's definition of "playing the fool," then, involves being unwilling to give oneself up to the forms others would give one's life. (In this sense holy foolishness provides a context for interpreting Nastasya Filippovna as well; and the novel, for the later Bakhtin, becomes the holy fool among narrative forms.)

In Myshkin, "playing the fool" goes so far as to include rejection of that most constrictive of givens, one's own body. Myshkin's epileptic fits are just such a casting off of the body, as seen and perceived as whole by others: from the outside, Dostoevsky's narrator explains, the face appears distorted, the body is entirely taken over by convulsions, and the sufferer emits an unimaginable, inhuman howl (195); in the category of the other, *for* the other, the fit is a disturbing, uncanny event, a monstrosity. But the moment before the onset of a fit, with all its apocalyptic and revelatory implications, is the very summit of "I-for-myself" experience: "The feeling of life, of self-knowledge [*samopoznanie*], increased almost tenfold in these moments which lasted about as long as a flash of lighting" (188).

The second has to do with Myshkin's fascination with death. It is significant that the stories about capital punishment Myshkin tells at the Epanchin home attempt to represent the *internal* perspective on death; as he tells the Epanchins' servant,

"But you see the chief, most intense pain, might not come from the wounds, but from the fact that you know for sure that in an hour, then in ten minutes, then in half a minute, then now, right now—your soul will fly from your body, and you won't be a person any longer, and that all this is for sure; the chief thing is that it's *for sure*. When you put your head under the actual blade and hear it sliding above your head, now those seconds are the most frightening of all." (20)

Rather than depicting the death of the convicted man as others see it, he approaches the impossible—he attempts to relate death as an event experienced by an "I-for-myself." But as Bakhtin writes, in what has become a popular citation:

In the life I live and experience from within myself, my own birth and death are events which I am in principle incapable of experiencing; birth and death as *mine* are incapable of becoming events of my own life. Just as in the case of outward appearance, the point here is not merely the impossibility of experiencing these events in fact; the point is first of all that I lack any essential axiological approach to them. ("Author," 104; *Estetika*, 92)

Myshkin observes this limit in his storytelling, unlike, by way of example, Tolstoy in "Death of Ivan Ilych,"[41] and also unlike Ippolit in *The Idiot*; the latter's attempt to stage his own death, to finalize himself and transform his life into a self-authored aesthetic event becomes one of Dostoevsky's "scandal scenes." But while observing these limits, Myshkin nonetheless tests them, he pushes them to the brink, and this is one of his defining characteristics. It can be seen, to be sure, in his stories about capital punishment; but his story about the braying ass offers a situation no less extreme: if in his stories regarding capital punishment he steps into the paradox of representing that which can never be related to another person, human consciousness perceiving itself at the moment of its extinction, with the story of the braying ass he represents just as paradoxical a moment—the self witnessing its birth of consciousness. For he had been sent to Switzerland as a complete idiot, in a darkness from which, he impossibly *remembers*, he "was completely awakened by the ass's braying" (48).

In addressing the "I-for-myself" in others, whatever changes Myshkin is able to effect are only temporary, never decisive (Bakhtin, *Problems*, 242). Only an authoritative perspective from the *outside* is capable of consummating one as an aesthetic whole; and even then, unless one is dead or a hero in a relationship to an author (or God) who can see one's life-story as a whole, one's experiences of one's self will inevitably exceed the boundaries of the aesthetic form given by the other. The penetrative word, it seems, can only be a thing of a moment, a flash in which Nastasya Filippovna's "spirit" (her inner self as she lives it) recognizes itself in the image of her "soul" (her inner life as Myshkin has summed it up from the outside);[42] but so long as Nastasya Filippovna is alive, she cannot help but rebel against—or perhaps simply live beyond the bounds of—the aesthetic form Myshkin has given her soul: "Spirit breaks up soul from within . . . [*Tak dukh razlagaet vo mne samom dushu*]" ("Author," 126; *Estetika,* 111). Myshkin cannot join with her bodily; nor can he stand over her as creator, the author-restorer of her life-story, as he did to Marie, for to redeem her life as a consummated whole she must be, like Marie, dead. In this sense, it is Myshkin's attitude toward Nastasya Filippovna throughout the novel that presses her on to her violent death. What is really needed here is not aesthetic, but open-ended ethical activity.[43] But Myshkin's education in the Swiss dream-world has confounded the two.

4 The Swiss Connection: Dostoevsky and Rousseau

In Switzerland Myshkin's creative, transformative act was successful; transposed to Petersburg, however, it appears absurd, and its failure is of tragic consequence. Myshkin approaches the Petersburg milieu in a distinctively literary manner, he attempts to apply the Switzerland story, as a generic model, to his Petersburg characters. Of course it does not work: whereas the others Myshkin authored in Switzerland were children, and Myshkin himself was not far from being a child there,[44] the child is out of place in a novel of Petersburg. The ensuing narrative structure of redemption proves as fragile as the Chinese vase, and it too shatters under the heterogeneous forces brought to bear by Petersburg characters and their desires.

Such an implicit critique of the story of Marie and Myshkin's reeducation is in some senses puzzling: why should Dostoevsky wish to negate themes of forgiveness and love and the essential innocence of children? It is not these values as such that are criticized in the novel, however, so much as the way they come to be extracted from that very complex and ambivalent cluster of motifs, of soteriological significance, surrounding the image of the ass; the expurgation of those values of corporality grounded in the axiological position of the other; and their codification in the monologic generic model represented by the Swiss story. This generic model may be described as an idyllic, Rousseauean novel of education—a "didactic-pedagogic novel" in Bakhtin's words ("Forms of Time," 224–36).[45]

Dostoevsky's intellectual involvement with Rousseau was characteristic of his generation. Writes Iurii Lotman: "Dostoevsky was irrepressibly drawn to Rousseau, but he resisted that attraction and all his life debated with Rousseau, just as all his life he carried on a polemical dialogue with Belinsky" ("Russo," 603).[46] The most overt reference to Rousseau in *The Idiot* is the cycle of confessional stories told at Nastasya Filippovna's name-day party; unmistakable in this regard is Ferdyshchenko's tale, which closely resembles the "theft of the blue ribbon" episode in Rousseau's *The Confessions* (I. Lotman, "Russo," 604 n.).[47] *The Idiot*'s connection with Rousseau is broader than this one episode from *The Confessions*, however.

For a start, there is at least one further episode from *The Confessions* that is echoed in *The Idiot*, and which proves to be more central to the overarching plot of Dostoevsky's work. Toward the end of *The Confessions* (Book 12, 1764), Rousseau describes his friendship with de Sauttern, a young Hungarian who visited him at Motiers "in order to learn virtue in his youth through intercourse with me" (568). Shortly after this fellow leaves Motiers, Rousseau learns that "the so-called baron had imposed on me with a heap of lies." Rousseau was still unwilling to believe those who warned him that the Hungarian had been sent to spy on him, however, and in the following paragraph describes an episode in which he, Rousseau, attempted to come to the defense of de Sauttern. The situation he describes cannot but recall Myshkin's own "Swiss story," and deserves to be cited at length:

> Immediately after his departure the maid at the inn at Motiers, where he dined, declared that she was pregnant by him. She was such a dirty slut, and Sauttern, who was generally esteemed and respected as a decent and well-behaved young man, so particularly prided himself on his cleanliness, that everyone was shocked by her effrontery. The most attractive women in the district, who had vainly lavished their charms upon him, were furious, and I was beside myself with indignation. I made every effort to get the impudent woman arrested, offering to pay all expenses and go bail for Sauttersheim. I wrote to him strong in the conviction, not only that her pregnancy was not of his doing, but that

> it was a pretence, and that the whole business was nothing but a trick on the part of his enemies and mine. I asked him to return to the district to confound the creature and whoever was prompting her. I was surprised at the weakness of his reply. He wrote to the pastor whose parishioner the slut was, and tried to hush the affair up. In view of which I ceased to interest myself in the matter, being greatly surprised that so debauched a man could have had sufficient control of himself to make me believe in his decency throughout our very close intimacy. (Rousseau, 570)

If indeed Dostoevsky had Rousseau's *The Confessions* in mind as he wrote *The Idiot*, it hardly seems possible this episode would have escaped his attention. Here is a story, the facts of which are quite like those in the story of Marie: a local girl is seduced and made pregnant by a man who leaves town. But what a difference between the reactions of Myshkin, and those of the self-proclaimed virtuous man, Jean-Jacques! In the end, Rousseau says nothing of the fate of the abandoned woman, but excuses his former friend on grounds that would be repugnant to Dostoevsky: "But while I deplore the fate of that unhappy young man, I shall never cease to believe that he was a gentleman by birth, and that his disreputable behaviour was only the effect of the situations into which he fell" (Rousseau, 571).

Rousseau's *The Confessions* are an extreme attempt at representing the self "for-oneself": "For I decided to make it [*The Confessions*] a work unique and unparalleled in its truthfulness, so that for once at least the world might behold a man as he was *within*" (Rousseau, 478; italics mine). A major thrust of *The Idiot*, we have suggested, was to demonstrate the bankruptcy of such a project (the same motivation is even more obvious in the I-narrated "Notes from the Underground" and *The Adolescent*). Any reader of *The Confessions* is likely to draw the same conclusion, given the work's inconsistencies and omissions, its polemicism, and perhaps even Rousseau's nagging problems with his own body.

At a more general level, in choosing Switzerland for the setting of Myshkin's education and the tale of Marie, Dostoevsky provokes association with Rousseau as a theorist of education and citizen of Geneva.[48] It may be no accident that Dostoevsky, who had been thinking about his next novel as he traveled in Western Europe, began actual work on *The Idiot* after arriving in Geneva ("Primechaniia," *Pss* 9:338).

Myshkin's recovery comes about through walks in nature: it is a process of transition from feeling outside the movement of a nature in which all is alien, "*chuzhoe*," to a feeling of oneness; that is, it follows a model of transformation reflecting the values of the idyll of pre-Romanticism or Sentimentalism. Through the work of the Swiss author, Salomon Gessner, this genre became associated with Switzerland more than with any other Western European nation; and it hosted that constellation of values which fed directly into Rousseau's theories regarding "natural man" (see Hibberd, esp. 2, 53), yet another context within which the notion of idiocy (as opposed to education and worldliness) can take on positive value. In typical fashion, Dostoevsky puts the words of truth into one of the least intelligent, most roguish characters in his novel when he has Keller reproach the prince: "Oh, Prince, how brightly and innocently, one might even say pastorally, you still look at life!" and "Oh, Prince, to what a degree you still understand people in a Swiss manner, so to speak" (257).

The opposition between Switzerland and Petersburg in *The Idiot* thus comes to reflect Rousseau's opposition between nature and culture. Myshkin in his Swiss story also asserts that telling the children the whole truth about Marie — that is, educating them about sex at a tender age — is the proper thing to do; his story advances the notion that people are by nature good, and in general replicates the nature-culture opposition we associate with Rousseau.[49] This opposition is playfully manipulated and rendered ambivalent in the body of *The Idiot*, however: Dostoevsky has much of the novel's action take place on the boundary between the two categories, such as in the park of Pavlovsk and on verandas; indeed, Pavlovsk itself, where a Petersburg population inhabits a green space with Swiss architecture, can be seen as an ambivalent combination of Swiss and Petersburg features.[50]

But perhaps the broadest association with Rousseau may be found in the central metaphors of execution and apocalypse operating in the novel.[51] As an author-figure, Myshkin seeks immediately to impress his addressees with a highly privileged knowledge. He speaks to the Epanchin women of the special experience of living through one's own death, of being certain one is to die, then surviving. The description of how it feels to suffer an epileptic fit — narrated in free indirect discourse, attached to Myshkin's consciousness (187–89) — suggests that the fits provide a revelatory experience every bit as valid as death. That Dostoevsky spoke of his own fits in very similar terms is well known:

S. V. Kovalevskaia has cited this utterance of Dostoevsky's: "All you healthy people [. . .] don't even suspect that there is such a sense of happiness as what we epileptics experience a second before an attack. Mohammed assures us in his Koran that he has seen and been in heaven. All those wise fools are convinced that he is simply a liar and fraud. But no! He isn't lying! He really was in heaven during a fit of the epilepsy from which he suffered, as do I." ("Primechaniia," *Pss* 9:442)[52]

It is not as an ominous bearer of bad tidings that Myshkin arrives in Petersburg armed with tales of death; rather, the tales are his claim to a certain authority, to wisdom: this extreme, otherworldly experience is what gives Myshkin the right to speak and to teach[53] (recall his admission, "I may really be a philosopher, and who knows, maybe I actually intend to teach..." [51]).

It has been shown that Myshkin's tales about the last moments of men condemned to death are modeled on Hugo's *Le dernier jour d'un condamné* (1829).[54] The extreme, paradoxical goal of Myshkin's discourse distinguishes this episode in *The Idiot* from Hugo's text, however. Hugo's short novel is written in the first person, and was originally published with a preface that suggested the work might actually be the writings of a man condemned to death. As such, there is at least an attempt to coordinate the time and conditions of the condemned man's writing with the events he describes: the narrative is broken off as the condemned man writes that he hears the steps of those coming to take him to the guillotine. While there are moments in which the narrator anticipates his death—writing, for instance, of how the blade will cut through his neck muscles and vertebrae—this moment cannot be the *end* of his narrative, as it is for Myshkin's.

We have already discussed the manner in which the tale about the braying ass performs the same limit-stretching function in regard to beginnings. David Bethea has aptly called Myshkin "a character of beginnings (he offers Nastasya Filippovna 'new life') and ends (he is obsessed by thoughts of execution and death); but not the continuous middle" (*Shape of the Apocalypse*, 124). The attempt to ground an authoritative discourse in the experience of such extreme moments can also be associated with Rousseau. As Alex de Jonge puts it, Rousseau deserves the title of "founding father of the *intensity cult.* While placing as his [Rousseau's] supreme good the notion of authenticity of experience, he [Rousseau] suggests that it is intensity of emotional experience that provides the means of authentication. Authenticity and emotional experience are inseparable" (221). In Rousseau's *The Confessions*, there are several instances in which Rousseau, convinced that he is on the verge of death, resolves to change his life and alter his relations with others. This is not the case of an agnostic who senses the proximity of death, catches a fright, and turns to prayer; rather, an acute awareness of his own death gives meaning to Rousseau's life and weight to his words: "I can well say that I did not begin to live until I looked on myself as a dead man" (218; see also 337, 460).

Dostoevsky's own extreme life-experiences and his attraction to Hugo's *Last Day* (to which he alluded while himself on the scaffold; see note 54 above), show that he certainly had an investment in this aspect of Rousseau's life and thought; witness once again the letter to Dostoevsky's brother of December 22, 1849:

> It's true! That head which acknowledged and grew accustomed to the lofty demands of the spirit, that head has already been cleft from my shoulders. What remains is memory and forms which I have created but not yet incarnated. They are tormenting me, it's true! But in me have remained a heart and the same flesh and blood that can also love and suffer and desire and remember, and that is still life! On voit le soleil! (*Pss* 28[1]:162)

Seeking to explain the radical change that has taken place in his life, he writes: "You see, today I was in the presence of death, I lived three-quarters of an hour with that thought, I was living my last moment, and now I live once again!" (*Pss* 28[1]:163).

Early in *The Idiot* Myshkin tells the Epanchin women of an acquaintance who, quite like Dostoevsky, was sentenced to death and then spared at the last moment.

> But he said that nothing was harder for him at the time than the constant thought: "What if I did not have to die! What if life were returned to me—what an eternity! And it would all be mine! I would keep an account of every minute, I would waste nothing!" He said that that thought degenerated into such anger in him that he began to wish that they would shoot him sooner. (52)

Aglaya asks: " 'Well, what did he do with this wealth afterwards? Did he "account" for every minute?' 'Oh no, he told me himself—I asked him about it—he didn't live like that at all and lost a many, many minutes' " (53). In this dialogue it emerges, however, that the prince believes that he could live up to such an oath. This conviction, and the linkage of death, discursive authenticity, and a new life is rendered problematic as the novel proceeds: every attempt to wield a final word on the basis of such intense experiences (each more parodic and ridiculous than the last) fails.

Indeed, a whole series of character-storytellers in the novel attempt to base authoritative discourses aspiring to a "final word" on their own apocalyptic visions. Such is the case with Ippolit's suicide speech, "My necessary explanation," in which "there won't be one word of a lie, but all a single truth, final and triumphant"; Lebedev's occupation with the biblical Book of the Apocalypse is another instance. Myshkin's own Petersburg authoring is grounded in his "death" and "rebirth" in Switzerland. It is therefore telling that, after breaking the Chinese vase, Myshkin feels compelled to relate the whole "truth" to the people around him, a communicative gesture no less absurd than Ippolit's.

This fragile and precious vase may be seen as a symbol of Myshkin's own life in the Petersburg world, via an implicit allusion to 2 Corinthians 4:7: "We are no better than pots of earthenware to contain this treasure." Thus, when the vase is shattered, Madame Epanchin remarks: "What a disaster! Even a person's life must come to an end, and here we've gotten upset over a clay pot!" (455); and later, when Aglaya and Nastasya Filippovna confront one another in Myshkin's presence, Nastasya says: "Well, take your *treasure*..." (474; emphasis mine).[55] The biblical figure of speech presents just the sort of problematic regarding incarnation we have found central to Myshkin's character. Moreover, Myshkin's strongest sensation as the vase breaks is one of a "prophecy fulfilled" (451), which echoes Myshkin's (and Dostoevsky's own) reference to the epileptic Mohammed, to whom were revealed the dwellings of Allah in less time than it took for a spilled pitcher to empty its contents (189). At the same time, this "prophecy fulfilled" is but the realization of Aglaya's warning, and the apocalyptic moment collapses into another scandal scene.

Michael Holquist writes of *The Idiot*:

> The constant collapse of privileged moments gives a special meaning to that other central metaphor of the book, the Apocalypse of St. John. It is present in Dostoevsky's book not because of the flaming end it prophesizes. The horror consists rather in the discovering that there *are* no ends that give meaning, just as there are no beginnings." (113)

If we recall the series of stories Myshkin tells at the Epanchin home, they were *all* about beginnings and endings that gave meaning; and precisely for this reason, as Holquist suggests, they all "collapse." These stories, a calling card brought from Switzerland, gained the prince entry to Petersburg society, but proved inadequate as models for new stories to be authored in this rougher environment.

Myshkin's failure in Petersburg is the failure of an author who has employed an inadequate genre and corresponding worldview. For Dostoevsky, not just this inadequate genre but the sort of enterprise we have described, *as a mode of operation*—the codification and reapplication in the Russian context of a story that worked in the west—is also associated with the name of Rousseau; writing to Strakhov about the Paris Commune in May of 1871, for instance, Dostoevsky remarks: "In essence it's all that same Rousseau and the dream of re-creating the world through reason and experience (positivism)" (*Pss* 29[1]:214).[56]

5 The Petersburg Connection: Dostoevsky and Gogol

In the very first pages of the novel Rogozhin had warned Myshkin that the cloak which kept him warm in Switzerland would not suffice for the harsh Russian climate. Now we might suspect that this coat is charged with literary significance, and that on the novel's plane of metapoetic meaning Rogozhin's warning was equivalent to stating that a Swiss generic framework simply will not do for a Petersburg tale. Here Rogozhin is a teacher offering both a lesson on how to treat the body and a lesson in poetics. It is a moment that leads us to consider a connection with Dostoevsky's own most significant native literary teacher, an author for whom the issue of corporality took on fatal importance—Nikolai Gogol.

Myshkin's delight in the mechanics of writing associates him with Akaky Akakievich, hero of the paradigmatic Petersburg tale (and object of parody in Dostoevsky's first novel), Gogol's "The Overcoat";[57] so too does Myshkin's projected marriage to Aglaya Epanchin: "*epancha*" is a kind of cloak, and in Gogol's tale Akaky looks upon his new overcoat as a wife. In part 4 of *The Idiot*, especially, allusions to Gogol proliferate. Some are overt, like the narrator's discussion of Podkolesin, hero of Gogol's "Marriage" ("Zhenit'ba"), and General Ivolgin's quotation from *Dead Souls* at the onset of his stroke (383, 418); others are less overt, such as Gania's solitary Chichikovian entrechat, danced to celebrate his renewed prospects with Aglaya (400).

Gogol himself experienced, or claimed to experience, a revelational change in his life while living in the Catholic West (Rome), after which he returned to Russia to teach. In a letter to Sergei Aksakov, which was available to Dostoevsky in the collection of reminiscences and letters published in 1856 by Kulish, Gogol used the very same vase metaphor from 2 Corinthians 4:7 echoed in the Chinese vase scene to describe his own condition: "I hear and know glorious moments" he said regarding his work on *Dead Souls*; "The holy will of God has become clear to me here" (Aksakov, 50; Kulish, 272). In asking for Aksakov's help he claimed to "have the right, and feel so in my soul" (Aksakov, 50; Kulish, 272). He requested that Aksakov's son Konstantin and Mikhail Shchepkin come to Rome and bring him back to Moscow: "They will bring with themselves a clay vase; of course, this vase is now all cracked, rather old, and barely holding together, but in this vase is contained a treasure, one which must be preserved" (Aksakov, 51; Kulish, 273). The tragedy of Myshkin as a teacher and self-declared prophet thus reflects the tragedy of Gogol.

In Dostoevsky's metapoetic novel, Petersburg becomes the dialogizing and ultimately destructive context for the Rousseauean tale of Marie. When the ending does come for Myshkin, it is not of his own making. The plot he has sought to author has been subsumed by the plot that is to be realized in spite of himself, Dostoevsky's plot. In this sense the powerful scene of Rogozhin and Myshkin going mad beside the slain Nastasya Filippovna—a very pictorial passage, and in its graphic details reminiscent of the Holbein painting—calls to mind the situation of Christ in Gethsemane, or that of the *liricheskii geroi* (lyric hero or poetic persona) in Pasternak's "Gamlet" ("Hamlet"), where the author has become a hero in his father's plot.

4

Aesthetics and Ethics in Tolstoy's *Anna Karenina*

Dostoevsky's *The Idiot* and Tolstoy's *Anna Karenina* are two peaks of the nineteenth-century Russian novel, and as scholars have long hinted with a footnote here, a few paragraphs there, each novel includes allusions to the other's author. In *The Idiot* Myshkin's name and patronymic match those of Tolstoy,[1] while his connections with the figure of Rousseau (see preceding chapter) recall Tolstoy's own widely acknowledged affinities.[2] General Ivolgin's imaginative tales about the Napoleonic invasion probably poke fun at the author of analogous historical fictions in *War and Peace*, the last parts of which were still emerging as Dostoevsky wrote *The Idiot.*

To be sure, parodic operations of this sort are far more characteristic of Dostoevsky than of Tolstoy,[3] and only with prodigious imaginative effort could *Anna Karenina* be read as chiefly a response to *The Idiot.* Yet, Tolstoy's novel about a fallen woman and a positive male hero who has set himself the task of living correctly echoes Dostoevsky's in a number of respects, not least of which are the structural roles given to motifs of the railroad and horses.[4] In Tolstoy's next (and last) full-length novel, *Resurrection*, Nekhliudov's attempt to redeem a fallen woman, and the eccentric and self-sacrificing path he takes to accomplish this feat (making him something of a *iurodivyi* [God's fool] in the eyes of others), recall *The Idiot* even more strongly; *Resurrection* could indeed be read as a belated, yet positive response to the ethical problems set out in *The Idiot.*[5] Finally, Dostoevsky devoted an unprecedented amount of space to a discussion of *Anna Karenina* in his *Diary of a Writer* (February and July–August 1877), even though as a rule he "endeavored to speak as little as possible about the current events in Russian literature" in this forum (*Diary*, 609; *Pss* 25:51).[6]

The two authors never met or corresponded, but they appear to have loomed large in one another's consciousness.[7] This suggests that their reciprocal attitudes might disclose something of each author's notions regarding his own poetics. The psychologist and scholar A. L. Bem has formulated these attitudes concisely: Tolstoy tried to "place Dostoevsky outside of art" ("Tolstoi v otsenke," 190), while Dostoevsky considered Tolstoy a consummate artist, but one lacking in moral insight.[8] Each admired the other in a backhanded way, praising features in the other's art that surpassed his own capabilities, yet viewing these same features as symptomatic of the other's shortcomings.

But how Tolstoy felt about Dostoevsky is of less importance to the present chapter—which is not a study in Tolstoevsky—than what is revealed by how he managed those feelings. In Tolstoy's stance Bem discerns a defensive reaction. His very unwillingness to come to terms with Dostoevsky as an artist, rather than as just a religious and philosophical thinker, reveals "a curious feature. . . . On the outside entirely immersed in questions of a religious-philosophical order, on the inside he answers first and foremost to questions of art" (Bem, "Tolstoi v otsenke," 189). Tolstoy's artistic activity, Bem suggests, can be split into two opposing aspects: an exoteric, referential dimension concerned with moral issues on the one hand, and an internal, perhaps hidden, metapoetic dimension on the other. Reams have been written on the first; I propose to show how the latter is manifest in *Anna Karenina*, and how the two aspects are related to one another in ways far more dynamic and complex than the model of surface and interiority indicates.

I will begin by tracing a series of overtly metapoetic passages portraying Anna Karenina as both reader and writer, and then proceed to the novel's more extensive treatment of the visual arts. Over the past twenty years—since, roughly, the invention of the term *metafiction*—a tradition of metaliterary interpretation has developed in Tolstoy studies regarding this aspect of the novel; my reading is more inclusive than previous studies, and it reaches different conclusions. Last, I will pursue the implicit—and at certain points explicitly thematized—interartistic comparison involved in the metaphoric association between literature and painting. In each instance, the pursuit of these metapoetic concerns results in a pressing need to deal with Tolstoy's ethical concerns—rather as was the case with Dostoevsky. Indeed, Tolstoy very deliberately makes it impossible to separate the metapoetic from the referential; " 'Ethics and aesthetics,' Tolstoy used to say, 'are two shoulders: one is raised, the other lowers—they ought to be kept even' " (Al'tman, *Chitaia Tolstogo*, 65).

I Anna Reading, Anna Writing

Two overtly metaliterary passages, one depicting Anna as a reader, the second, as an authoress, occur at highly marked moments in the plot structure of *Anna Karenina.*

The shift in Anna's psyche that makes the adulterous affair with Vronsky possible is associated with her act of reading an English novel on the train from Moscow to Petersburg. Tolstoy's treatment of Anna's projective reading opens a theme of the "pathology of novel reading" (notoriously associated with Emma of *Madame Bovary*[10]): "When she read of a member of Parliament making a speech, she wished to make that speech; when she read how Lady Mary rode to hounds, teased the bride, and astonished everybody by her boldness—she wanted to do it herself" (I, xxxix; 92).[11] But Anna is drawn beyond a temporary identification with literary characters. In the following passage Anna's thoughts about her own life are spliced with the novel she is reading:

> The hero of the novel had nearly attained to his English happiness of a baronetcy and an estate, and Anna wanted to go to the estate with him, when she suddenly felt that he must have been ashamed, and that she was ashamed of the same thing,—but what was she ashamed of? 'What am I ashamed of?' she asked herself with indignant surprise. She put down her book, leaned back, and clasped the paper-knife tightly in both hands. There was nothing to be ashamed of. She called up all her Moscow memories. They were all good and pleasant. She recalled the ball and Vronsky and his humble, enamoured gaze, and their relations with one another; there was nothing to be ashamed of. (I, xxix; 92)

The passage continues in the same vein, with Anna pathologically crossing the boundaries between the fiction she has been reading and her own life. And then: "She passed her paper-knife over the window-pane, then pressed its cold smooth surface against her cheek and almost laughed aloud, suddenly overcome with unreasoning joy." She has been using this knife to cut the pages of her book, and now she presses it to her cheek as though she were the book whose pages needed cutting.[12] Reading novels is thus implicated in what is arguably the *zaviazka* (tying of the knot) of Anna's relationship with Vronsky.

As Anna's life grows increasingly complex and contrary to the code of behavior customary in her circles, it also becomes worthy of treatment in a novel. Thus Betsy at one point tells Anna that Liza Merkalova "said that you are a real heroine for a novel" (III, xvii; 271). Later, while Dolly travels to visit Anna at Vronsky's estate, her fantasies en route repeat the scene of Anna's train ride, with the difference that Dolly's fantasies take Anna's romantic and novel-like life as their model: "[W]hile thinking of Anna's romance she invented an almost similar romance for herself with an imaginary, composite man who was in love with her" (VI, xvi; 552). If Anna had earlier fantasized about being Lady Mary, who "rode to the hounds," Dolly now encounters an Anna who is out riding (VI, xvii; 553), on an estate where "Tout-à-fait à l'anglaise" (VI, xx; 562).

By the time Anna dies, her mimetic desires have been realized — even if differently from how she had wished — or so the figures of speech Tolstoy attach to her suicide would suggest: "The candle, by the light of which she had been reading that book filled with anxieties, deceptions, griefs, and evil, flared up with a brighter light than before, lit up for her all that had before been dark, flickered, began to grow dim, and went out for ever" (VII, xxxi; 695). In this elaborate metaphor Anna's life is *both* the light and that which is being read by the light. Her life in the world has been articulated into a narrative shape on par with those presented in the novels she used to consume with envy, and she has herself been reading this narrative by the light that now goes out. The figure of speech thus only consummates what the nearly delirious entanglement of her life with those of the English novel she read on the train had begun.

No less significant is what has been omitted from the depiction of Anna's death. Compared with those of Ivan Ilych, Prince Andrei, or even Anna at the end of Book I when it appears she is mortally ill, this scene of final accounting lacks the motifs of revelation Tolstoy typically attaches to the death of major characters.[13] Not that the rhetoric of revelation is altogether absent: "[S]uddenly the darkness, that obscured everything for her, broke, and life showed itself to her for an instant with all its bright past joy"; and the candle's spurt of light before dying lights up for her "all that had before been dark." But her vision is quite different from what Ivan Ilych of "The Death of Ivan Ilych" or Prince Andrei of *War and Peace* see in their final moments. What has been revealed is circumscribed by Anna's own life; she flips back through the pages, but never reaches beyond the bounds of her own life, a life tainted even here with bookishness.[14]

The second instance occurs during the episode where Levin meets Anna and the two talk about art—certainly a critical moment in the novel's structure, this unique juncture of its Anna and Levin plot lines. Here it is disclosed that Anna has taken up writing children's literature (VII, ix; 629 and VII, x; 633–34). No mention is made of the content of her one composition to date, however, nor of its reception, nor, indeed, whether any children have ever seen it. We know only that the book is bound in morocco leather, inappropriate for a children's book and, given the lack of other information, a damning detail.

At the moment this book clearly serves as a prop with which the self-involved Anna presents herself to her visitors. Its function is akin to that of the portrait of Anna viewed by Levin before he meets Anna in the flesh: one is an iconic representation of the self Anna wishes to present to the world, the other an indexical sign valued for what it signifies to guests in her salon about the woman who has produced it. Any discussion of the book's capacity to educate and entertain children would be hypothetical and irrelevant. Anna herself likens the work to "those little baskets and carvings made in prisons" (VII, x; 633), an analogy both revealing and deceptive: revealing as a token of self-consciousness and a complaint against the society that has shut her out ("the hardships of her situation," as Levin perceives it [VII, x; 634]); deceptive because there is something theatrical in this allusion to her role of an outcast, and also because it is a transparently conventional gesture of humility. The latter point is underlined through a juxtaposition of this scene with one occurring a very short time before, in which Kitty's brother-in-law Lvov utters similarly self-denigrating words; here, however, the narrator calls Lvov "not in the least affected from desire to appear, or even to be, modest, but . . . quite sincere" (VII, iv; 616).

These are but a central two of the widely scattered episodes and individual motifs connected with the making and consumption of art. Together they comprise a systematic treatment of questions of art, which emerges most widely in regard to the pictorial arts. Through his representation of the production and consumption of painting, Tolstoy inscribes into *Anna Ka-*

renina an extensive metapoetic commentary, the center of which are the chapters portraying the Russian artist Mikhailov in Italy.

2 The Author as Painter

It has been asserted that the character of Mikhailov was born of Tolstoy's contact with the painter Ivan Kramskoy, who completed two portraits of Tolstoy—one for Pavel Tetriakov, the other for Tolstoy—during the early stages of *Anna Karenina*'s composition. For a month in early fall of 1873, there were daily sittings and long conversations about religion and art. Soon after the novel appeared, the painter Ilya Repin wrote in a letter: "Yes, a man who was able to crawl into the soul of 'Mikhailov', and live his life, can of course figure us sinners out without much trouble. But you know, his Mikhailov looks an awful lot like Kramskoy" (Repin and Stasov, 29; see also Gol'dshtein, 139).[15]

But there are resemblances to others as well. Golenishchev attributes to Mikhailov an "Ivanov-Strauss-Renan" attitude toward Christ and religious art, thus associating Mikhailov with the Russian painter, Aleksandr Ivanov, whom Gogol had befriended in Rome some three decades before the fictional time frame of *Anna Karenina.*[16] In Shklovsky's novelistic reconstruction of the conversations between Kramskoy and Tolstoy, Tolstoy describes the work of Gogol's favorite painter in the same terms as are applied to Mikhailov: "It seems to me that it's as though Ivanov would remove the covers from his subject. Those covers, because of which the subject is not entirely visible. In removing the covers he tried not to harm the subject itself" (Shklovskii, *Lev Tolstoi*, 353). Mikhailov's statement, "I could not paint a Christ whom I had not in my soul" (V, xi; 429), is also reminiscent of words Gogol wrote about Ivanov in *Selected Passages*: "An artist can only depict what he has *felt*, and about which a full idea has already formed in his head" (Gogol, *Pss* 8:330).[17]

From the perspective of our study, this theme of painting begs to be understood as bearing metapoetic significance. It is therefore quite revealing that in a letter where Tolstoy informed Strakhov of both his progress with the novel and his new status as the subject for another artist's project, he compares himself to a painter: "As a painter needs light for the finishing touches, so I need inner light, of which I always feel the lack in autumn"

(*Tolstoy's Letters*, 265; *Pss* 62:49). The Mikhailov episode has in fact received deserved notice from a number of interpreters of *Anna Karenina*; a few have claimed it is a key to the work.[18] But readers have tended to be satisfied with pointing out a metaphoric association between the authoring of *Anna Karenina* and the authoring of Anna's portrait without exploring the implications of this self-reflexive moment in depth. As with any metaphor, there are differences to be accounted for as well as similarities, and in this case Tolstoy appears to have mobilized these differences quite deliberately. Positing a simple metaphoric equivalence between Mikhailov and his painting and Tolstoy and his novel greatly diminishes the metapoetic plane of meaning in *Anna Karenina.* The one does not simply stand for the other: there is an implicit comparison of Anna's various renditions, in portrait painting and in a novel, and the juxtaposition of these interartistic translations cannot help but lead to reflections on the semiotic capabilities and limitations of the respective art forms.

Tolstoy's complex system of juxtapositions appears to operate by a rule of three: three artists are depicted as characters in the novel (the consumptive artist Petrov, whom Kitty befriends abroad; Mikhailov, who paints Anna in Rome; and Vronsky); three of Mikhailov's paintings are described by the narrator, and so too is their reception by Anna, Vronsky, and Golenishchev; and there are three portraits of Anna (Mikhailov's, Vronsky's, and the one hanging in Karenin's office, painted by an unnamed and undescribed Petersburg artist). All these series of juxtapositions will be considered en route to a fuller understanding of the metapoetic significance of painting in *Anna Karenina.*

As one activity of the privileged class portrayed in the novel, and as grist for the mill of social talk, the theme of art is part of the novel's represented world; that is to say, the tastes of characters who consume art, and the aesthetic theories of characters who produce and criticize it, reflect the moral and intellectual qualities of these characters.

Vronsky takes up painting chiefly out of "a desire for desires — boredom" (V, viii; 422). Rather than a vocation, making, buying, and talking about paintings is one feature of the refined decadence of aristocrats living in a cultural playground. What other meaning could such creative activity hold in the context of a life where a day's most significant (and pleasurable) decision involves choosing the room in which to have supper (in a draft version; *Pss* 20:397)? When Vronsky's pursuit of an errant "poetics" is related, then, it is not just a commentary on poetics; it is also—perhaps chiefly—of characterological significance. Vronsky's entire mode of life dictates that he will be a poor artist by Tolstoy's standards, that "he could not imagine that it is possible to be quite ignorant of the different kinds of art and to be inspired directly by what is in one's own soul, regardless of whether what one paints belongs to any particular school" (423), and that "he found inspiration very readily and easily, and equally readily and easily produced paintings very similar to the school of art he wished to imitate." Vronsky is a master of convention, *comme il faut* in everything he approaches in a world where such behavior is prized, and painting is no exception.[19]

Mikhailov is in every respect Vronsky's opposite:

> He often heard the word *technique* mentioned, and did not at all understand what was meant by it. He knew it meant a mechanical capacity to paint and draw, quite independent of the subject-matter. He had often noticed—as now when his picture was being praised—that technique was contrasted with inner quality, as if it were possible to paint well something that was bad. He knew that much attention and care were needed not to injure one's work when removing the wrappings that obscure the idea, and that all wrappings must be removed, but as to the art of painting, the technique, it did not exist. If the things he saw had been revealed to a little child, or to his cook, they would have been able to remove the outer shell from their idea. And the most experienced and technical painter could never paint anything by means of mechanical skill alone, if the outline of the subject-matter did not first reveal itself to his mind. Moreover, he saw that if technique were spoken of, then he could not be praised for it. In all he painted and ever had painted he saw defects that were an eyesore to him, the results of carelessness in removing the shell of the idea, which he could not now remedy without spoiling the work as a whole. And in almost all the figures and faces he saw traces of wrappings that had not been entirely removed and that spoilt the picture. (V, xi; 431)

In this passage Tolstoy offers two competing views of artistic activity; where the Golenishchev-Vronsky view is described with overt irony, the accumulation of phrases such as "he saw" and "he knew" in the reporting of Mikhailov's thoughts supports the many readers who have inferred that Mikhailov's views express Tolstoy's own. Mikhailov is uneducated and uncomfortable in society; he knows nothing of "conventions," and his art is the better for it.[20] In the face of the above passage, Golenishchev's evaluation of Mikhailov—especially his notion that Mikhailov's ill-humor is due to jealousy of Vronsky's talent—is characteristic of the self-assured and shallow critic.

There is a provocative similarity between this scene of criticism and the treatment Tolstoy received from critics spanning the ideological spectrum (including Dostoevsky, as noted above): they saw him as a master of technique with little to say. Of *Anna Karenina* the radical critic Tkachev, for instance, wrote: ". . . I am not at all surprised that in his latest novel the writer with his usual brilliance and the perfection of the novelist's art has distinguished himself by an unbelievable—one might almost say scandalous—lack of content: but an author with the philosophy of the creator of 'War and Peace' must logically come to writing 'Anna Karenina' " (*Tolstoy: The Critical Heritage*, 253). The antiradical writer V. G. Avseenko departed from a different position, but reached similar conclusions:

> [Y]ou will not only fail to see in this wonderful novel the main trends of contemporary life, you will not only fail to meet a single character who would be typical of modern society (with the exception of Nikolai Levin . . .), but you will feel that all these people and their lives are organically opposed to the bases of our present-day reality and its main facet—the intelligent and moral middle class. (*Tolstoy: The Critical Heritage*, 263)[21]

Even the remarks about Mikhailov's lack of education, a traditional reproach against the practitioners of the figural arts (Hagstrum, 66), are relevant to Tolstoy, for by the standards of the "men of the forties" Tolstoy the autodidact was poorly educated.[22] In representing the confrontation between artist and critics, Tolstoy has done something analogous to what Pushkin did in "The Little House in Kolomna," though more directly and humorlessly.[23]

The issues raised in Golenishchev's critique of Mikhailov reemerge during Levin's visit to Anna in Moscow:

> The conversation touched on the new direction taken by art and the new illustrations of the Bible by a French artist. Vorkuev accused the artist of realism pushed to coarseness. Levin said the French had carried conventionality in art further than anyone else, and therefore attributed special merit to realism. In the fact that they had left off lying they perceived poetry. (VII, x; 632)

Eikhenbaum interpreted this comment metapoetically when he suggested that it reflected Tolstoy's own fear of falling into a vulgar realism or naturalism in *Anna Karenina*—a threat not faced in *War and Peace*, thanks to "the fact that all the family and domestic events and their sequels appeared against a background of historical events and philosophical discourses" (133). The implication is that Levin's words are Tolstoy's as well, and that for both a desirable poetics searches out a middle ground between the conventionality characteristic of an entrenched neoclassical tradition and literary naturalism. In both instances art forms are ranked on the basis of their referential function. At the same time, the implicit premises of Levin's remark—like those of Tolstoy's later theory of art—are heavily oriented toward the conative function of literature: he addresses issues of reception, especially the ethical effect of art. A tradition of lies deadens the addressees of art to "truth," it has a consciousness-lowering effect not unlike that assigned to automatization in the poetics of the Russian Formalists.

Nevertheless, the very fact that Levin's bon mot is well-received in Anna's drawing room problematizes any attempt to identify the view he expresses there with Tolstoy's. One must consider suspect a discussion of art and conventionality that takes place in the context of a seduction scene, as Levin's encounter with Anna is revealed to have been after the fact, and as are all of Anna's encounters with young men at this time. Here Levin in effect philosophizes in a whorehouse, since his tipsy entry to Anna's flat, which has followed an extravagant meal and gambling at the club, is described with overtones associating it unmistakably with a visit to a brothel.[24] The entire stay in Moscow is a stumble in the lives of Kitty and Levin, their own "fall," and Levin touches bottom when, briefly infatuated with Anna, he seeks to impress her with witty pronouncements about art.

Levin's opinions take on added irony if we consider that his visit to Anna is itself a breach of *social* convention; might not the peculiar emotional stimulation he feels this evening be the product of a psychological dynamic analogous to the one he attributes to the French in the realm of the arts? He has "left off lying," and in this he "perceives poetry." All the more so, since in the city Levin and Kitty have fallen into precisely the sort of reprehensible, conventional pattern of life that Levin has avoided until now. Only against the background of such a life could this visit be so delightful. What proved true of Vronsky's views on art, then, is no less the case with Levin: there is an intimate connection between the whole mode of life of this man, so awkward in society, so ill at ease with the conventions of courting and churchgoing and contemporary political life, and his understanding of the role of convention in art.

If, on the other hand, we are to discount the pragmatic orientation of Levin's remark and evaluate it on its own terms as a kind of incipient reception-theory of art, there remain some troublesome questions. Especially problematic in Levin's assertion, and in Tolstoy generally, is the very notion that in art it is *possible* to leave off lying altogether, that is, to abandon convention.[25] Tolstoy was not blind to his dependence on previous conventions in writing *Anna Karenina*: he wrote to Strakhov in May of 1873 that he was writing his "first novel" in a strict sense ("*Roman etot – imenno roman, pervyi v moei zhizni . . .*" [*Tolstoy's Letters*, 261; *Pss* 62:25]), that is, his first novel in a *conventional* sense[26] (which certainly cannot be said of *War and Peace*).

Nevertheless, it has been suggested that Tolstoy's whole signifying practice is an attempt to repudiate the inevitable role of convention in art. Krystyna Pomorska traced the operation of this practice at the lexical level in Tolstoy and found a tendency toward substituting iconic or "natural" signs, which indicate their referent by means of resemblance, for signs acquiring significance through the mediation of convention ("Tolstoy," 385). "For Tolstoy," she writes, "desirable communication occurs when the sign matches exactly the 'thing,' or, ideally, when signs are altogether absent" (387). The Tolstoyan quest for a simple, natural, and correct life is thus carried through to his literary language; in semiotic terms, "Tolstoy's attacks against highly developed culture can be viewed as a protest against overextended semiosis" (384).

This line of argument would lead one to expect in Tolstoy a certain privileging of the iconic arts — represented in the novel by painting — over literature and music, both of which are dominated by conventional signs. However paradoxical it might seem, according to such a ranking of the arts Mikhailov's Anna would be of a value superior to Tolstoy's own version, tainted as it is by the medium of verbal art; and one might expect Tolstoy to strive for pictorial effects in his representation of Anna and other characters. Indeed, the Platonic eye of Tolstoy's illiterate painter makes the creation of an image of the original an "unwrapping" and penetration of its outer shell;[27] the sign does not merely point to its referent by means of convention and resemblance, but *reveals* something not apparent even in the breathing original: "The only thing that showed she was not alive was that she was more beautiful than a living woman could be."[28]

Yet, one would not wish to overstate the special artistic vision of Mikhailov. It suffices to compare Tolstoy's painter with those of Gogol, who either are, or were once capable of becoming, artists in the high Romantic sense, in touch with a realm of transcendental, religious meaning—and for whom, recalling Chertkov of "The Portrait," easy profits from portrait painting were the devil's temptation.[29] Mikhailov is firmly grounded in this world, as the details of his domestic life, his concern over money, and his irritability all demonstrate. This is even more true of the other painters represented in the novel: of Vronsky nothing more needs to be added, while the consumptive artist Petrov, who paints a portrait of Kitty at the spa in Germany, not only fails to discover his subject's true, inner self, but falls in love with precisely that newly assumed and artificial persona of "ministering angel" which the healthy Kitty will discard.

What Mikhailov's portrait discloses in Anna is nothing transcendental, but the properties of a woman living entirely in this world—her sweetness, her seductiveness. Moreover, there has been something inherently pictorial about Anna from the start, as the description of her at the ball in Moscow, narrated from Kitty's perspective, suggests: "And her black velvet with rich lace was not at all conspicuous, but served only as a *frame*; she alone was noticeable—simple, natural, elegant and at the same time merry and animated" (I, xxii; 72; italics mine). Kitty finds her "simple" and "elegant"; and yet the figure of speech framing these words associates Anna with a portrait in a frame, not a natural, live object, but an aesthetic one.

Near the novel's beginning Levin had told Oblonsky: "I have never seen any charming fallen creatures, and never shall see any, and people like that *painted Frenchwoman* with her curls out there by the counter, are an abomination to me, and all these fallen ones are like her" (I, xi; 38); now, in the presence of a fallen woman who has been painted, Levin is enchanted. Mikhailov's portrait thus has the negative ethical value of assisting in Levin's temporary capitulation to Anna's charms.[30] However impressive the result, for Mikhailov, too, painting Anna was something of a fall—he found the sittings unpleasant, and the project diverted him from his major project depicting Pilate's Admonition.

3 The Sister Arts

The interartistic comparison staged in *Anna Karenina* has to be prejudiced by the circumstance that it is enacted entirely in language. No reader of the novel ever *sees* the portraits of Anna; Mikhailov's painting is but a fictive iconic sign represented by the conventional linguistic signs of a prose novel. It is, moreover, scantily described, and in such distinctively nonvisual terms that the term "ekphrasis" hardly seems applicable. Tolstoy's strategy for circumventing this dilemma is evident: instead of attempting to imitate in words the pictorial imitation of Anna, he emphasizes the effect the painting has on various viewers. This attention to the vicissitudes of viewer response is at once an evasion of certain insurpassable obstacles, and the implicit injection of an additional issue into the traditional comparativist project: one must deal with more than formal properties and inherent semiotic capabilities, Tolstoy suggests; one must take into account the addressee's responses as well, and they can be quite idiosyncratic.

This strategy of representing the production and consumption of figural art, while at the same time skirting what is implicitly recognized as the distinctive domain of the sister art, is in keeping with the thrust of Tolstoy's later writings on the theory of art. It also agrees with the views Levin expresses. During the intermission of the concert to which he has escorted his sister-in-law, Levin criticizes the new piece of music, which is based on *King Lear*:

> Levin maintained that the mistake of Wagner and of all his followers lay in trying to make music enter the domain of another art, and that poetry commits the same error when it depicts the features of a face, which should be done by painting, and, as an example of this kind of error, he mentioned a sculptor who carved in marble certain poetic phantasms arising round the pedestal of his statue of a poet. (VII, v; 620)

It is no accident that the passage cited above should recall an argument made by Gotthold Ephraim Lessing in *Laocoön*.[31] Also central to the novel's plane of metapoetic meaning is Lessing's famous distinction between the temporal and spatial dimensions in which the two arts operate:

> But if painting, by virtue of its symbols or means of imitation, which it can combine in space only, must renounce the element of time entirely, progressive actions, by the very fact that they are progressive, cannot be considered to belong among its subjects. Paint-

ing must be content with coexistent actions or with mere bodies which, by their position, permit us to conjecture an action. Poetry on the other hand . . . (Lessing, 77)

What makes this timeworn opposition interesting in *Anna Karenina* is the way Tolstoy has associated its terms with certain metaphysical and moral values and limitations.[32] Closer examination of Tolstoy's juxtaposition of the paintings described in the novel reveals that Levin's observation on the integrity of individual art forms might be missing the mark, and that, in spite of overt statements suggesting the contrary, Tolstoy finds a cunning merit in their mixture.

Three quite diverse paintings by Mikhailov are described: the large canvas in progress depicting Christ before Pilate; the portrait of Anna; and the painting of two boys fishing, which Anna and Vronsky purchase. The painting of Christ before Pilate is to be Mikhailov's masterpiece; of the three it is clearly the most significant to its painter, if only because it occupies him now.

Two chief, and not entirely distinct, issues raised by the painting emerge as central to the whole novel as well, and in this sense take on metapoetic significance. The first concerns the painting's abandonment of the traditional code of religious art. Golenishchev criticizes Mikhailov's "error" of depicting Christ as a historical figure, as "a revolutionary or a sage"; he claims that Mikhailov's realistic technique has made Christ "a man-God, not a God-man" (V, ix; 424). The artist's answer is simple: "I could not paint a Christ whom I had not in my soul" (V, xi; 429). His painting is virtually a natural phenomenon, it comes from the "soul," not from convention—a counterexample to Vronsky the painter and man of the world. Mikhailov's spontaneity and honesty in art is underlined in the little episode where his daughter splatters a discarded sketch with tallow, and this gives him an idea for righting the figure in the sketch (V, x; 426–27).[33]

The second issue arises from the situation depicted in the painting. There are some precise indications as to what this moment from Christ's life meant for Tolstoy. Roughly fifteen years after writing *Anna Karenina*, Tolstoy took a great interest in the painting of Nikolai Ge, "What is Truth," which represented Christ before Pilate in a manner recalling that of the fictional Mikhailov.[34] For Tolstoy, who wrote letters to promote and explain this painting, the encounter of Christ and Pilate portrayed there represents the meeting of two value systems, one true and one false. One man "sees" and "expresses the essence of his teaching," the other is "impenetrable," "a very kindly fellow who is not concerned with Christ or the Jews, still less with any truth explained to him" (*Tolstoy's Letters*, 463); in the failure of communication that ensues, the man representing false values turns his back, confident and self-sufficient in his lying world.[35] And through depicting the encounter of these two worlds, rather than emphasizing Christ's pictorial image, Ge resolves the problem in religious aesthetics posed by Golenishchev in *Anna Karenina*—how to represent Christ when the traditions of religious painting are no longer satisfactory, but when the current aesthetics of naturalism would destroy that which is most essential about Christ (see *Pss* 65:108 and 124–26).

Tolstoy asserted that Ge's painting represented more than a single, narratable event in the story of Christ's life on earth. Its subject is outside the bounds of time, it has recurred over and again, and is happening even now in many different societies.[36] In this sense Mikhailov's painting can also be said to reflect the fate of its own author: a clash of the wealthy, powerful, and self-satisfied with a bearer of truth—this describes Mikhailov's relations with Vronsky, Anna, and Golenishchev. After the portrait is finished, Vronsky and Golenishchev continue to believe that they know more about art than Mikhailov, and they suspect Mikhailov of artistic jealousy. Anna and Vronsky remain on the whole indifferent to Mikhailov's religious painting, and this lack of a response speaks volumes—not, as has been claimed, about the lesser value of the painting (Mandelker, 8), but about the moral state of Anna and Vronsky.

One could further argue that the momentary crossing of two life lines and the corresponding juxtaposition of two value systems represented in the painting diagrammatically repeat a fundamental aspect of the structure of *Anna Karenina*.[37] The Anna plot line—in the space it travels through, the values held by the people that move in this space—is summed up in the figure of Pilate; the Levin plot line, in Christ. This is not to say that Levin, a doubter, is in the same sense as Dostoevsky's Myshkin a Christ figure, but rather that as a positive Tolstoyan hero, a seeker, he belongs to the world of values represented by the Christ in Tolstoy's discussion of Ge's painting. This interpretation is reinforced by a series of juxtapositions in the novel between contemporary Russia and the Roman Empire, especially evident in the horse-race scene, where the track is repeatedly associated with the circus of ancient Rome.[38]

But there is yet another sense in which Mikhailov's painting is emblematic of *Anna Karenina.* When Golenishchev complains that if Christ is to be treated as a historical figure, it would be better to choose a different historical theme, Mikhailov responds, "But if this is the highest theme open to art?" (V, xi; 432). The presentation of Western man's highest religious ideals in the imagery of current everyday life offends Golenishchev. In this respect, the Mikhailov episode is an inverted parallel of the situation of Tolstoy at work on *Anna Karenina*: Tolstoy takes the *lowest*, most mundane theme open to art — an adulterous wife, the stuff of farce[39] — and places it in a novel that opens with an epigraph from the Gospels; that is, he frames it with a religious meaning. And the epigraph is not just any passage from the Bible, it is one in which the Lord speaks: "Vengeance is mine; I will repay." The novel opens with the voice of God, only to turn immediately to Oblonsky's dream of "little decanters that were really women"; and this shocking contiguity prefigures the whole novel's poetics.

Two other paintings by Mikhailov are discussed in some detail. The first was painted three years before this meeting.

> It represented two boys angling in the shade of a willow. The elder had just thrown the line and, quite absorbed in his preoccupation, was carefully drawing the float from behind a bush; the younger one lay in the grass, leaning on his elbows with his fair tousled head in his hands, and with dreamy blue eyes gazing at the water. What was he thinking about? (V, xii; 432)

Anna and Vronsky are captivated: " 'Oh, how charming! How charming! Wonderful! Charming!' he [Vronsky] and Anna began both at once" (V, xii; 432). That they prefer to contemplate this idyllic scene over that of Christ before Pilate reveals the central feature of their present mode of life: it is all idleness and daydreams, an attempt to distance and forget precisely those issues of responsibility, sin, and guilt raised by the painting of Pilate and Christ. It is true that the notion of forgetfulness is ambivalently charged in the novel; the engrossment experienced by the boys in Mikhailov's painting might be likened to Levin's "blessed moments" of oblivion while mowing, which are valued very positively (III,v; 230; see esp. Gustafson, 420–27). But it matters what is forgotten, and through what means. Levin's mowing is useful labor, it establishes good relations with his peasants, and the vexations it displaces are those produced by his overactive, overrationalizing mind (and his philosopher brother). Anna and Vronsky flee Russia and assume false rhythms of life and styles of dress (in essence, costumes) in pursuit of peace from the consciousness of their own moral transgressions. Art helps them do this, and that, for Tolstoy, is bad; in time Anna will turn to morphine drops for the same purpose.

In the novel's draft Anna and Vronsky are captured by a different painting. There

> [a]n Italian beauty sat on a doorstep and breast-fed her baby. With one hand she was carefully holding his little hand, which he was pressing against her white breast; she hadn't covered her other breast, but wanted to cover the bared breast and was peacefully and rapturously looking at a man with a scythe who had stopped before her and was admiring the baby.
>
> Whether he was her husband, lover, or stranger, he was obviously praising the child, and she was proud and satisfied. (*Pss* 20:399–400)

On returning home, still under the painting's effect, Anna attends to her little daughter and loves her like never before or since; she "repents" of the way she has cooled toward children, and she contemplates a visit to Serezha. It is a clear case of "infectiousness" in art, and quite ironic, given Golenishchev's evaluation of Mikhailov as having technique rather than talent, and not understanding what he does.

But Tolstoy replaced this painting and the reactions it aroused with the painting of the two boys, and one wonders why. Certainly the portrait of the two youths better reflects the mind-set of Anna and Vronsky during their Rome sojourn; they have become enchanted with a painting that reflects their present situation and their desire to live in idyllic oblivion. In having them react to this painting rather than the painting of mother and child in the draft version, Tolstoy underlines the couple's self-centeredness and blindness to moral duty, and denies them even the momentary spiritual reinvigoration the painting of mother and child provokes in the draft.

The third work by Mikhailov is one of three portraits of Anna described in the novel, and should be discussed in the context of both the Anna series and the Mikhailov series of paintings. The other two paintings of Anna are the one Karenin commissioned of a Petersburg artist and Vronsky's unfinished effort.

Vronsky's portrait is described in very few words: "He liked the graceful and effective French School of painting best, and in that style began painting a portrait of Anna dressed as an Italian, and he, as well as every one else who saw it, considered the portrait a great success" (V, vii; 423). The artistic method described here is the inverse of Mikhailov's: where the genuine artist removes the "wrappings" to disclose something true about Anna, Vronsky dresses her in the artificial wrappings of an Italian woman and depicts her in an arbitrarily chosen generic style. Vronsky is struck by Mikhailov's portrait of Anna: "It was strange that Mikhailov had been able to discover that special beauty. 'One needed to know and love her as I love her, to find just that sweetest spiritual expression of hers,' thought Vronsky, though he himself had only learnt to know that 'sweetest spiritual expression' through the portrait" (V, xiii; 434). Further: "Anna's portrait, the same subject painted from nature by both of them, should have shown him the difference between Mikhailov and himself; but Vronsky did not see it. He merely left off painting Anna, deciding that it would be superfluous now" (V, xiii; 435). Vronsky soon quits painting altogether, however, in an implicit recognition of the "difference" between himself and Mikhailov.

The painting hanging in Karenin's study is described only in brief, and this just after Anna has informed her husband that she is Vronsky's mistress:

> Above the arm-chair hung a beautifully painted portrait of Anna by a celebrated artist. To Karenin the splendidly painted black lace on the head, the black hair, and the beautiful white hand with many rings on the third finger, suggested something intolerably bold and provocative. After looking at the portrait for about a minute he shuddered and his lips trembled and made a sound like 'brr' as he turned away. (III, xiv; 259)

In this short passage two perspectives on the painting are presented, first that of the detached narrator who declares it "beautifully painted," then the anguished husband's. Karenin's attention falls on adornments and body parts, for him signs of a feminine sensuality that will not be arrested in a portrait and kept safely and lawfully in his home. The portrait is more than an unpleasant reminder of marital discord; it produces a physical reaction in him — the tremble and "brr" — a reaction not unlike what one would expect to experience upon touching a corpse.

There is a sharp contrast between this act of viewing and Levin's later appreciation of Mikhailov's portrait:

> Another reflector-lamp fixed to the wall illuminated a large full-length portrait of a woman, which attracted Levin's involuntary attention. It was Anna's portrait painted in Italy by Mikhailov. . . . Levin looked at the portrait, which in the bright illumination

seemed to step out of its frame, and he could not tear himself away from it. He forgot where he was, and without listening to what was being said gazed fixedly at the wonderful portrait. It was not a picture, but a living and charming woman with curly black hair, bare shoulders and arms, and a dreamy half-smile on lips covered with elegant down, looking at him victoriously and tenderly with eyes that troubled him. The only thing that showed she was not alive was that she was more beautiful than a living woman could be. (VII, ix; 630)

Like Karenin's, Levin's gaze first falls on those physical features traditionally standing for feminine sensuality—hair, shoulders, lips; but he also peers into Anna's eyes and searches her facial expression for signs of her inner life.

In Tolstoy's series of juxtapositions involving Anna as the subject of a portrait, three different painters, and three different scenes of viewing portraits, the sources of the viewers' responses are ambiguous: each respective artist's penetration of his subject bears some responsibility, but the difference in attitude toward Anna with which Vronsky, Karenin, and Levin approach the portraits must also be a determining factor. This painting's infectious effect on Levin is doubtless: it takes him out of the present moment and place; presumably, it causes him to see Anna as Mikhailov saw her—one aspect of what good art should do, according to Tolstoy's later theories.[40]

Levin forgets where he is while viewing the portrait; to the extent that he participates in the inner life of the Anna depicted there, he is absorbed into the time and space of the painting. It is as though he has met Anna in Italy, at the height of her relationship with Vronsky, when the two lovers suspended time for a short interval in an artificial life of their own composition. And this life is reflected in the static art of painting, indeed, in the still more static genre of portraiture.

If we consider the three paintings by Mikhailov as a group, time and narrativity prove to be a distinctive feature differentiating the works. Time is also key to the metasemiotic juxtaposition of the painted Anna with the Anna of Tolstoy's novel. This might appear a banal point; as Jakobson succinctly reformulates Lessing's distinction between the verbal and pictorial arts, "Both visual and auditory perception obviously occur in space and time, but the spatial dimension takes priority for visual signs and the temporal one for auditory signs" ("Visual and Auditory Signs," 336).[41] Verbal arts and music can more "naturally" represent time; the pictorial arts, space. To the extent that this principle is a semiotic fact of art, its operation in Tolstoy's novel is of no special significance. But Tolstoy deliberately foregrounds this distinction, and he does it in a way that brings out certain ethical ramifications.

The painting of Christ and Pilate captures a turning point in Christ's life, the culmination of one series of events and the beginning of another, both of which are familiar to every viewer. And the ending of the narrative to which this painting alludes is no less well known. Little wonder that Anna and Vronsky turn away from this canvas: the whole purpose of their present place and mode of life is to freeze the inevitable "progressive action," to recall Lessing's phrase, of the adultery plot they are living, and so to defer the consequences of their own actions. Karenin had rightly warned his wife: "Our lives are bound together not by men but by God. This bond can only be broken by a crime, and that kind of crime brings its punishment" (II, ix; 133); and later, ". . . you can yourself foresee what awaits you and your son" (III, xiv; 258).

In the painting of the two boys, time is suspended in idyllic surroundings. Yet the painting's effect—indeed, that of the whole generic complex of the idyll—arguably relies upon a viewer's own harried temporal sensations: the expression of the boy lost in reverie would have no meaning were it not perceived against the backdrop of a viewer's awareness of passing time, pressing events, and the imperative of labor. We have suggested that its attraction to Anna and Vronsky resides in its ability to serve as an objective correlative of their own wishes for life in Italy.

Anna's portrait, on the other hand, is truly a static, timeless rendition, describable but not narratable; it may be situated within a series of events, as it is in the novel, but unlike the other two canvases by Mikhailov, it depicts none. Its spatial and temporal values are directly opposed to those of the novel as a whole, where, as Nabokov maintained, "What really seduces the average reader is the gift Tolstoy had of endowing his fiction with such time-values as correspond exactly to our sense of time" (*Lectures*, 141). And beyond Tolstoy's "mysterious accomplishment" (Nabokov, *Lectures*, 141) of mimicking a reader's sense of passing time, a narrative, unlike a painting—especially unlike a portrait—needs an ending. What Wendy Steiner writes of poetry is thus no less true of Tolstoy's novel: "The very perception of a literary work is thus a reminder of temporal impermanence with the poem, unlike the physical canvas, sharing in this impermanence of humanity itself" (42).

It is under the pressure of time that Anna and Vronsky grow estranged and Anna disintegrates emotionally. The burning candle imagery associated with Anna, especially at her death, repeats the motif of time pressing on to an inevitable end; the much-interpreted nightmare she and Vronsky share, with its loud noises and frenetic activity, acquires a portion of its menacing significance merely through its placement against the background of the lovers' quest for stillness.

But the attractions of permanence are not limited to Vronsky and Anna. Three men in love — Karenin, Petrov, Vronsky — paint or commission portraits of the objects of their affections. The gesture is one signifying possession (which in part explains the uncanny effect on Karenin of Anna's portrait now that she is in no practical sense any longer his); and as a gift to the beloved of her own idealized reflection *as the one who is loved*, it validates the lover's desires through an appeal to the other's narcissism (quite effective in Anna's case).

Levin, in contrast to these three unfortunate men, has no portrait painted of Kitty; but this is not to say that he is immune to the art's charms, as his reaction to Anna's portrait shows. Long before the incident at Anna's flat, Tolstoy associates Levin's attraction to Kitty and his wish to create a family life with the allurements of the pictorial arts: at the skating rink where Levin first encounters Kitty after his long absence from Moscow, he finds her "more beautiful than he had imagined her"; whereupon follows a description of his ability to "vividly picture to himself her entire person," most especially "the expression of her eyes — mild, calm, and truthful, — and above all her smile, which carried him into a fairyland where he felt softened and filled with tenderness — as he remembered feeling on rare occasions in his early childhood" (I, ix; 26). When at Stiva's request he visits Dolly and her children in the country (later he will call on Anna, also at Stiva's request), "[o]n seeing her he found himself before one of the pictures of family life he had imagined for himself in the future" (III, ix; 243). But Levin suffers a deep depression in the period after the birth of his son. "What he felt toward this little creature was not at all what he had anticipated. There was nothing merry or joyful in it; on the contrary, there was a new and distressing sense of fear" (VII, xvi; 650). Levin's disillusionment that family life has not resolved the spiritual problems of living becomes the positive awareness of that which a static and finalized idyllic *picture* of family life could not possibly convey.[42]

Levin's epiphanic revelation at the novel's end involves discovering that such imagined pictures, as a goal toward which he once yearned—and thus the motivation or "cause" of his actions and the end or "reward" for which he strove—have at best a false connection with that which is really worth living for: "goodness [*dobro*]."

> I and millions of men who lived centuries ago and those who are living now . . . we all agree on that one thing: what we should live for, and what is good. I, and all other men, know only one thing firmly, clearly, and certainly, and this knowledge cannot be explained by reason: it is outside reason, has no cause and can have no consequences.
>
> If goodness has a cause, it is no longer goodness; if it has a consequence—a reward, it is also not goodness. Therefore goodness is beyond the chain of cause and effect. (VIII, xii; 720)

These conclusions follow Levin's conversation with the peasant Theodore (Fëdor), who has passed moral judgment on two other peasants—one good, one bad—based upon how they live. The immediacy and the sureness of Theodore's evaluation reassures Levin: he decides, first, that we all already know that goodness is what makes life worth living as well as what this goodness is, so that an abstract codification of ethical rules is unnecessary; and second, that goodness involves *how* one lives—not what one lives *for*.

Levin's formula about "goodness" is the crowning argument in a philosophy of life, but it is also the penultimate step in Tolstoy's metapoetic treatment of the aesthetic problems we have been discussing. If "goodness" is beyond the chain of cause and effect, then it is also beyond the metonymic series ("progressive action") making up a narrative; ultimately, Levin says, goodness cannot, like the "moral of the story," be the endpoint of an action: what Levin finds in this revelatory moment has nothing to do with the arc of the novel's action from its beginning to its end—he knew it all along.

Two interpretive questions regarding, respectively, the novel's beginning and end have perennially troubled the novel's readers: the contextual meaning of the epigraph ("Vengeance is mine, I shall repay"), and the coherence of the ending (part 8), which culminates in this moment of revelation, with the rest of the novel. Here these two questions fold into one. Levin's formula about "goodness" both echoes and reverses the novel's epigraph, and thereby enacts two highly significant transformations: it inverts the semantic theme of transgression and punishment, resulting in a theme of goodness and reward; and it negates the terrifying grammar, or metonymic logic, of the epigraph, which declares that transgressions will be avenged and which makes Anna's fate, as the heroine of an adultery plot, inevitable. The epigraph, itself a miniature narrative, serves to prefigure the Anna plot line (and, indeed, preceded the Levin-Kitty line in Tolstoy's drafts [Eikhenbaum, 146]); this counter-epigraph, an antinarrative embedded in the text near the novel's end, undermines our conventional narratological sense of an ending's meaning. No wonder virtually every student in courses where I have taught this novel has found the ending "unsatisfying."

Our discussion has come full circle, only to doubly contradict itself. In rejecting time and cause and effect—the metonymic principle found by Jakobson to be the chief structural feature of the realistic prose novel ("Two Aspects," 255–58)—this counter-epigraph devalues precisely that which, in connection with our discussion of Mikhailov's paintings and Lessing, appeared key to the proper ethical effect of a pictorial aesthetics. Tolstoy approved of Ge's painting of Pilate and Christ because of the way it verged on narrative: in his judgment the canvas's representation of an event, the conflict between two value systems, was more important than its representation of Christ, which by itself could not have helped but fail. At the same time, Tolstoy "denied the meaning of color, the role of paints, which at times hindered the perception of the purely literary side of the picture" (I. Brodskii, introduction to *L. N. Tolstoi i khudozhniki*, 27).

Second, to achieve an understanding of this thing Levin calls "goodness," which is outside of time and the chain of cause and effect, narrative proves to be the necessary tool. Indeed, the revelation that does finally bring peace of mind to Levin—however unconvincingly—results from a series of *stories* Levin tells himself and interprets, parables drawn from life around him. In addition to Theodore's parable of the "good peasant" and the "bad peasant," he recalls the incident when Dolly's children tried to cook berries in cups over a candle and pour milk into one another's mouth as from a fountain (VIII, xiii; 722–24).

Recent scholarship has engaged this contradiction between parable and plot (or causality) in the novel. In his article on prosaics and *Anna Karenina*, Morson asserts that the prosy and undramatic breadth of Tolstoy's novel, so rich in the meaningless and "messy" details of everyday life, dissolves the "chain of cause and effect" associated with plot. In discussing the scene where Dolly bathes with her children, he concludes: "Tolstoy's point here is that these are the most important events of the book and of life generally, even though — in fact precisely because — they are too prosaic and ordinary to have any dramatic interest. Where plot is, 'true life' isn't" (5). But when Levin recalls the children's meaningless, messy play with the teacups, he does so in order to assign it a parabolic meaning, which means that it is no longer "prosaic" in the sense I understand Morson to mean the term. Rather, it has been recuperated as the verbal vehicle for a complex allegorical statement. In the most literal sense, Levin here makes meaning out of mess — and the meaning is not in his ethical response to this unexpected event, but in his aestheticization of it into a parable about the givenness of our knowledge about right and wrong, and the dangers of reasoning about it philosophically.

For Mandelker, the solution is to be found in the very consciousness of both the irrepressible urge to project one's life into static pictures, and the dangers of doing so: ". . . Levin, at the novel's conclusion, acknowledges both the dangers of framing and the potential for salvation in such visions" (17). At stake is more than a higher degree of self-consciousness, however: Levin now uses language and images in a fundamentally different way than he did before. It is the difference between ekphrasis and allegory or parable. Both achieve iconicity within the medium of language, and both are articulated in time, as verbal signs must be; but the ekphrastic composition remains a sum of conventional linguistic signs, which in essence negates the temporal aspect of verbal art, while allegory requires a genuine detour through time to mean something other, or something more, than the sum of its designations. Just as the eye need not begin its scan of a pictorial sign at any particular spot to arrive at a mental image of the whole, the ekphrastic verbal construction could, in principle, have the order of its noun phrases jumbled and still convey the same image; the ekphrastic passage requires adverbs of place, but not of time. Allegory, by contrast, relies upon time and the chain of cause and effect for its meaning.

Gustafson reads Tolstoy's art as a reflection of his theological beliefs, and has written of Tolstoy's own propensity to read allegorically, to approach the world around him as does Levin in this moment of revelation: "[F]or Tolstoy the world is the expression of the Divine. Reality is God's language. His word and His world. Life is revelation, and reality is emblematic" (203). How is it, though, that the actual revelation at which Levin arrives proves so unsatisfying to readers? Placed in the context of Tolstoy's biography and thought, the resolution of Levin's spiritual crisis can only be interpreted as a *wished-for* resolution, one that certainly did not "stick" for Tolstoy.

Perhaps the *activity* by means of which Levin extricates himself from his spiritual predicament—isolating sequences of events from the life around him, and interpreting them as allegorical stories—is of greater significance than the conclusions he reaches. The pictures of Anna and of family life seduced him, led him astray; reading life about him parabolically discloses the proper path. In seeking meaning that eclipses the contingencies, causes, and effects of his life, Levin's revelation about atemporal "goodness" must also be achieved out of time, rather than outside of time, as a sort of second-degree iconicity. Approached metapoetically rather than theologically, the processes of revelation emerge, appropriately enough, as akin to Jakobson's definition of the poetic function in verbal art—the projection of a similarity (Levin's allegorical interpretation) onto a contiguity (the story of the teacups); that is to say, Levin discerns a constructive principle of parallelism in his life, and in this culminating episode he unearths and interprets parallels at a fast and furious pace.

Finally, what appears contradictory in Tolstoy's recension of Lessing's distinction between the verbal and pictorial arts is in fact consistent in its anti-aesthetic intent. He insistently introduces the "progression of events" into painting; he asserts that it is the atemporal system of parallels (or "linkages," as Tolstoy called them in his famous letter) that matter in his prose novel: in each case his deformation of the aesthetic experience is a means of raising the ethical shoulder of art.[43]

In many respects, then, metapoetics in the novel emerges as inseparable from metaphysics, and aesthetics inseparable from ethics. So it is that Levin's revelation becomes one last counterpart to all the other episodes in the novel portraying the reception of a work of art. Indeed, here Levin provides the definitive model for how to approach *Anna Karenina*, and it is a model which Tolstoy makes pay off immediately: as Levin deliberates on the need to live to serve others, he helps an insect make its way up a stalk of grass; as he links his thoughts together in a convincing series, he ties blades of grass together into knots, "trying not to break them" (VIII, xii; 721). While following Levin's thought processes as he approaches "truth" through a process of allegorical interpretation, the reader of *Anna Karenina* is also confronted with passages depicting Levin from the outside which beg to be interpreted in the same fashion. Is this not a metapoetic invitation to read the entire novel as an allegory?

5

Chekhov's "The Steppe": A Metapoetic Journey

"The Steppe" (1888) was Anton Chekhov's first serious *povest'*-length work,[1] the first of his long works to appear unserialized, and the first to appear in a prestigious "thick journal." In the eyes of Chekhov, his contemporaries, and virtually all Chekhov scholars ever since, this story signals the emergence of a mature and ambitious author. And yet "The Steppe" has proven problematic from the perspective of the mature Chekhov's poetics. Readers find it long, inefficient, lyrical, and dreamy—by no means the usual Chekhov tale. This very oddness, and the deliberate engagement of the Russian prose tradition and the norms and expectations of the reading public it entails, tends to compel readers to think about the story in terms of poetics.

We, however, are interested in the metapoetic *representation* of these and other aspects of a work's own poetics. On what grounds might such a reading of "The Steppe" be pursued? In the preceding four chapters, the texts considered were either overtly metapoetic or else included prominent themes of artistic creation and storytelling; regarding each of these works there is also a certain critical tradition of metapoetic reading. Not so with "The Steppe," the most covertly metapoetic of all the texts treated here. In fact, such an interpretive approach goes very much against the grain of the dominant understanding of Chekhov, who—with, perhaps, the exception of his dramatic masterpieces, especially *The Seagull* (*Chaika*)—is still most often read as consummating the poetics of Russian realism.

This chapter begins by recapping what past readers have said about how

"The Steppe" violates conventional expectations, and then proceeds to demonstrate how, in each such instance, the story actually represents the relevant problem of poetics in a covert, symbolic way.

I Problems in the Poetics of "The Steppe"

"The Steppe" describes the journey of a nine-year-old boy, Egorushka, as he is taken across the steppe to a major city where he will be boarded with an old friend of his mother's and enrolled in school. He begins the trip in the company of his uncle and a priest, who are traveling to sell wool, but along the way is transferred to the cart train conveying the wool; for the rest of the journey he is among the peasant carters. Besides these peasants, his uncle (Kuzmichov) and the priest (Father Khristofor), Egorushka meets a number of new and striking personalities, among whom are: two Jewish brothers (Moisei and Solomon) who run a hostel where Egorushka, Kuzmichov, and Father Khristofor stop for tea; an attractive female landowner (the Countess Dranitskaya); the wealthy, industrious, and commanding Varlamov, whom all seem to need and fear; and a Great Russian shopkeeper. Although the story is episodic in nature, it does display a certain dramatic movement. Separation from home and mother (his father is dead), the steppe's mind-boggling vastness,[2] and new acquaintances who have been broken by life's vicissitudes combine with intimations of death and a nascent sexuality to shape the journey into a critical turning point in Egorushka's life, marked by the crisis of a terrifying thunderstorm and a brief illness.

But "The Steppe" is not only *about* one life's critical junctures, it *is* such a juncture: Chekhov, a transitional figure in Russian literature, wrote this story to create and commemorate a turning point in his own career. His letters of the time show him at work with great deliberation. Responding to encouragement from a prominent author of Dostoevsky's era, Dmitrii Grigorovich, Chekhov described the story he was writing in January of 1888:

> Each chapter is a separate story, but all the chapters are as interconnected and closely related as the five figures of a quadrille. I'm trying to give them a common aroma and a common tone, and the better to accomplish this I follow one character through all the chapters. I feel I've made a lot of headway and that there are passages that smell of hay, but on the whole I'm ending up with something rather odd and much too original. Since

I'm not used to writing anything long and am constantly, as is my wont, afraid of writing too much, I've gone to the other extreme. All the pages come out compact, as if they had been condensed, and impressions keep crowding each other, piling up, and pushing one another out of the way. The short scenes, or, as you call them, spangles, are squeezed tightly together; they move in an unbroken chain and are therefore fatiguing; instead of a scene, I end up with a dry, detailed list of impressions, very much like an outline; instead of an artistically integrated depiction of the steppe, I offer the reader an encyclopaedia of the steppe. (*Anton Chekhov's Life*, 91–92; *Pis'ma* 2:173)[3]

In letters to such distinguished literary elders Chekhov repeatedly pointed out the story's deficiencies, hoping perhaps to anticipate criticism; yet in a letter to his contemporary Aleksandr Lazarev he called "The Steppe" his "masterpiece": "I cannot do better," he wrote (*Pis'ma* 2:187).[4]

Subsequent criticism of "The Steppe" has for the most part followed the same contradictory lines found in those letters. Variety in modes of writing, de-emphasis of plot, and a strange multiplicity of narrative voice are some of the story's most striking features. At times one finds, true to the author's confession, dictionary-like catalogues of steppe wildlife; long lyrical digressions might follow. There is also the haunting, dreamlike repetition of certain motifs throughout the story. Such repetition goes far in maintaining the "uniform tone" mentioned in Chekhov's letter; it also underlines the monotony of a journey across the steppe (though less charitable readers have found that repetition replicates that dullness).[5] But this feature alone has not mitigated many readers' dissatisfaction with what they perceive as a lack of coherence.

"Unity" and "artistic integration" are terms invoking the rhetoric of a normalizing and totalizing poetics of formalist bent. But Chekhov himself established the pattern of approaching "The Steppe" with an orientation toward issues of the formal integrity traditionally expected of mid-length prose fictions, and it is no surprise that attentive readers such as Nils Åke Nilsson, who has examined in depth the tone and narrative voice of "The Steppe," have confirmed Chekhov's worst fears.[6] Still, even Chekhov's own criticisms of the story's structure are less valuable as definitive evaluations than as calls for attention to the composition's challenges to the norms of prose fiction, to its deliberate upsetting of the expected hierarchy of components.

For readers who focus on the story's poetic texture, on the other hand, the significance of such structural aberrations diminishes or changes. Writes Petr Bitsilli: " 'The Steppe' as a whole has to do with poetry; that is, to assimilate it otherwise than having read it with one breath, still grasping every word, is impossible, because the general 'form' is composed by means of the subtlest verbal suggestions" (*Tvorchestvo*, 64). Bitsilli and Abram Derman both discuss rhythm and counterpoint in "The Steppe," finding that the story's unity is of a musical nature.[7]

The story's superficial lacks have also provoked readers to probe for indirect, symbolic planes of meaning. Bitsilli makes such an interpretation, likening the road across the steppe to "life's path"; for him, the baffling multiplicity and arbitrariness of "The Steppe" are entirely appropriate, since "chance, and not 'elective affinities' brings together and disperses people" (*Tvorchestvo*, 66).[8]

One gathers from all these comments a threefold view of the story: its overall shape or surface is irregular and flawed; its discourse works in a poetic, even musical fashion, lending the story a sense of unity which, however, tends to defy any precise articulation; and, perhaps in spite of Chekhov's intentions, the story not only reflects the beauty of the steppe while telling the story of a young child in crisis, but is symbolic of something greater as well. Examining these three aspects will show that discontinuities in the story's surface are corners around which the hydra-like complexity of Chekhov's design lies in wait. As the nature of that design emerges, so too does a symbolic meaning giving the story an astonishing degree of unity, though of an odd and complex sort. One overriding structural principle of "The Steppe" turns out to be the figuration of its own structure (in this instance very much like Dällenbach's *mise en abyme*). Why this should occur in Chekhov's landmark story, and why it should be so hidden, will be taken up toward the end of the chapter.

2 From Poetics to Metapoetics

Nilsson and others have shown that the surface or external form of "The Steppe" lacks a number of expected unifying features. At certain moments the story appears to break down in terms of its chronological and actional structures and the nature of its narrative voice. But discovering how these features are integrated into the larger whole reveals them to be deliberately placed false leads, rather than evidence of Chekhov's failure to create an "artistically integrated" text; and in each case, this situation is reflected metapoetically.

The temporal structure of "The Steppe" lacks any obvious complexity. The plan Chekhov outlined in his letter to Grigorovich was to "follow one character through all the chapters," and his handling of time appears to be entirely linear: day follows day and remembrances never sidetrack the narrative for long. As Nilsson points out, the very title, "The Steppe," suggests a constant setting and dictionary-like facet to the story, while the subtitle, "The Story of a Journey" ("Istoriia odnoi poezdki"), implies a chronological "line of continuity" that will allow smooth transitions and order the story (66), much as (extending Chekhov's analogy) the alphabet orders dictionaries.

The rate of passage along the story's time-line, however, is not at all constant. If the narrative is divided into twenty-four-hour sequences, from one morning to the next, each of the first two days makes up some three-eighths of the story, while the last two days divide evenly the remaining quarter. That is, time passes much more rapidly in the story's final chapters than it does at the start. Furthermore, because so much of "The Steppe" is narrated from Egorushka's point of view, time in the story is quite subjectivized. One repeatedly finds a retardation of time associated with boredom: "It seemed that since morning one hundred years had passed..." (26); there are also accelerations accompanying heightened interest in surroundings or events: "The boy gazed at the familiar places, but the hated carriage ran on and left everything behind" (14). For the reader accustomed to reading for the plot, time must often hang as heavily as it does for Egorushka and the peasant drivers crossing the steppe. Even so, one might maintain that sequential time, warped by its juncture with the portrayal of the steppe and a child's view of the world, is the principal unifying feature of "The Steppe"; or, to say it differently, the story is to be read primarily as the chronicle of a boy's journey across the steppe.

But how then is one to understand the many passages that find no place on even a warped time-line? Inserted narratives told by characters in "The Steppe," though they are all quite brief and though the reader never forgets their narrative context, do complicate the overall time structure of the story. These fictions and tales of events long past affect the very movement of "The Steppe." They become a part of Egorushka's present experience, his journey, and so are causally related to Egorushka's subsequent illness and crisis. What happened once before occurs again now, so that instead of a "this time" and a "that time" there is the sense of all time at once.

Lyrical digressions like the following also subvert the story's apparent time structure:

> And now a lone poplar appears on a hill; who planted it and why it is there—God alone knows. To tear one's eyes away from its shapely figure and green clothing is hard. Is that beauty happy? In the summer there is oppressive heat, in the winter, frost and blizzards, in the fall, frightening nights when you see only darkness and can't hear a thing except the aimless, angrily howling wind; but mainly, your whole life you are alone, alone... (17)

The image presented here becomes a vision of timelessness. Even the ellipsis ending the passage suggests discontinuity, a thoughtful pause in the story's narration; and what takes place in the space of this pause is a departure from the temporal "line of continuity," for the poplar is presented in terms of its cyclical, seasonal life. The very lyricism of such passages is also a forgetting of time, like that of a laborer who, falling into a reverie and forgetting the work before him, stands motionless, his tool still poised to strike.

Chekhov's departures from a consistent narrative voice may be related to the disruptions in the story's linear time flow. As lyrical descriptions of nature displace the sequential in favor of the cyclical, so retrospective musings and what Nilsson calls "philosophical parentheses" indicate that some process of recollection, a repetition and reordering of time, takes place alongside the consecutive presentation of events (42).[9] Most significant in this respect are those passages anticipating the viewpoint of a Egorushka aged beyond the temporal limits of "The Steppe": "Russians love to reminisce, but do not like to live; Egorushka did not yet know this" (64). A collection of older, more experienced narrative voices coexist with the naive point of view of Egorushka, so that what seems new in Chekhov's text is always, at the same time, the repetition or recollection of something old and well known.

Reading "The Steppe" on the chronological plane, then, as a journal recording successive impressions of the steppe, fails to make sense of some of the more crucial passages in the story. But to understand these discontinuities as flaws is shortsighted. Rather, these are moments when the story's chronological aspect is absorbed by the plane of *motifs*, and that is where a more rewarding vantage point for the examination of "The Steppe" is found. Timelessness, for example, is a notion associable with the oft-repeated motif of death. One senses an undercurrent of seasonal, cyclical time in Egorushka's recollections of the graveyard where his grandmother is buried: "Egorushka recalled that when the cherry tree flowers, these white spots mix with the cherry blossoms into a white sea; but when it ripens, the white monuments and crosses become strewn with crimson, bloodlike spots" (14). The Egorushka who departs on this journey is still unable to comprehend his own mortality and so can only view his life as eternal: "For himself, personally, he did not admit the possibility of death, and felt that he would never die" (66).

Similarly, if the stories told by characters within "The Steppe" disrupt the story's apparent chronos, this is because storytelling is more than a feature of steppe travel duly reflected by the author; these stories serve to repeat and intensify certain configurations of motifs in accordance with a more inclusive plan. A motif is, by definition, that which recurs in a literary text. On the plane of motifs "The Steppe" constantly repeats itself, as it were, while its temporal line of continuity is really something of a ruse, determining the story's structure only insofar as the author has troubled to construct this deceptively linear surface.

The very concept of linear time finds itself expressed on the plane of motifs. Following the theme of maturation, for instance, Egorushka's progression from the enclosed, familiar, grammatically feminine carriage (*brichka*) to the exposed, masculine cart (*voz*) of the peasants, and then to reliance on his own two feet, portrays the workings of sequential time better than the narrative calendar-clock discussed in the preceding paragraphs. After Egorushka's transfer from the carriage to the cart, the road before him widens and, through the appearance of telegraph poles, gains a vertical dimension; the city that is the journey's end, with its multistory buildings and other new features, is figuratively speaking a further widening of the road; and the soiling of Egorushka's coat can signify the irreversible passage of time and the gain of experience.

There is in "The Steppe" a whole series of images echoing iconically the way both time and narrative voice function in the story. One of the many images in "The Steppe" involving circular motion, the windmill, can serve as a natural symbol of the story's narrative voice. This windmill is first encountered, "waving its wings," toward the end of chapter 1: "[O]ne could distinctly make out its two wings. One wing was old, all patched up; the other, only recently made of new wood, glistened in the sun" (19). Through this image is evoked the cyclical, repetitive nature of the story's narration; and one sees the common axis of rotation, the juncture and thus the unity, of the young narrative voice with the old. Both voices, like the old and new wings, pass through the same space—but at different times. This windmill also performs a certain labor; figuratively speaking, it spins out the narrative of "The Steppe." Several details support this notion of the windmill as a symbol bearing metapoetical significance: the mill was built by the farmer Boltva for his son, and the name "Boltva" provokes association with the Russian for "chatter" or "idle talk," *boltovnia*; the relationship between father and son is presumably one of experience with naïveté; and the windmill seems to follow Egorushka, now hiding itself, now showing up a little closer or at a greater distance, like a narrator shadowing his character.

Similarly, time in "The Steppe" is much like the gate and fence encountered at Nastasya Toskunova's house: "On both sides of this very old, grey gate stretched a grey fence with wide chinks: the right part of the fence listed heavily forward and threatened collapse, the left sank backwards into the yard; but the gate stood up straight, still choosing, it seemed, whether it would be more convenient to fall forward or backward" (101). The fence is a recurrent motif in "The Steppe," demarcating pieces of land in the same way that linear, sequential time makes events discrete: there is the graveyard, and the time when Egorushka's grandmother was buried there; there is the prison, and the time when Egorushka took gifts to the prisoners held there; and so on. The processes of recollection and anticipation—falling backward or forward in time—allow passage through the gate.

These metapoetic symbols are two of a series we shall be extending throughout this chapter. The full significance (not to mention the validity) of each individual interpretation can emerge only in retrospect, after a complete set of such images accumulates and the scope of the story's metapoetic dimension reveals itself.

Much of "The Steppe" is devoted to searches of one sort or another. Egorushka's uncle and Father Khristofor must find Varlamov to sell their wool, for instance, but there are other, briefer segments where the device of suspense comes into play. In such instances the narrative is enlivened and the reader kept engaged by the question: how will this problem be solved, what will happen next? Let us now survey the limits within which the compositional principles of mystery, adventure, and suspense unify the story.

The narrative's authorially manipulated order and the reader's sense of the story's unfolding — its plot dynamics — intersect with a broad thematic notion, which we might call "things in their proper places." Narrated events are related to one another by means other than the distance separating them in the reader's time or in fictional time. Expectations are constantly aroused in the reader, played with, and perhaps satisfied. These expectations are based on a reader's understanding or misunderstanding of literary norms, norms of behavior in the social milieu that might be reflected in a narrative, psychological law, the logically determinable causal relationships between events, and so on. Each narrative step taken will therefore determine what succeeding steps can "properly" take place. For this reason, themes of propriety and social hierarchy can be considered alongside the story's actional structure (in which a journey is expected to reach its end and mysteries are expected to be solved); for our understanding of these themes will have a large part in conditioning our expectations from the plot.

The interaction of Egorushka's uncle and his driver Deniska during the first day's rest stop ably illustrates this conjunction of plot significance and social hierarchy. Kuzmichov consumes a small feast while Deniska, though hungry, feigns indifference to the food and passes time swatting the flies on his horses; only when Kuzmichov has finished his meal can the servant Deniska eat. Social hierarchy is thus connected with suspense: Kuzmichov holds Deniska in the servant's proper place and reaffirms his own superior position while Deniska, made to wait for satisfaction, kills flies.[10]

The mystery facet of "The Steppe," largely associated with the search for Varlamov, peaks at the hostel of Moisei Moiseich. The enigma surrounding Varlamov's figure has by now been intensified, so that the next chapter begins: "Just who, finally, is this elusive, mysterious Varlamov, about whom they say so much, whom Solomon scorns, and whom even the beautiful countess needs?" (43). Social hierarchy is also articulated in this passage, through the bowing and scraping of Moisei and through the motifs of money and hats. The unprosperous Moisei is so embarrassed at the sight of Kuzmichov's money that he leaves his own room (36). Hats too show a character's place in "The Steppe." Egorushka wears a hat newly purchased for his trip across the steppe and thus metonymically associated with his step upward into the adult world. The two features of the hat specified, its coachman's styling and peacock feather, evoke that world of labor and male sexuality the child is about to enter. And Moisei invokes the conventional gesture of deference involving hats, saying to Egorushka, "You'll leave school such a gentleman, we'll all be taking our hats off to you!" (34).

But these devices of suspense and the reflection of social hierarchy lend a semblance of cohesion to the surface of "The Steppe" which eventually collapses; they comprise a series of false moves masking the inner movement of the story. Thus the passage that begins chapter 4, while noting the suspense surrounding the figure of Varlamov, initiates the process through which that character is shifted to the story's periphery: "For some reason Egorushka wanted to think only about Varlamov and about the countess, especially about the latter" (44). Egorushka finally sees the mythical Varlamov, but does not recognize "Varlamovness" in this rather short and unremarkable fellow. When Pantelei reveals the mysterious man's identity during what should be the climactic scene of recognition, Egorushka reflects: "My God! . . . In this short gray little fellow, shod in large boots, sitting on an ugly little horse and conversing with peasants at a time when normal people sleep, it was hard to recognize the secret, elusive Varlamov, whom all sought, who was always circling about, and who had far more money than the Countess Dranitskaya" (79). Earlier Father Khristofor had assured Kuzmichov that Varlamov was a man, not the proverbial "needle," and that "We'll find him" (22). He is found, but there hardly seems to have been a search; moreover, once he is found, nothing special happens, and as the story proceeds he is all but forgotten. Such an understated outcome to the Varlamov mystery negates the entire suspense facet of "The Steppe."[11]

A new sequence of conflict and rising tension begins after Egorushka joins the carters. Upon first meeting Dymov, Egorushka determines that the young carter is a "wicked person"; he "already hated his light brown head, clean face, and strength with all his soul, listened to his laugh with repulsion and was thinking about what chosen word he might say to him in revenge" (55). This conflict culminates just before the natural culmination of the thunderstorm. There Egorushka curses Dymov and, in perhaps the story's tautest moment, invites the rest of the carters to beat this "naughty person [*ozornik*]" (83). Egorushka's moral indignation at Dymov's violation of the code of acceptable behavior, his naming of Dymov as "naughty one," is very much related to the theme of "things in their proper places." But this code is a weapon available to all, and so is used by Dymov to scold his fellow travelers: he picks a fight with Emelyan when the latter dips his spoon into the dinner pot before the others (81–82), and he rebukes Egorushka for eating with his hat on (65).[12]

Here too a denouement is lacking, however. There is a displacement of the tension growing between these characters whereby the violent outburst anticipated from the story's characters takes place, instead, in nature. While a certain catharsis is achieved through the storm, one could argue that this move on Chekhov's part is more an interruption and shelving of the story's dramatic possibilities than an exploitation of such possibilities on a metaphorical plane.

Consistent with this pattern of providing zero endings to sequences of adventure and suspense, of always substituting an anticlimax for the climax, is the outcome of Kuzmichov's and Father Khristofor's commercial mission. The negotiations surrounding the sale of their wool take place outside the story's narrative, and the great need these two men are said to have for Varlamov comes to play no functional role in the narrative's development. This lack of completion is a calculated inattentiveness, however, a false move made possible by constraining the various narrators of the story to stay at Egorushka's side. If following only Egorushka's path across the steppe is a restriction that helps unify the narrative of "The Steppe," it also justifies certain deliberate omissions; it frustrates the reader, providing less in the end than he has been given reason to expect.[13]

Even the narrative sequence embracing the whole story, the journey itself, ends negatively, in understatement. The peasant's life proves intolerably dull to Egorushka, and because the journey has left him ill, he views the new, wondrous details of that journey's endpoint with complete indifference. When Egorushka, now recovered, recalls the steamer, locomotive, and wide river he had seen the day before, he grows curious and sets out to see them again (97); he is interrupted by the return of Father Khristofor, however, so that while retaining a dim recollection of his discovery of these new things, he never really sees them with fresh eyes. Most significantly, just how Egorushka will adjust to his new life remains beyond the narrative. The story's last words, "What sort of life will it be?" (104), suggest a new beginning with heightened uncertainty rather than a resolution and ending.

On the thematic plane, too, motifs that seem to mark a character's place in the story's social order become, through contextual associations, charged with meanings undermining that order. Thus, the king-making motif of money is associated with death in the tales of robbery and murder told by Pantelei.

This simultaneous movement toward both creating and undermining order finds emblematic expression in the world of Moisei Moiseich's inn. One reader has suggested that the hostel "can be viewed as a microcosm of the steppe, complete with a small windmill in the garden" (Maxwell, 148); the hostel can also be seen as a parodical microcosm of "The Steppe." Notions of propriety and convention are manifest in the painfully excessive hospitality of Moisei; they are also ridiculed by his brother, Solomon. Moisei wants badly to serve his customers in proper fashion. He observes carefully the conventions of his trade and in every word or gesture stays well within his lowly social position. The homebred existentialist Solomon, by contrast, has adopted a negationist attitude toward conventions of any kind. Moisei is always referred to by name *and* patronymic, Moiseich; Solomon, his brother, by first name only.

If the opposition between these two brothers reflects a particular structural feature of "The Steppe," then the two prints hanging on the walls of Moisei Moiseich's guest room represent—as in *mise en abyme*—that same opposition:

> There was nothing akin to decoration on either walls or windows. Nevertheless, on one wall, in a gray wooden frame, hung some sort of regulations with a two-headed eagle, while on the other, in the same sort of frame, hung some sort of engraving with the title: "The Indifference of People." To what people were indifferent was impossible to understand, though, since the engraving had largely faded from time and was lavishly flyblown. (32)

Each brother's name and character associates him with one of the prints: Moisei, the family patriarch, recalls the Old Testament's great patriarch and receiver of the law, Moses, and so can be linked with the print of the Czarist symbol and list of regulations. Solomon is a sophist whose thought reflects the existential sensibilities of King Solomon, author of the Book of Ecclesiastes. His response to the laws or regulations that make a slave of him is perverse indifference, and this aspect of his character finds reflection in the flyblown print.[14]

Related to the aspect of "The Steppe" in which any movement toward order is accompanied by the undermining of that order is the point that Solomon, once a successful storyteller, no longer cares to take on that role. There is an intimate connection between Solomon's cynicism and his abandoned talent. Solomon voices contempt for conventions of hierarchy: "I am my brother's lackey, my brother is the lackey of passersby, the passersby are the lackeys of Varlamov, and if I had ten million, then Varlamov would be my lackey" (39). Order is a function of capital, and Solomon, scornful of both, has burned his father's legacy in order to avoid taking the place which, by convention, this money assigns him. But narrative, it should be pointed out, is also ordered and held together by conventions;[15] such is the assumption behind any notion of poetics, and certainly behind this discussion of metapoesis in "The Steppe." When finally, as though against his own will, Solomon assumes the role of storyteller, his tales provoke an angry response from the easygoing Father Khristofor: "If you don't like your faith, then change it, but to laugh is a sin; it's the last man who mocks his own faith" (40). Solomon has repudiated even that system of rules which keeps whole the social self.[16]

The aspect of "The Steppe" that deliberately disrupts the story's apparent order can therefore be called "Solomonesque." Similarly, the tendency to present a surface continuous and ordered in a traditionally acceptable way can be associated with the figures of Varlamov and Moisei, the lawgiver and the law-receiver. Solomon and Varlamov then become personifications of the two opposing principles whose interplay delineates the story's irregular surface structure.

3 The Composition of Motifs

The deceptive, discontinuous nature of the surface structure of "The Steppe" can be alluring: what seems misshapen draws one more deeply into the story's structure, in search of a viewpoint from which even the erratic will make sense. It jolts the reader into contemplating the story's poetics, as the secondary literature on "The Steppe" indicates. On the plane of motifs in "The Steppe" there are two striking appearances of deformity: the carter and naturalist, Vasya, whose jaw is horribly malformed (the symptom of a disease contracted while working in a match factory); and Moisei's inn, with its pitted, cracked floor and odd, uncomfortably shaped furniture. We will return to Vasya shortly; but the malformed chairs and deteriorating floor — the artifices, in a sense, of Moisei's hotel, itself a microcosm of "The Steppe" — can symbolize the story's own apparently inadequate artifices.

The chapter depicting Egorushka's stay at the inn (chapter 3) is correlated with the passage in chapter 5 describing the Great Russian's shop, which Egorushka visits alone after leaving the peasant carters in church. The shopkeeper's character positively combines the opposing tendencies represented in Moisei and Solomon, and in the prints on their wall: "His face reflected complete indifference, but in each sigh one heard, 'Just wait, I'm gonna give it to you!' " (62). The man is authoritarian and can do as he pleases — even his sighs sound like threats — yet he acts kindly, inviting Egorushka to tea. His face is free of both Solomon's scorn and Varlamov's anger, and though the shopkeeper serves others, he does so without the obsequiousness of Moisei; his kindness is not oppressive to Egorushka, as was the Jew's.

Egorushka establishes the correlation between the two episodes when he takes the cookie Roza gave him out of his pocket and compares it to those for sale in the Great Russian's shop. It is revealed that the honeycake he has been carrying is worth more than any of the cookies in the shop, a puzzling development. The two-word paragraph that follows, "Silence ensued" (62), provides a space during which all of chapter 4 can be recalled.

There even turns out to be something Jewish about the Great Russian's shop: "The floor in the shop was poured [*polit*];[17] it was probably a great dreamer and free-thinker who poured it, because the whole thing was covered with figures and kabbalistic signs" (61–62). The introduction of these signs of kabbalistic magic recalls the exclamation provoked by the view of Boltva's windmill, "What a wizard!" (20). Just as this windmill symbolizes the alternating narrative voices in "The Steppe," so the shopkeeper's floor can be seen to represent the composition of motifs in the story. Egorushka carried away from the cramped, squalid Jewish world of the inn something that turned out to be of surprising value. Similarly, Chekhov has transferred something of value to his own Russian context: a particular attitude toward the word, epitomized by the kabbalistic tradition; and as the cookie's heart shape would seem to imply, this attitude can be seen as the story's organic center. "Kabbalah" is but one name given to many, often divergent traditions, and it is unlikely that Chekhov had more than a common idea what these esoteric traditions involved.[18] Still, a few general comments seem called for by the appearance of this kabbalistic motif in the story.

For kabbalists, language is far more than a communicative code; it is the agent of which reality itself is created. As an interpretive discipline, Kabbalah views all the world as a text awaiting decipherment. This is especially true of the Torah or Pentateuch, which, as the direct word of God, holds a privileged position in the hierarchy of this world. One undertakes this interpretive task not merely to get some message, but to attain revelation of the mysteries of creation; to *see* God as He reveals himself in creation. In Gershom Scholem's words, "The main basis of the kabbalistic attitude toward the Torah is . . . the fundamental belief in the correspondence between creation and revelation" (169). What is more, the laws governing creation and, if one understands them, permitting revelation, are those of language: "The hidden processes of the universe . . . can themselves be regarded as essentially linguistic in nature" (Scholem, 177). In referring to kabbalah, then, Chekhov invokes a cosmic principle of metapoesis.

In Kabbalah, however, revelation can come about only in an indirect, symbolic way, and to achieve it a reader's vision must penetrate beyond the literal, referential surface to see figures entirely internal to a text. To cite Scholem again:

> The kabbalistic attitude to the Pentateuch, and in a somewhat lesser degree to the Bible as a whole, was a natural corollary of the overall kabbalistic belief in the symbolic character of all earthly phenomena. There was literally nothing . . . which in addition to its exterior aspect did not also possess an interior aspect in which there existed a hidden, inner reality on various levels. (168)

It is just this "interior aspect" of Chekhov's story that we wish to comprehend and articulate.

Worth noting is a kabbalistic parallel to our claim that the flaws in the surface structure of "The Steppe" only add significance to the text's hidden, internal aspects:

> The author of the *Zohar* [the canonical kabbalistic text], whose belief in the primacy of kabbalistic interpretation was extreme, actually expressed the opinion that had the Torah simply been intended as a series of literal narratives, he and his contemporaries would have been able to compose a better book! Occasionally kabbalistic interpretations would deliberately choose to stress certain words or verses that seemed insignificant on the surface and to attribute to them profound symbolic importance. (173)

Chekhov's letter of January 18, 1888, to Ia. P. Polonsky, suggests that readers of "The Steppe" take such extreme measures: "There are many places that will be understood by neither critics nor the public; they will seem trifling to both, not meriting attention, but I anticipate with pleasure the two or three literary epicurians that will understand and value these same places, and that is enough for me" (*Pis'ma* 2:178). We can expect, then, that apparently unimportant places will become highly significant when the text's internal processes — the processional association of motifs through puns, metaphor, and metonymy — are revealed.

The kabbalistic floor, itself a text of sorts, thus becomes a model for the interpretation of "The Steppe." One thinks of a floor as stationary and flat, but the participle used to describe it, "*polit*" (poured), suggests an essentially fluid nature. In the letter cited at the start of this chapter, Chekhov describes the separate stories making up "The Steppe" as being "as closely related as five figures in a quadrille." One can see how this analogy with dance echoes Chekhov's compositional method: through the process of figuration, those kabbalistic signs cast into the Great Russian's floor — esoteric symbols concealed in Chekhov's text, but found when our eye was drawn to the malformed floor of Moisei's inn — are allowed a lifelike freedom of movement. Why not? In the *Zohar*, the very letters of the word for God are personified, copulate, and give birth to other letters, thus creating the whole of His name. The various Hebrew names of God, as well as their anagrams and other such configurations, are all considered to retain the mystical powers associated with his His figure. And Chekhov himself animates stones, bushes, and windmills throughout the narrative of "The Steppe." [19]

To pursue Chekhov's analogy: on the plane of motifs the movement of "The Steppe" is like a dance that leaves traces, one in which each step is remembered. As the story proceeds, motifs are repeated in new contexts or coupled with other motifs through the use of figurative language. In these unions each gathers semantic value from the other, even as it gives some up, and by this mutual exchange meaning is constantly accumulated and made more complex. There is a dramatic movement to this process, in which the essential element of conflict can be found in the polarized, anti-"Steppe" world of Moisei's inn; there motifs are combined that prove incompatible. As Egorushka sits at Moisei's table and struggles to remain awake, his thoughts are said to be tangled "like knots" (37). The congruity between this simile and the classical formulation of dramatic structure as the tying and untying of a knot is no accident, for this scene is the turning point in the underlying dramatic movement of "The Steppe." Also appearing at this critical moment is the story's biblical theme: Egorushka notices the odor of rotten apples, a motif that recalls the forbidden fruit whose consumption is itself the turning point in the story of man's Fall.[20]

A word play found in "The Steppe" illustrates this process of expansion and crisis nicely. The Russian word "*tochno*" can denote both "precisely" and "as though," two rather divergent significations. Things that exist "precisely" as themselves are related to one another through "as though" in a process of figuration specific to language. A rock looks as though it is a man (45), Moisei has a birdlike figure (30), and so on. In such a tightly composed, poetic text as "The Steppe," such associations are not accidental; as they accumulate, so too does the obvious difference between the terms of such associations, which in turn makes itself known as tension within the meaning of these terms. The end of this process, surfacing at the level of characterization in Egorushka, is sickness and nausea. In Russian, "*toshnota*" denotes sickness, and is just subtly divergent from the word "*tochno.*" To sum up: discrete, "precise" things (*tochno*) are related through figurative language ("as though," *tochno*) until the difference accumulated in this process as tension causes crisis in meaning and sickness (*toshnota*).[21] So, in the spirit of Kabbalah, might one summarize "The Steppe."

In Egorushka the violent agitation of the storm and illness sever, or at least displace from consciousness, the contradictory associations that have developed in the course of a journey through the steppe. Thus the heart-shaped honeycake, a token of Egorushka's stay at the Jewish inn and all that took place there, grows waterlogged during the storm, loses its shape, and is finally eaten by a big white dog. This storm was promised in the story's very first chapter: during its thunderous downpour the breakdown anticipated by the "thunder" the carriage produces and its "readiness to fall apart" (13) is finally realized.

Following a few major motifs through significant passages illustrates the scheme outlined above. Since cookies are so freshly in mind, let us first discuss the motif of food.

Early in "The Steppe," Egorushka recalls the sweets his grandmother used to make for him, and reference is made to the content faces and full bellies of Kuzmichov and Father Khristofor. These recollections of meals already taken, along with the midday rest stop of chapter 2, have an expository function. In the latter passage, the search for Varlamov is discussed, notions of hierarchy are reflected in Kuzmichov's treatment of Deniska, and the stories Father Khristofor tells of his own education serve as paradigms through which the purpose (or purposelessness) of Egorushka's journey can be understood; here too the countess is prefigured in the singing peasant woman.

An element of conflict within the motif of food is introduced through its unpleasant associations at Moisei's inn. There sweets are unfavorably compared to the delicacies of Egorushka's home, and money smells like rotten apples and kerosene. Tension rises during each successive meal, reaching a high point when the wandering Konstantin brings to the "table" a freshly killed bird—that is, raw and indigestable food. Then the motif of food is coupled with the knife motif, through the metallic taste of the melon Egorushka eats during the storm, after which, in the story's denouement, the sick child vomits.

Implicit in Egorushka's ability to digest what Father Khristofor brings him toward the end is physical recovery and a resolution of the food motif; and in the story's epilogue, meals are taken in the child's new home, perhaps suggesting that food has recovered its original associations of home and security, perhaps suggesting a new beginning to the cycle outlined here.

The knife motif follows a similar pattern of development. The description of mowers early in "The Steppe" appears as a touch of local color; the peasants and their scythes, a common sight, produce no alarm in Egorushka. Indeed, the blades of these tools are said to "glisten gaily" (17). But the very same scythes turn to "long knives" and peasants become murderers in the nighttime stories of robbery and death told later in "The Steppe." While the tales are told, moreover, all are aware of the two graves that lie just outside their campsite. A merchant and his son, murdered by mowers with scythes, lie buried there.

Once again, the first intimations of an association between the knife motif and the motif of a violent death are found in Moisei's hostel. There are no "long knives" here, but there are a number of references to the "long nose" of Solomon; and in Russian, "long knife" (*dlinnyi nozh*) and "long nose" (*dlinnyi nos*) differ by only a minimal phonological distinction. What is more, Solomon reminds Egorushka of something like an "unclean spirit" (*nechistii dukh*, 41), and ghosts, the unclean spirits of murderers, figure heavily in the stories told by Dymov and Pantelei. During the storm Egorushka thinks he sees giants following him with picks, in his hallucination equivalent to very long knives (87). Shortly thereafter he is given a piece of melon to eat, but tastes only the knife which cut it—a knife "very similar to those knives with which robbers slash merchants in hostels" (89)—and is overcome by nausea. Varlamov is also associated with this knife motif, though in an indirect and negative way. Father Khristofor asserts that Varlamov will be found because he "is not a needle" (98).

The storytelling motif traces the same pattern of development. Toward the beginning of "The Steppe," Father Khristofor offers tales of his own erudite youth in order to soothe Egorushka and create a sense of this journey's value. During the first day's rest stop, there is also mention of Defoe's *Robinson Crusoe* (23); perhaps Egorushka's predicament can be understood in terms of the famous castaway's story. Finally, Egorushka associates the wide road that takes him across the steppe with those of the Russian folk epic: "Who could need such space? It was incomprehensible and strange. One could actually think that those widely stepping giants like Ilya Muromets and Solovei Razboinik still existed in Russia, and that the steeds of giant heroes [*bogatyry*] had not all died out" (48).

Nevertheless, in none of these instances do stories subvert what is presented as reality. Egorushka pays little attention to the priest's rather absurd, paradoxical tales; the allusion to *Robinson Crusoe* neither confuses Egorushka's image of the old priest nor provides any sort of key for understanding his own, unhappy situation; and last, the folk tales are explicitly recognized as fictions and their heroes as purely imaginary figures: "And how fitting to the face of the steppe and the road these figures would be, if they had existed!" (48).

Yet Egorushka soon comes to take the tales narrated by Pantelei as "freshly minted coins" (72), and through this error the logic of nightmares prevails over the logic of conscious, rational thought. Story after story about robbery, murder, and the intervention of otherworldly forces somehow implant in Egorushka the notion of his own imminent death.

Throughout "The Steppe" the real and the unreal exist together, and characters fictionalize their own lives at will. This feature of life on the steppe is taken up in a digression from the passage describing the evening of storytelling: "Life is terrible and wondrous, and therefore no matter what kind of terrible story you tell in Russia, no matter how you embellish it with robber's dens, long knives, and wonders, it always echoes with reality in the listener's soul—save perhaps the strongly literate, skeptically inclined sort of person, and even he will be silent" (72). In "The Steppe," Solomon is the most "skeptically inclined person"; for Egorushka he is a prototypical storyteller as well: "About two years ago, Egorushka well remembered, Solomon . . . narrated scenes from Jewish life and achieved great success" (33). The notion that storytelling must reflect real events can thus be traced back to Moisei's inn and the figure of Solomon.

This unraveling and extraction of motifs has an unavoidable degree of arbitrariness to it; one could isolate more and different motifs in a process with limitless variations. Yet there is a common form to each "history of motif"; one sees the manner in which motifs couple, as well as the nodal function of the chapter concerning Moisei's inn.

This interpretive strategy also provides insight into Egorushka's characterization. Egorushka's crises are a part of his struggle to comprehend an expanding world through language; his problem is one of reading and establishing meaning. Earlier the Russian word "*tochno*" was punned to create a model for the process of expanding motifs. Through the use of "as though," "like," and other verbal devices that create figures of speech, new things are grasped, conceptualized, and read, so to speak, through the preexisting text of memory. But the associations one makes in language, it could be argued, often have far more to do with language itself than with the phenomena they are meant to fence in (unless, that is, one is a poet or mystic). It seems only natural, then, that moments when the conceptual links established between the terms of a figurative association are concretized should be moments of crisis; that crises should occur when life takes on a poetic texture. Thus, while Egorushka is ill Father Khristofor is referred to directly as "Robinson Crusoe," realizing the figurative association made near the beginning of "The Steppe" (96). Likewise, during the thunderstorm Emelyan, who has covered himself with a rug and so taken a triangular shape, is metonymically named "triangle" (*treugol'nik*, 88).

Throughout the story the conceptual assimilation of new phenomena is related to the digestive process. Father Khristofor, for instance, calls his own philosophizing "spiritual food" (22). This is yet another case of a single word having two meanings — the assimilation of food and the assimilation of impressions — the juncture and interplay of which gives rise to a textual tension and, at the level of character, crisis.[22] In the final pages of "The Steppe," one reads the parenthetically enclosed (and therefore unique in the story) statement: "All red-haired dogs bark in a tenor" (101). Here Egorushka, overfed with impressions, has given palatable form to something inedible. This encapsulated, precociously reasoned bit of wisdom is like a piece of food that looks good—it is grammatically and, so far as Egorushka can recall, empirically a correct statement—but it is indigestible, false, so that in the place of an indication of the wisdom Egorushka has gained through his journey, which one might well expect at the story's conclusion, we find the negation of wisdom and a foreshadowing of Egorushka's next crisis.

4 The Steppe as Literary Space

The metapoetic images we have been unearthing in "The Steppe" reflect just those features of the story's structure that readers have found most troublesome. They provide a perspective on the story's unity which, because it relies on figures internal to "The Steppe," acquires a special authenticity.[23] But the whole story can also be seen as such an image, with the steppe serving as a metaphor for literary space. Each attempt to articulate some structural feature of the story has led to a passage iconically representing that feature because the description of its own poetics is an overriding narrative principle of "The Steppe."

The story is abundant with imagery which, added to the passages of metapoetic significance already discussed, helps orient this allegorical reading. When Egorushka awakens on the morning after his transfer from the buggy of his uncle to the cart train, the steppe's vastness "aroused bewilderment in him and led him to fairy-tale thoughts" (48); here the physical spaciousness of the steppe is linked with spaciousness of imagination. In the following paragraph one reads: "Along the whole length of the right side of the road stood telegraph poles with two lines. Growing smaller and smaller, they disappeared behind greenery and huts near a town, and then reappeared in the lilac distance, in the form of very small, thin sticks that looked like pencils stuck in the ground" (48–49). The equivalence behind the simile associating telegraph poles with pencils suggests that the earth of the steppe is like text.

In a passage discussed earlier the narrator makes the explicitly metaliterary statement, "Life is terrible and wondrous, and therefore no matter what kind of terrible story you tell of Russia, no matter how you embellish it with robber's dens, long knives, and wonders, it always echoes with reality in the listener's soul . . ." (72–73). Although these words refer to the tales of thieves and murders told around the campfire during Egorushka's travels, they still define the steppe — indeed, all of Russia — as something more than geopolitical space: it is literary space as well.

The journey Egorushka and his uncle take on foot through the maze of streets leading to the home of Nastasya Toskunova culminates and, in a sense, repeats the journey across the steppe. At one point Chekhov writes: "When their feet and tongue had brought them to Malaya Nizhnaya ["Little Lower"] Street, they were both red and, taking off their hats, they wiped away the sweat" (100). The word "*iazyk*" can be understood to signify both "tongue" and "language." The immediate context suggests that here it refers to the directions Kuzmichov asks for as he and Egorushka make their way across town,[24] but this also happens to be the end of the whole journey described in "The Steppe."

As a final example, there is the simile with which Chekhov describes Moisei's beard: it is black "like Indian ink" (*kak tush'*, 30). While the comparison to Indian ink is but one of many available synonyms for *very* black, the vast choice of such possibilities confers a special significance to this selection. Moreover, we can clearly see a pattern in "The Steppe" of using figurative language to introduce meanings associated with the semantic field of reading and writing, making the present instance anything but arbitrary.

Chekhov's letters are also full of comments which, through their play with those same motifs found in "The Steppe," suggest that the story be read as an allegory. In a letter to Pleshcheev, Chekhov makes use of the earth/text as a metaphor when he warns that the story is likely to be a "field for disappointments" (*pole dlia razocharovanii*, 182). In the very same letter, he says that he should write a schoolbook titled "Theory of Literature," and that he will definitely hurry to this task upon finishing "The Steppe." This statement shows, at the very least, that Chekhov was interested in the more theoretical aspects of writing fiction during the period when he wrote "The Steppe"; it is also possible that he was giving Pleshcheev a joking hint regarding the true nature of "The Steppe," for the idea of a schoolbook or primer containing a theory of literature parallels our notion of "The Steppe" as the story of a child which also embodies a discussion of its own poetics.

Before "The Steppe" was written, many of Chekhov's literary acquaintances had urged the young author of humorous sketches to take his work more seriously. While writing the story, Chekhov sent a letter to one such acquaintance, Vladimir Korolenko, in which he said: "Not just you, from a pure heart, have set me on the true path, and you can understand how ashamed I am" (*Pis'ma* 2:170). Here the writing of a serious work is associated with the initiation of a journey. Note also the element of coercion present here, as in Egorushka's situation.

As Bitsilli writes, " 'The Steppe' is the most brilliant, most demonstrative specimen of Chekhov's compositional manner . . ." (*Tvorchestvo*, 68). Chekhov's poetics is most apparent in this story because poetics is the subject of the story. Recalling the letter to Grigorovich cited at this chapter's start, it even seems possible to call "The Steppe" an encyclopaedia of Chekhovian poetics. We ask next what the story's metapoetic commentary reveals about certain cardinal features of Chekhov's poetics, namely laconicity and musicality (especially relevant here because of the length and lyricism of "The Steppe"); and we will speculate as to why Chekhov felt compelled to present such an "encyclopaedia" in the work marking his emergence as an author to be taken seriously.

5 Chekhov on Chekhov's Poetics

Chekhov's maxim regarding laconicity is widely known: if there is mention of a gun in a story or play, then it is necessary that in the end the gun go off. Explains Bitsilli: "For him, every work of verbal art is ideally its own sort of system, where all elements are connected with one another and where nothing can replace anything else; otherwise, the whole system disintegrates. This is laconicity" (*Tvorchestvo*, 27). Chekhov demands that every detail in a story be necessary and related to other details.

It is easy to see, however, that laconicity is a two-sided issue; indeed, while our point of departure for interpreting "The Steppe" was the postulation of a systematic nature to the story, we have also had to contend with a perverse tendency in the story undermining those laws by which everything is necessary and related to everything else. Recalling the steppe at night, when "everything presents itself as that which it is not," one might say that as a system "The Steppe" functions by means of just such substitutions, by freeing the semantic loads of words to wander from one vehicle to another, all the while remembering this complex process of exchange. What is more, if a story is to seem at all original, its order must somehow be disguised, known only in retrospect, and those laws of necessity governing the function of detail must be masked. Chekhov remarks on the originality of "The Steppe" again and again in his letters, often calling this characteristic "frightful"; yet there can be no doubt that this was precisely the effect he sought.[25]

Though laconicity is clearly not the same as brevity, the two are related such that to achieve some measure of laconicity becomes a greater task as a work's length increases. Discounting his early serialized potboiler *The Shooting Party* (*Drama na okhote*), "The Steppe" was Chekhov's first long story, and his letters show that maintaining creative standards throughout the piece was an ordeal: "I sin involuntarily, because, as it now turns out, I am not yet able to write long things" (*Pis'ma* 2:174). The subject of the steppe—terrain that verges on being an utterly useless desert—together with the role repetition plays in the story's unique composition, the travelers' boredom, and the story's concealment of its inner movement all make laconicity especially difficult. The story's narration cannot be likened to a straight road running from Egorushka's home to the journey's end, since this "Story of a Journey" describes, more than anything else, rest stops and side trips away from that journey. Digression is thus not only allowed, but essential, so that we cannot even discuss laconicity without discussing superfluity and excess as well.

The Countess Dranitskaya is the very paradigm of that which is digressive in "The Steppe." Her home is a pleasure palace with extravagant parties and exotic foods, while her name provokes association with the Russian adjective "*dranyi*" (torn, ragged), the colloquial "*dran'e*" (worn-out or torn clothing),[26] or perhaps even further, with "*drian'*" (rubbish, refuse)—in a word, that which is utterly without use. Nevertheless, the countess provokes in all a vague and impossible desire, a wistfulness that can in turn be productive. She has no plot function; and yet the characters all orient themselves toward her. This lyrical digression, presented as Egorushka sleeps, illustrates the special force associated with the countess's figure. In the story's original version it occurs as Egorushka dreams about the countess, at night, when the steppe—like the countess—is clothed in black; it refers to both the steppe and the countess:

> And then, in the chirping of insects, in the suspicious figures and mounds, in the blue heavens, in the moonlight, in the flight of the night bird, in all that you see and hear, there

> begins to appear the exultation of beauty, youth, the blossom of strength and the fervent thirst for life. The soul gives a response to the fine, harsh native land and you want to fly over the steppe together with the night bird. And in the exultation of beauty, in the excess of happiness, you feel agitation and longing, as though the steppe recognizes that she is lonely, that her richness and her inspiration perish to the world in vain, unnoticed and unneeded by anyone, and through the joyful hum you hear her melancholy, hopeless appeal: a bard! a bard! (46)

In this lyrical passage the steppe does find its bard. Excess and superfluity have in fact led to an act of artistic creation. Rather than making everything clearly functional, laconicity maintains a tense interplay between the necessary and the unnecessary, both mutually vital, correlative features of the steppe.

This interplay is iconically represented in the description of the Great Russian's store. Half the store is devoted to the necessities of labor and, significantly, to the kind of labor binding things together: here one finds tar and yokes. The store's other half is devoted to knickknacks, beautiful things, and sweets (61). These two halves sit on a common floor, however, and it is this floor with kabbalistic signs that provides mediation between the excessive and the necessary, both in the Great Russian's store and in Chekhov's "The Steppe."

In letters Chekhov underlined the musical aspect of his work. To V. M. Sobolevsky he wrote, "I read proofs not to correct the exterior of a story . . . but to . . . finish off a story and correct it, so to speak, from the musical side" (*Pis'ma* 7:101). Recall that his letter to Grigorovich likens the internal unity of "The Steppe" to that of the quadrille, a dance accompanied by a certain kind of music. One might approach the relationship of "The Steppe" to music by pointing out correlations between the poetics of music and of this story. One could also search for patterns of alliteration, consonance, rhyming, or the calling into play of some sort of meter. The contrapuntal presentation of motifs such as boredom and discovery can be called musical;[27] what is more, this aspect of the story may be related to the French quadrille—a dance that probably has its origins in *contredanse* (Raffe, 403–4)—mentioned in Chekhov's letters. In view of the story's self-descriptive tendency, however, it seems most promising to approach Chekhov's musicality through an examination of the motif of music in "The Steppe."

The motif of music in "The Steppe" invariably appears together with the motif of water, so the two must be discussed together. Chekhov likely borrowed this association from Goncharov, whose *The Frigate Pallada* (*Frigat Pallada*), the journal of a round-the-world voyage by sea, is clearly echoed in the climactic, lyrical description of the steppe ending in a plea for a bard (cited above; Bitsilli, *Tvorchestvo*, 7–8).[28] Goncharov's sea becomes a complementary metaphor for Chekhov's steppe: in "The Steppe" the night conceals and oppresses the steppe and its riches, while in *The Frigate Pallada* the quiet, empty sea is said to squander a night that should be filled with "serenades," "sighs," "whispers of love," and "nightingales." Both of these passages end with pleas for a song. This metaphorical relationship between the steppe and the sea underlies the whole of "The Steppe," but surfaces at both the most pleasant moment of Egorushka's journey and at the most horrible, during his swim (57) and during the crisis of the thunderstorm (85–88).

The motif of music first appears at an earlier, more tentative surfacing of the sea/steppe metaphor. During the midday rest stop on the first traveling day, Egorushka hears the song of a peasant woman just after he drinks from a spring. When in chapter 5 Egorushka and the carters bathe in a stream, music is associated with the ecstatic relief of a swim: "On a hot day, when there is nowhere to hide from the heat and stuffiness, the splash of water and the loud gasps of a swimmer act on the ear like fine music" (56). Here music touches and relieves, but like every motif already discussed, the motif of music is given ambivalent meaning in "The Steppe." Water took the music-loving Emelyan's voice away from him: he lost it when he caught cold after swimming. And the monotonous, mournful song of the peasant woman only intensifies Egorushka's sense of oppression.

In the end, what musicality cannot do may best define its function in Chekhov's poetics. The musical aspect of "The Steppe" is absolutely incapable of communicating experience or relating wisdom. Konstantin, when narrating the tale that culminates the cycle of storytelling in chapter 6, forgets his story's most critical detail: Dymov asks what words, after three years of refusal, persuaded Konstantin's beloved to marry. "Words? I don't remember... And what's to remember? Then it was like water from a gutter, without a breath: ta-ta-ta! And now I can't repeat one word..." (77). Here musicality is associated with a direct outpouring of desire, a flow apart from any conscious meaning and unmediated by the conventional signification of words.

Konstantin imparts no knowledge of the world to the carters and Egorushka. He entertains them for a short while, then leaves, in the end only infecting them with a heightened sense of boredom and longing. This longing is in a sense the very goal of Egorushka's journey: he will live in the home of Nastasya Toskunova, whose name cannot help but suggest the Russian "*toska*" (mournful longing, wistfulness).

In following the motif of water, one finds that "The Steppe" presents an allegory of its own reading and misreading. Toward the end of chapter 4 the cart train pauses near a well:

> Lowering his bucket into the well, the black-bearded Kiriukha lay with his stomach on the framework, and thrust a part of his chest into the dark hole, so that only his short legs, barely touching the ground, were visible to Egorushka; seeing his head reflected in the well's bottom from a distance, he grew pleased and poured forth a stupid, deep-voiced laughter, and the well's echo answered him with like; when he got up, his face and neck were red, like calico. (54)

Dymov takes his turn at the well, finishes, then utters "loudly, for the whole steppe, about five obscenities" (54). If in "The Steppe" the steppe is figuratively likened to literary space, while water is a metaphoric counterpart to the steppe, it follows that water too can serve as a figure for text. And the well provides an opportunity to look deeply into the earth, beyond the textual surface.

The image of reflection here also suggests reading this passage as being about reading. Both Dymov and Kiriukha are presented as simple-minded, violent men. We first meet them as they are killing a grass snake (51–52), and Dymov listens to the stories of Pantelei with an even more fearful, literal-minded, and childish attitude than that of Egorushka. One might therefore see these two characters as simple-minded, violent readers as well. They stare into a well of the steppe but see only themselves; and they respond to the steppe with obscenities, the most thoughtless, conventional words available to them. For them, in short, reading is a superficial, specular reflection; it is all surface, it forgets what lies beneath.

Musicality adds a depth to Chekhov's texts like the depth of the stream in which the carters bathe: "The water, deep because the heavens were reflected in it, passionately beckoned to itself" (56). The verb used here, "*manit'*" (to beckon), recalls the "deceptive steppe" and that motif of wizardry and magic in which the windmill and kabbalistic floor each play a part (in Russian, "to deceive" [*obmanut'*] and "to beckon" [*manit'*] share the same root). If this stream, like the well, serves as a figure for text, then Egorushka's swim can be seen as a correlate to the passage about Kiriukha and Dymov at the well.

Egorushka dives as deeply into the stream as he can:

> . . . some power, cold and pleasant to the touch, caught hold of him and carried him back upwards. He emerged and, snorting and making bubbles, opened his eyes; but the sun was reflected on the river right near his face. In the beginning blinding sparks, then rainbows and dark patches passed before his eyes; he hurried to dive again, opened his eyes under water, and saw something murky green, like the sky on a moonlit night. Again that same force, not allowing him to touch bottom and stay in the cool, carried him upwards; he emerged and sighed so deeply that it grew spacious and fresh not only in his chest, but even in his stomach. (57)

The image of "something murky green, like the sky on a moonlit night," is linked to the countess, by way of the vision Egorushka has later, while gazing at the sky on a moonlit night: "The quiet, warm night lowered itself upon him and whispered something in his ear, and it seemed to him that that beautiful woman [he has been thinking of the countess] bent down to him with a smile, and wanted to kiss..." (78). The color green also recalls the green, shapely poplar tree that Egorushka remembers when he first meets the countess. This ecstatic moment under water is presented as the inverse of Egorushka's crisis: here his stomach is "fresh," whereas during the storm he suffers nausea.

Egorushka never touches the bottom of this stream, and the image he finds while immersed *reflects* nothing from outer reality. It represents no one thing, though it can be associated with many. One would never expect music to reflect something in the way Kiriukha's face is reflected by the well-water's surface, however. The same process of association that makes Egorushka sick and provides a climax to the story, the free play of Egorushka's memory, produces at this peaceful moment an image associable with the figure of the countess. Words transmit messages only insofar as they have meanings which are relatively stable and known to a given circle of communicants. Music, on the other hand, can at best provoke in them a mnemonic play of signifiers which, in turn, gives rise to a shared sense of "return." The fixed significations of words are like fences barring entry to this text of memory, where words do not signify so much as resonate.

Chekhov's wish to be musical is a wish to pass through this fence into a realm where words conduct themselves with an always-innocent semantic promiscuity, freeing themselves of loud, obscene, and restrictive signifieds. Such a mythic, Edenic realm would in "The Steppe" be associated with the Countess Dranitskaya.

Egorushka thinks of the countess after hearing Konstantin's story: "[W]ith such a woman, probably, it would be very pleasant to live; he [Egorushka] would perhaps marry her with pleasure, if it were not so shameful" (78). What might be allowable inside Eden is shameful outside its gates. The force that tugs Egorushka back up to the stream's surface and the curses resounding over "the whole steppe" — Chekhov's whole text — are reminders that musicality, like Egorushka's vision, is but a wish or dream embedded in "The Steppe." The story realizes this wish to the degree that it manages, beneath and in spite of a conventionally signifying surface, to extend itself through a process of figuration rather than, or in addition to, affording the "stupid glee" of recognizing one's own reflection.

Musicality is thus a site where opposing forces clash: the wish to dive deeply into the musical possibilities of language, and the force of lexical meaning that always draws one toward the surface. Like laconicity and every other structural feature of "The Steppe" already discussed, this contradiction is represented in the story. In the passage likening telegraph poles to pencils (cited earlier), Chekhov proceeds to describe birds sitting on the pair of wires that run from pole to pole. These wires resemble, in this image, the staff on which music is written, and — as in a child's musical primer — the birds perched on them are like notes. They disappear into the "greenery" (remember Egorushka's underwater vision) and reemerge in the "lilac distance" as "thin sticks" which are, in turn, likened to pencils. It is an iconic reconciliation, above the steppe, of word and music.

6 Why Metapoesis?

In one of his letters to Grigorovich Chekhov concretized the metaphor of the steppe as literary space, and, tongue in cheek, he named Gogol as landowner: "I know that in the other world Gogol will get angry with me. He is the czar of the steppe in our literature. I've stolen onto his property with good intentions, but I've talked a lot of nonsense" (Feb. 5, 1888;

Pis'ma 2:190). How indeed did Chekhov, the most belated of nineteenth-century Russian authors, feel as he stepped onto the lands of the authors who preceded him? Here after all was an author who, with a few rare exceptions, refused to publish under his own name, to formally identify himself before his reading public as a Russian author, for the first six years of his publishing career. Might there still have been something of Moisei in him, something of Egorushka when he sees giants behind him—the anxieties of a transgressor and sheer fear? It is surely no coincidence that Egorushka's age of "about nine years" roughly corresponds to the length of Chekhov's writing career when he wrote "The Steppe."

We have seen this aspect of the story's poesis thematized on the story's metapoetic plane, through the figuration of a whole series of encounters with readers. To these should be added the diseased carter Vasya, who of all the characters in "The Steppe" has the best eyesight. His vision penetrates into faraway places, and he can see the creatures of the steppe when they are off guard, at play in their homes: "Thanks to such sharp vision, Vasya had, in addition to the world everybody saw, his own, accessible to nobody else and probably very fine, because when he gazed and was enraptured, it was hard not to envy him" (56). Vasya sees animals as they "wash their paws," "preen their feathers," and "beat out their 'points'."[29] Vasya at times behaves more like an animal than a man: when the carters are preparing a meal from their catch of fish, he eats a live grudgeon. In short, one could call Vasya a true naturalist of the steppe. If this scene of "looking" is correlated with the passage in which Egorushka opens his eyes under water, and with the one in which Dymov and Kiriukha stare into a well, Vasya appears as a privileged reader, perhaps a figure for the author as reader; for Vasya can see the author's creations even when they are "nested" in the most hidden facets of their world, "The Steppe," and he can see what they do: they play, they wash their hands (relieve guilt?), they preen themselves (show pride?), and they demarcate their territory and express desire, all under cover, all in safety. Read metapoetically, this passage evokes a sense of creative vulnerability, and it appeals for a reader's delicacy; it is a counterexample to the killing of the grass snake.

But the story also offers a complex of imagery implying the possibility of bold and triumphant confrontations. When Egorushka visits Moisei's inn, he is taken into the family's bedroom. There, huddled in the bed—the nest of this steppe species—he sees the innkeeper's children: "If Egorushka had possessed a rich imagination, he could have thought that under the blanket lay a hundred-headed hydra" (39). Again we are offered an image juxtaposing surface and depth, with what cannot be perceived on the surface by Egorushka's naked eye made present through a different faculty — the narrator, explaining what Egorushka *might* have, or *ought* to have seen. And the narrator casts this natural domestic scene as one providing an opportunity for heroic feats (slaying the hydra), and an interpretive challenge: how to conceive of the manifold, manifestly present surface phenomena as being unified, as issuing from a common source. "The Steppe" resembles this hydra, with its separate faces joined deep within a nest, hidden from the reader's vision; and the story's complexity does indeed recall that of the mythical creature which grows two heads for each one lopped off, or so suggests our analysis of individual motifs in the story.

There is quite a bit of play in "The Steppe" with this serpent motif. The grass snake that Dymov kills, to Vasya's horror, can be seen as one pathetic refiguration of the mythical and dangerous hydra-head. Varlamov, through a subtle bit of word play, is also figured into this motif. When Pantelei reveals Varlamov to Egorushka, he says, "*on uzh na nogakh*," and "*Etot uzh ne upustit dela*" (79). Translated as the immediate context would seem to indicate, these statements read: "He is already on his feet," and "That fellow doesn't let his affairs get out of hand"; but the Russian word for grass snake, "*uzh*," is a homonym of the word for "already" used here, and if this second meaning of "*uzh*" is permitted to slither into Pantelei's comments — an operation requiring no grammatical or lexical changes — they can be read, "He is a grass snake on feet," and "This grass snake doesn't let his affairs get out of hand." [30] Thus Varlamov is linked with the serpent of Eden (who, until his prank, was a snake with feet), and with the myth of the Fall, one of the many slippery thematic lines in "The Steppe."

Even Egorushka's name calls into play this figure for the story's serpentine unity. Immediately before Dymov kills the grass snake, Pantelei notes that Egorushka's name is derived from that of Saint George the Dragonslayer (51). Egorushka's meeting with Varlamov — landlord of the steppe — thus becomes that battle with a dragon promised by the hero's name. Recalling their anticlimactic encounter, however, we see that this is yet another of those events in "The Steppe" that are promised but do not take place. Moreover, much as Chekhov treats the biblical figures of Moses and Solomon, the order of things suggested by the traditional story of Saint

George and the Dragon is overturned in the process of its integration into "The Steppe": here the serpent rather than the hero rides a horse.[31]

We have seen this irreverence in Chekhov's handling of other subtexts in "The Steppe," and such parodic operations represent nothing new for Chekhov: in his early humorous tales they are often central.[32] And yet one wonders if the role of parody and metapoesis in the work where Chekhov was "stepping out *originally*" (emphasis mine) can remain the same as in those early works. Affirming one's originality must involve a new relationship to tradition. The subtexts we have broached — St. George, the Old and New Testaments, Gogol's *Dead Souls*, Goncharov's *Frigat Pallada*, works of classical antiquity and traditions of Russian folklore — deserve more attention.[33]

Donald Rayfield has remarked that Chekhov's years of writing for the subliterary popular press postponed his confrontation with Russia's "high" literary tradition until his authorial ego was prepared: "Unlike Dostoevsky or Maupassant, Chekhov did not have to spend years working Gogol or Flaubert out of his system" ("Anton Chekhov," 35). And yet one is inclined to take seriously Chekhov's joke regarding the Gogolian influence on "The Steppe." In a letter to Suvorin several years after that remark, Chekhov contrasted his own generation of authors with its more impressive predecessors: "If you lift up the skirts of our muse, all you see is a flat area"; while of the more virile elders he wrote, "[T]hey have a certain goal, like the ghost of Hamlet's father" (Nov. 25, 1892; *Anton Chekhov's Life*, 243). If Chekhov suffered "anxiety of influence," he was also a conscious theorist of it (a supposition reinforced by his triangular and metaliterary *Seagull* [*Chaika*]).[34]

One suspects that metapoesis in "The Steppe" was a latecomer's way of dealing with these issues, of addressing and securing admission to the Russian prose tradition. Metapoesis in the story is covert — more so than in any other work taken up here — and therefore sets up a communication situation in which the addressee is split, as in "The Little House in Kolomna." But here there is no single "insider" addressee, nor has Chekhov set out to explore as a subtheme the metaphysical and ethical ramifications of authorship in ways that, we have observed, Dostoevsky and Tolstoy did. Instead, Chekhov constitutes himself as a practitioner in the tradition by the act of speaking its special language. He does so covertly in this career-making work — as opposed to the light-hearted spoofs of his earlier years —

perhaps because he is still working in the context of a literary system where the norm for serious literature calls for maximum transparency of literary convention and is therefore inhospitable to metaliterary play. A few years later, when he writes *The Seagull* for the stage, he will be much more bold. Finally, if (as letters suggest) Chekhov was anxious about stepping out ambitiously, about claiming the status of Russian author, surely he could not help but reflect deeply on the writing process in which he was engaged; and this reflection became figured into the text of "The Steppe."

A Conclusion:
Metapoesis and Tradition

When Edmund Wilson sent Vladimir Nabokov the gift of a new translation (which Nabokov found "dreadful") of stories by Chekhov, Nabokov wrote back, "Thanks for my predecessor's book" (*Nabokov-Wilson Letters*, 297–98). In what precise sense Nabokov considered Chekhov his predecessor remains provocatively unexplained, though Nabokov mentions "attention to the specific detail, to the unique image, without which—as you know as well as I do—there can be no art, no genius, no terror, no tenderness, and no surprise" (298). Simon Karlinsky, who has edited and annotated letters of both Chekhov and Nabokov, suggests that Nabokov had in mind Chekhov's courageous bucking of categories fixed by the dominant trends in literary criticism of the previous half-century (here we return to Chernyshevsky), his resumption of the "tradition of objective and independent literary art, not subservient to ideology, nationalism or religion" ("Nabokov and Chekhov," 15).[1] The preceding chapter suggests yet another reason for viewing Chekhov as Nabokov's predecessor: the latter certainly continued and arguably capped the Russian prose tradition of foregrounding the metapoetic function.[2]

These five works represent far too small a sampling to prove the literary-historical theses mentioned in the introduction, although they certainly advance the case. To recall, it was suggested that metapoesis constitutes a tradition extending through the nineteenth century; that it manifests the persistence of Romantic irony even after the poetics of Romanticism take a subordinate position in the Russian literary sytem; that in the diachronic series examined here, and in the specific instance of Pushkin's "Little House," one can see metapoesis "going underground," that is, becoming covert; and that metapoesis has special bearing on Russian literature's sense of itself as *Russian* literature, that it speaks to the well-traveled but still vital theme of "Russianness" (here the mixed metaphor is very much to the point).

Only a massive comparativist study could show that there is something distinctively Russian about this tradition. What is more, such a study would ultimately fail if it depended upon contrasting an absence of metapoesis in Western European literature of the Realist period with its marked presence in Russia. And yet it is clear that the very notion of tradition is inextricably bound to that of metapoesis. The author who writes metapoetically foregrounds the issue of literary tradition—the code, understood in its historical, social, and individual-psychological contexts—and therefore cannot help but intervene in the creation of a distinctive national literary tradition. As a cultural phenomenon Russian literature is an institution which is constantly being made and remade, and in regard to which every act of writing puts into question an author's inclusionary or exclusionary status; metapoesis is both symptom and agent of these processes.

To be sure, these processes play out differently in the belated Chekhov than they do in Pushkin, the heroic originator of this tradition who writes with foreign models in view (and yet, as Belinsky said, succeeds in rendering them distinctively Russian [Belinskii, "*Eugene Onegin*"]). Perhaps Dostoevsky's juxtaposition in *The Idiot* of the very Russian genre of the Petersburg tale with Western European Sentimentalist genres most clearly demonstrates the nexus between metapoesis and Russianness; indeed, this was the procedure in the work with which his career began, *Poor Folk* (*Bednye liudi*, 1846). Pushkin's characterization of Eugene Onegin as a "parody" and a "Russian in Childe Harolde's Cloak" does the same, though to a more equivocal end.

Metapoesis is not just a "mirror in the text," it is discourse pitched at a particular addressee. Whether intended as an aggressive challenge to readers, pedagogic glossing, self-defense, proof to those in the know that one shares their esoteric knowledge, play—or, in Russian literature after the Revolution, a "safe passage" (*okhrannaia gramota*) to preserve tradition and insure its transport to some future, more auspicious communication situation (Segal)—literary discourse in which the metapoetic function is foregrounded will at the very least pursue or reaffirm one's own inclusion, and perhaps others' exclusion, from a certain privileged community of readers and writers.

It is certainly true that all the authors we have discussed here felt that there was something special about being a *Russian* author. Too often the distinctive feature identifying such a personage has been understood, precisely, as "subservien[ce] to ideology, nationalism, or religion"; but now it may be possible to adduce another: metapoesis plays a great role in making Russian literature "Russian"—not as a feature that marks the Russian author as such, but as a dynamic discursive process situating the author in regard to a tradition.

This is perhaps most evident in Chekhov's "The Steppe," for all its hiddenness. It was to be expected, since Chekhov—the most accomplished and discrete literary thief among our five authors—arrives at the end of the century's distinguished prose tradition, and writes "The Steppe" as his ticket of admission. It is well to recall that his publishing career began in Moscow in the immense shadow of the Pushkin celebration of 1880, a landmark event in the formation of the sense of a native literary tradition in the broader Russian cultural consciousness.[3] In the letters he wrote to Grigorovich and Pleshcheev while laboring over the story, he addressed two of the living representatives of that tradition, and he indicated to them that they were his privileged addressees; through metapoesis in the story he addressed the tradition as such; and in the story about a child crossing the most Russian of landscapes, the narrator emerges to make broad generalizations about Russia and Russians (such as "Russians love to reminisce, but do not like to live...").

With Pushkin's "Little House," by contrast, the tradition to be mastered is less the Russian than the broader Western European one. And though the poem comprises a competition with its selected addressee precisely regarding literary mastery, a high degree of competence on the part of both the author and his secret addressee is never in doubt. Pushkin situates himself and his interlocutor in that tradition—in particular, identifying himself with Aesop, whose very figure, as presented in "The Life of Aesop," can be understood as a rumination upon the persona of the poet[4]—and meditates on the position of the poet in current Russian reality.

In the works by Gogol, Dostoevsky, and Tolstoy, metapoesis is implicated in the theme of Russia and the West, and more particularly, the Russian abroad. The first version of Gogol's self-defensive "Leaving the Theater" was begun on the eve of his own hasty departure from St. Petersburg, and the playlet was completed some six years later in Rome. This context of self-imposed exile is precisely what renders comprehensible the author's mania for feedback from his readers; great geographic distance also makes possible the peculiar "all-seeing" (Stilman) perspective Gogol attributes to the author in that playlet, and wishes for himself.

Our reading of Dostoevsky's *The Idiot* ascribes Myshkin's failure as an author to the choice of Western generic models inadequate for dealing with Russian reality; and there is a link between this failure and the moment sealing his fate as a character in the represented social world of the novel—his catastrophic Slavophile diatribe at Belokonskaya's salon. The novel's last words, in spite of the humorous accent they receive by being spoken by Madame Epanchin, manifest just this connection: "And all this being abroad, all this Europe of yours is only a fantasy, and all of us, when we're abroad, we are only a fantasy. Mark my words, you'll see for yourself."

In Tolstoy's *Anna Karenina*, as the biblical epigraph and "absolute language" of the novel's opening indicate, a very special addresser-addressee relationship is established—one that appears to address no particular reader from the point of view of absolute truth.[5] It is no exaggeration to say that the well-born and self-assured Tolstoy hardly deigned to address the Russian tradition in his metapoesis; he suffered no anxiety over the place of his art in Russian literature (where by the time of writing *Anna Karenina* he knew himself to be a "general"), even if he was wont to severely question his art in regard to what was true and good. And yet, it is no accident that some of the most overtly metapoetic moments in *Anna Karenina*—the discussions about art in Rome, Kitty's relationship with the painter Petrov—take place abroad. Here, as throughout nineteenth-century Russian literature, the Russian's travels abroad inevitably become a culturally self-reflexive moment, a moment foregrounding the question of what is distinctively Russian. And in *Anna Karenina* the two chief segments dealing with this subject—the Shcherbatsky family at the spa and Anna and Vronsky in Rome—involve encounters with artists of metapoetic significance.

We are in some senses the ideal addressees of such discourse. It is in large part because Nabokov, Borges, Calvino, and others like them have helped shape today's reader's literary sensibilities that one returns to Russian literature of the preceding century—including the great realistic novels—to examine whether and how it too reflected upon its own poesis. The interpretations offered here thus demonstrate the asymmetries of the communicative process, a feature of the communication situation duly emphasized by Jakobson (although not in "Linguistics and Poetics").[6] In terms of the communication situation model discussed in the introduction, the organization of communicative functions will be perceived differently depending upon whether one approaches the message from the point of view of the sender or of the receiver; and as was noted while discussing the poetic function, shifts in the context of reception also change a message's hierarchy of functions. This means that our metapoetic readings of "Leaving the Theater after the Presentation of a New Comedy," "The Little House in Kolomna," *The Idiot*, *Anna Karenina*, and "The Steppe" cannot help but enact such manipulations of each text's hierarchy of functions (as, indeed, all readings do). But as a practical matter, it was simply impossible to proceed in discussing each of the five texts without touching upon other features of the communication situation. In the end, it is the place of metapoesis within a dynamic interaction between the whole set of communicative functions that gives the metapoetic function its meaning.

Notes

Introduction

1 For some cardinal distinctions between the functions of self-reflexivity in Russian literature before and after the Revolution, see Segal. His major point, which is addressed again below, is that pre-Revolutionary metaliterature, as opposed to that following the cultural rupture of the Revolution, remains oriented toward extratextual reality, with strong referential ("modeling") and didactic or conative ("programming") functions ("Literatura kak okhrannaia gramota"). Segal calls *The Gift* "compositionally and semantically the richest example of a text about the creation of a literary work" (152).

2 Although it should be noted that Davydov is referring here specifically to an instance in which Chernyshevsky pseudonymously published a review of his own work.

3 See for instance Todd, *Fiction and Society*, 89.

4 This has recently been discussed by Moser (esp. 28–32), who cites the radical critic Nikolai Shelgunov's characteristic statement, "Novelists merely collect the firewood and stoke the engine of life, but the critic-journalist is the driver" (29; cited from "Dvoedushie esteticheskogo konservatizma," *Delo*, no. 10 [October 1870], 54–55).

5 In brief analyses, Morson has pointed out that Chernyshevsky, like so many authors of the period of realism, "framed his utopia [the genre of *What Is to Be Done?*] as a novel about the harmfulness of novels" (*The Boundaries of Genre*, 99); and Moser considers that *What Is to Be Done?* "subverts the entire genre of the novel as a prose fiction" (142).

6 Chernyshevsky's division of his implied readers into two groups is also discussed in Morson, *Boundaries of Genre*, 101–4.

7 As elaborated in Todd, *Fiction and Society*, esp. 55–72.

8 "Tsenzor (Basnia)," in P. A. Viazemskii, *Stikhotvoreniia*, ed. L. Ia. Ginzburg (Leningrad: Sovetskii pisatel', 1953), 160. This fable, censorship, and Aesopism in Russian literature find interesting treatment in Laura Wilhelm, "The Aesopic Legacy in Russian Literature" (unpublished manuscript).

9 For a discussion of Pushkin's metapoetry, see Erlich, *The Double Image.*

10 For a fascinating account of the way Chernyshevsky's supposed model of reality became a model for reality, see Paperno.

11 For a concise discussion of what is meant by the term "poetics," see V. V. Ivanov's contribution to *Kratkaia literaturnaia entsiklopediia*, "Poetika." For a short historical discussion of the concept of poetics, see "Poetics, Conceptions of" in *Princeton Encyclopedia of Poetry and Poetics*, 636–39.

12 Jakobson, in turn, departed from a model of language in communication elaborated by Karl Bühler ("Linguistics and Poetics," 24). For an elaboration of Jakobson's model, see Holenstein (153–64). For some critiques and refinements of Jakobson's theoretical description, see Scholes (22–40); Pratt (29–37); Attridge; Morson and Emerson (127–130); and Coste (75–83).

13 For a discussion of this point, see Todorov, "Three Conceptions of Poetic Language," where Jakobson's perspective on the poetic function and the concept of "poetic language" are contrasted with Iurii Tynianov's notion of "the literary fact," which can lose or gain literary status depending upon its historical context (144). See also Tynianov, "O literaturnom fakte," and "O literaturnoi evoliutsii"; discussed further in Jurij Striedter, "The Russian Formalist Theory of Literary Evolution," 7. The issue is also taken up in Barbara Herrnstein Smith's "On the Margins of Discourse."

For further elucidation of Jakobson's notion of a poetic function, as conceived within the six-function framework, see L. Waugh.

14 See also Pomorska, "On the Problem of Parallelism"; and Lodge, xii, 5–6, 90–93. If anything, Jakobson underplayed both the pervasiveness of the semiotic phenomenon he called the "poetic function" and its signifiying capacity, that is, its ability to do more than draw attention to the message and make it palpable; see Kristeva ("Ethics"), who echoes Jacques Lacan in her application of Jakobson's poetic function (in her article, *rhythm*) to the psychoanalytic concept of the unconscious, among others.

15 Scholes also grapples with this idea (29–31). One consequence of neglecting this distinction is evident in Todd's use of the communication scheme, which collapses the literary system into the linguistic: thus, while discussing the communication situation in the case of Trediakovsky's poetry, Todd puts "Old Church Slavonic" in the code slot and "Ode" in under message; that is, the language in which a literary work is written is taken for the literary code, and the genre is supposed to be the message, whereas the genre of a given poem properly belongs under the heading of literary code (*Fiction and Society*, 52).

16 Lotman, *Structure of the Artistic Text*; Todorov, "Reading as Construction," in *Genres in Discourse* (39–49).

17 See especially Bakhtin, "The Problem of Speech Genres," in *Speech Genres*; Bakhtin and Medvedev, *The Formal Method*; and Vygotsky, *Thought and Language.*

18 See also P. Steiner, 262–63. For this reason Todorov substitutes the term "translinguistics" for "metalinguistics," and calls Bakhtin "the modern founder of pragmatics as a discipline" (*Mikhail Bakhtin*, 24). Todorov also elaborates a comparison of Jakobson's model of the communication situation with the one implicit in the work of Bakhtin, Medvedev, and Voloshinov (*Mikhail Bakhtin*, 54–56).

19 See for instance "Discourse in the Novel," esp. 260–75, where Bakhtin does not reject structural linguistics so much as point out its limits and assumptions.
20 For an attempt to come to terms with this process, see Todorov, "The Origin of Genres," in *Genres in Discourse*, 13–26.
21 Cf. the following lines from Pope's *An Essay on Criticism*: "If, where the *Rules* not far enough extend, / (Since Rules were made but to promote their End) / Some Lucky LICENCE answers to the full / Th' Intent propos'd, *that Licence* is a *Rule*" (lines 146–49).
22 See Karcevskii; consider also the statement of Iurii Tynianov: "Strictly speaking, every use of a word in a different surrounding or context is a partial change of its meaning" (Tynianov, "O parodii," 294).
23 The same distinction is made in Dällenbach's definition of *mise en abyme* (48–51) and in Mukařovský's definition of the "aesthetic function" (in "Poetic Reference").
24 Jakobson's article "Shifters, Verbal Categories, and the Russian Verb," written a few years before "Linguistics and Poetics," in essence approaches this very topic from the opposite direction: it proceeds from certain linguistic categories to the aspects of the communication situation to which they refer. Interestingly, the factors involved in the speech situation are named and ordered somewhat differently than in "Linguistics and Poetics," and there is no reference to a poetic function or poetic speech—perhaps because the category under analysis here, the verb, could hardly be expected to display the immanent properties of "poetic" speech. And yet elsewhere, in his discussions of iconicity in language, Jakobson was keen to demonstrate "the projection of the principle of equivalence from the axis of selection into the axis of combination" at even such levels—that is, how "the 'system of diagrammatization,' patent and compulsory in the entire syntactic and morphological pattern of language, yet latent and virtual in its lexical aspect, invalidates Saussure's dogma of arbitrariness" ("Quest for the Essence of Language," 337).
25 According to P. Waugh (2), who also offers an extensive bibliography of secondary literature on metafiction (161–69).

See Gass's "Philosophy and the Form of Fiction": "There are metatheorems in mathematics and logic, ethics has its linguistic oversoul, everywhere lingos to converse about lingos are being contrived, and the case is no different in the novel. I don't mean those drearily predictable pieces about writers who are writing about what they are writing, but those, like some of the work of Borges, Barth, and Flann O'Brien, for example, in which the forms of fiction serve as the material upon which further forms can be imposed. Indeed, many of the so-called antinovels are really metafictions" (24–25).
26 Patricia Waugh's more recent definition ably stands for most of them, and its also manifests a fundamental distinction between metafiction and metapoesis. She writes: "*Metafiction* is a term given to fictional writing which self-consciously and systematically draws attention to its status as an artifact in order to pose questions about the relationship between fiction and reality. In providing a critique of their own methods of construction, such writings not only examine the fundamental structures of narrative fiction, they also explore the possible fictionality of the world outside the literary fictional text" (2).

27 See for instance Alter, who writes in his study of "the novel as a self-conscious genre": "If modern philosophy can be said to begin with Descartes's methodological skepticism, his making ontology essentially problematic, a whole tradition of the novel, as the paradigmatically modern narrative genre, is informed by that same critical-philosophical awareness, beginning almost half a century before Descartes with Cervantes. Ontological critique in the novel, moreover, is carried on typically not as discursive exposition but as a critical exploration through the technical manipulation of the very form that purports to represent reality" (x).

28 See the discussion in Todorov, "Introduction to Verisimilitude."

29 As J. L. Borges put it: "Why does it disturb us that the map be included in the map and the thousand and one nights in the book of the *Thousand and One Nights*? Why does it disturb us that Don Quixote be a reader of *Don Quixote* and Hamlet a spectator of *Hamlet*? I believe I have found the reason: these inversions suggest that if the characters of a fictional work can be readers or spectators, we, its readers or spectators, can be fictitious" ("Partial Magic," 231; cited also in Dällenbach, and as an epigraph to Alter's study).

30 David Shepherd's *Beyond Metafiction*, which treats self-consciousness in Soviet literature, appeared after this manuscript was complete and cannot be properly taken into account here. As is the case in my treatment of metapoesis, Shepherd—working within a Bakhtinian framework—demonstrates that metafictions cannot be understood outside their social, historical, and ideological contexts. Although it is a minor point in the context of his impressive study, I cannot help objecting to Shepherd's facile dismissal of Jakobsonian poetics (he singles out "Linguistics and Poetics"); in this tradition, he says, the term "metafiction" is "effectively a shorthand notation for the Jakobsonian view that the 'poetic function' of 'verbal art' is 'the . . . set toward the message as such, focus on the message for its own sake' " (11)—a rather reductive misconstrual, as I hope my discussion shows.

31 See also Linda Hutcheon, 16.

32 This is the position taken by René Wellek, for example; see "The Poet as Critic, the Critic as Poet, the Poet-Critic," where he writes of such "versified criticism": "In general, one can dismiss these poems, if we judge them as poetry, but one should recognize that some of them, particularly Pope's *Essay on Criticism*, display some aesthetic qualities: design, metrical skill, verbal wit" (260–61).

33 See Tynianov, "O literaturnom fakte," and "O literaturnoi evoliutsii"; discussed further in Striedter, "The Russian Formalist Theory of Literary Evolution," 7. This is also taken up by Barbara Herrnstein Smith, among many others.

34 Thus, precisely those features of "egocentrism," contingency, and self-defense for which T. S. Eliot faulted the poet-critic (Wellek, "The Poet as Critic," 254) are of interest to us.

35 I have benefited from Charles Isenberg's treatment of Dällenbach in "Figures for the Text," presented at the national convention of AATSEEL, December 1990 (unpublished), and from his discussion of the paper.

36 Strangely enough, Dällenbach does adduce as *mise en abyme* the entire chapter of the novel where Anna and Vronsky first meet at the train station and where the signal-

man is killed by a train (Dällenbach, 204 n). But can this meeting and the subsequent action be seen as a reflection of the *whole of the narrative*? Is it not rather a case of simple foreshadowing, a *parallelism* of the sort Dällenbach elsewhere (48–51) distinguishes from the *mise en abyme*?

37 See for instance the definition in Baldick (138).

38 See also the similar arguments in Furst (46–47) and Dällenbach (99–100).

39 Cited from Silbajoris, 23–24.

40 Schlegel did not use the term "Romantic irony" as it is used today; see the discussions in Furst, 29–30, and Immerwahr, 82–4.

41 For a treatment of the complex relationship between German Romanticism and philosophy, see Lacoue-Labarthe and Nancy; see also the discussions in Knox, Dällenbach (175–77), Furst, and Behler.

42 In particular, I avoid taking up the wide range of meanings that different Romantic writers actually attached to the notion of irony; for a historical typology of Romantic ironies, see Behler.

43 See Alter, chapter 4 ("The Self-Conscious Novel in Eclipse"), for a discussion of why self-reflexivity is counterindicated in the realistic novel.

44 See also Dällenbach's discussion of the *mise en abyme* in realism and naturalism (52–53).

1 Gogol's Metaplay, "Leaving the Theater after the Presentation of a New Comedy

1 See Debreczeny (17–29) for a discussion of the play's reception.

2 All translations from this and other Russian sources are mine unless otherwise indicated.

3 The intervention of Nicholas I was indeed responsible for allowing *The Government Inspector* to be staged in the first place.

4 See Debreczeny for elucidation of such echoes; see also the commentary to "Leaving the Theater" in *Pss* 5, esp. 495–98.

Iurii Mann points out that the "above seven years" which separate the author from the time when applause such as he has just heard "would have set my heart beating, would have made everything throb in me" and the present corresponds to the interval between Gogol's disastrous publication of *Gants Kiukhelgarten* and the production of *The Government Inspector* ("Dramaturgiia," 466); that is, the chronology of the author's career in "Leaving the Theater" is the same as that of Gogol at the time of *The Government Inspector*'s production.

5 "Leaving the Theater" was in fact staged at the Mariinsky Theatre in Petersburg in April of 1902, on the fiftieth anniversary of Gogol's death (Mann, "Dramaturgiia," 465 n).

6 Ludwig Tieck's *Puss in Boots* is often cited as the paradigm of self-reflexive Romantic dramaturgy.

7 "Gogol, being Gogol and living in a looking-glass world, had a knack of thoroughly planning his works *after* he had written and published them" (Nabokov, *Nikolai Gogol*, 57).
8 According to Debrezceny, "[F]irst, he [Gogol] maintained that it [*The Government Inspector*] had no social implications; then he accepted the critics' notions of its social implications and, as a result, rejected the play. Now, while he was working on *Dead Souls* abroad, the compromise led him to a third solution; the play *did* reflect Russian society in a critical manner, yet was a valuable work because its negations prepared the ground for the later positive message, just as the first volume of the novel [*Dead Souls*] would do. This third view of the play was to be replaced later by a fourth, with a religious bias" (24–25).
9 Thus, Donald Fanger writes: "To speak of unriddling is to follow Gogol himself, who insisted repeatedly that his existence was textual, and that the text constituted a riddle whose key lay in the future" ("Gogol and His Reader," 61).
10 The author's comment about laughter being the only honest character in the play (*Pss* 5:169) is quite often attributed directly to Gogol (see, for example, Fanger, "Gogol and His Reader," 86); see also David Magarshak, who writes that "a gentleman a little careless about literature" *is* Bulgarin, while the Second Lover of the Arts is "Gogol himself" (140–143).
11 Particularly in his "Peterburgskie zapiski 1836 goda" (*Pss* 8:177–90) and in the later "O teatre, ob odnostoronnem vzgliade na teatr i voobshche ob odnostoronnosti" (in *Vybrannye mesta iz perepiski s druz'iami* [*Pss* 8:267–77]).
12 Writes Krivonos: "The laughter of the *Writings* is a *radiant laughter*, which follows the definition of the play's Author; it awakens the sources of humanity in people, it prevents dozing off and the shallowing of life, the soul's encrustment in 'slime and mold' ([*Pss*,] V, 171). This is a laughter which restores and animates. Gogol's book, the positive hero of which is laughter (*radiant laughter* [*svetlyi smekh*]), itself became the quintessential instance of the history of laughter as the history of the constant rebirth of the human in man, of the human soul" (143). See pp. 133–48 for Krivonos's Bakhtinian discussion of laughter in Gogol.
13 See Krivonos (104–9) for a summary of such precedents, as well as for attribution of their discovery.
14 The italicized French term *vaudeville*, from which the Russian *vodevil'* is derived, is used here to avoid confusion with the form of entertainment Americans are accustomed to refer to as "vaudeville."
15 Gottlieb's book on Chekhov begins with a discussion of the *vaudeville* tradition. Other treatments of the genre consulted here include Chistova's article in *Istoriia russkoi dramaturgii*, Varneke (188–99), Karlinsky (*Russian Drama*, 269–77), and Wigzell.
16 See Karlinsky (*Russian Drama*, 228–62) for a treatment of this tradition. Karlinsky sees "Komediia protiv komedii" as an important model for "Leaving the Theater" (260). Chistova also discusses the use of *vaudeville* to settle literary disputes (415–18).
17 See also Uspenskii, 3–4.
18 As Krivonos points out, "The difference between the role of a reader and the role of a

theater-goer . . . did not interest Gogol in 'Leaving the Theater.' 'Leaving the Theater' is a work meant not for the stage, but for reading, and its characters (the theater-goers) are depicted by Gogol as bearing a reader's function" (110).

19 Chistova notes that eavesdropping was often the "mainspring" of a *vaudeville*'s plot (411).

20 Wrote Gippius: "It is essential to recognize that there is a hidden psychological reason why Gogol departed so decisively from the tradition in just this respect, a reason which biography, psychology and psychopathology have so far been incapable of revealing in all its aspects" (*Gogol*, 87). For a discussion of Gogol's life and works that delves into this question, see Karlinsky, *Sexual Labyrinth.*

21 Noted also by Chistova, 412.

22 Writes Mann, "The author's monologue in the finale trumps, as it were, all the other voices, embracing individual judgments with a higher truth" ("Dramaturgiia," 466).

23 For a discussion of the notion of "anti-genre," see Morson, *Boundaries of Genre*, 115–20.

24 Carl Proffer has argued, alternatively, that the 1842 version of "Leaving the Theater" was more an anticipatory defense of *Dead Souls* than a retrospective apology for *The Government Inspector*, and he offers a series of parallels between "Leaving the Theater" and the metapoetic digressions in *Dead Souls* as evidence. No doubt the general concerns that led to the writing of "Leaving the Theater" apply to *Dead Souls* as well, but so many of the issues raised in "Leaving the Theater" are specific to the situation of a dramaturgist (the gathering together of all readers, from all social classes, the ability to make them react as one, the very possibility of observing an addressee's reactions, and so on), that one suspects Proffer of overstating his case (see Proffer, 183–200).

25 See Robey's Ph.D. dissertation, *Pictorial Language in Gogol: Metaphor, Tableau, Intertext*, Indiana University, 1991.

26 See Mann, *Komediia* (68–77), for a discussion of the "*nemaia stsena*"; *Poetika Gogolia*, where this moment is discussed in greater detail as an exception to Gogol's general observance of the dramatic convention of the "fourth wall" (255–57); and his "*Uzhas okoval vsekh*," where Mann maintains that the dumb scene is "one of the nodes in which Gogol's creative philosophy is concentrated as a whole" (227).

27 It could of course be argued that the dramatic production of a play involves several factors intervening between the addresser and the addressee—namely, aspects of the production, which involve interpretation and recodification of the author's words. While this poses problems on a theoretical plane, in the instance of "Leaving the Theater" neither the audience-characters nor the comic makes a single remark regarding the new comedy's staging. There would be, therefore, no basis for incorporating a discussion of the new comedy's production in our discussion of the relationship between the author and his readers—this in spite of the fact that Gogol's own immediate reaction to the first production of *The Government Inspector* was that the actors had ruined his play. (See "Otryvok iz pis'ma, pisannogo avtorom vskore posle pervogo predstavleniia *Revizora* k odnomu literatoru" [*Pss* 4:99–104]. This fragment is supposed to have been addressed to Pushkin.)

28 As does Mann: "But in 'Leaving the Theatre . . .' each character does not propel the action so much as bring along his own 'color,' his own 'word' to the general aesthetic theme of the play" (*Poetika*, 272); and " 'Leaving the Theatre' is an intellectual and, one wants to say, theoretical play" (*Poetika*, 273). In "Dramaturgiia," however, Mann writes that "Leaving the Theater" was the most remarkable instance yet in Russian dramaturgy of a play which was *both* a theoretical and a more conventional, comic play (464).

29 See for example Gogol (*Pss* 14:82); Fanger (*Creation*, 198–99); and Erlich, who maintains that Gogol's incessant requests for "fullest possible reports on the public response to *Dead Souls*, with particular emphasis on hostile criticism . . . reflected . . . [a] neopenitent's desire for punishment . . . [and] insistence on self-castigation as a necessary prerequisite for purity, the desire to eavesdrop on anything that was said or whispered about him, however painful and injurious" (*Gogol*, 169).

30 As emphasized by the prefix *raz-* in "*raz"ezd.*"

31 On the metapoetry of Pushkin and in Romanticism generally, see Erlich, *The Double Image*, 1–37.

32 Pointed out to me by Vadim Liapunov.

33 Or, it could be argued, to reestablish that groundwork after the trauma of *The Government Inspector*'s reception, since there is plenty of didacticism in the earlier Gogol. Still, a distinction can be made between the nature of the authority Gogol establishes in "Leaving the Theater" and that which is claimed in, say, the essays published in his 1835 book *Arabesques*, where Gogol pretends to the scholarly knowledge of a historian.

2 The Aesopic Content of Pushkin's "The Little House in Kolomna"

1 The edited, first-published version of the poem is taken from Pushkin, *Polnoe sobranie sochinenii v shesti tomakh* (henceforth *Pss*), 2:430–40. Citations are given in the Russian original from that source, and as translated by Walter Arndt ("The Little House in Kolomna"), with occasional alterations.

2 See Briusov (91) or William Harkins, who writes: "[T]his great beauty who came from a needy family of gentle birth . . . had sacrificed herself to marry a rich old count of seventy, by which act she had recouped the family's fortunes and assured herself of a position in Petersburg society" ("The Little House in Kolomna," 65). See also Semjonow, 92–93.

3 See for example Stanza XVIII:

By winter dusk they had the shutters fastened,
But in the summer until late at night
The house stayed open. Pallid Dian's crescent
Long poured into the maiden's room her light.
(The writer's moon is never evanescent,
There is no novel where it's out of sight.)

At times the mother's snores had long been hissing
While daughter would still watch the moon, and listen

Эимою ставни закрывались рано,
Но летом до-ночи растворено
Всё было в доме. Бледная Диана
Глядела долго девушке в окно
(Без этого ни одного романа
Не обойдётся: так заведено!)
Бывало, мать давным давно храпела,
А дочка—на луну ещё смотрела.

Here note the shift from the "high" and periphrastic "Pallid Dian" to the blunt "moon"; note also the common and vulgar "snores" and the metapoetic statement hinting that this tale be read as a "novel."

4 The omitted stanzas are included in the editors' commentary ("Varianty i kommentarii"), *Pss* 2:595–98; they are integrated into the text of the poem in the version printed in *Biblioteka velikikh pisatelei*, 92–99.

The omitted stanzas were first published by P. V. Annenkov in *Materialy dlia biografii Aleksandra Sergeevicha Pushkina* (St. Petersburg, 1885). Several errors and omissions in this edition, some of which were carried through to *Biblioteka velikikh pisatelei*, are pointed out by Goffman (113–20).

All translations from these stanzas are my own.

5 Katenin wrote in "Pis'mo k izdatleliu": "For great authors form is not something arbitrary which can be altered without damaging the spirit of a composition; their tie is inseparable, and the distortion of one necessarily brings with it the loss of the other" (*Razmyshleniia*, 189). Rozanov speaks of Katenin's "constant striving . . . to make form strictly correspond to content" (130–31).

6 See Fomichev ("Oktavy") for further discussion of the octave in "Little House" and the Russian poetic tradition.

7 This was a quality in Katenin which Pushkin valued highly; see his review of Katenin's works (*Pss* 5:76–78; see also Rozanov, 104–5).

8 Viktor Vinogradov's reading of "Anchar" ("The Upas Tree") as Pushkin's response to Katenin should also be noted here; see "O stile Pushkina." Without contesting Vinogradov's reading of "Anchar," I hope to show that "Little House" constitutes a fuller response.

The recent article by M. L. Gasparov and V. M. Smirin comments on a number of polemical and parodistic allusions in "Little House," and concludes that Pushkin's chief target is himself, and that self-parody is the poem's chief organizing principle. I find the elucidation of allusions to other poets more useful than the notion of self-parody, and I think the Katenin connection is the most important.

Fomichev and Kurganov ("Iz real'nogo kommentariia") have deciphered a few additional interesting references to contemporary literary life.

9 Even for Valerii Briusov, who in the article cited above reads the poem as an attempt to create a Russian version of the "joking poem" of Byron and de Musset, the most significant aspect of the tale about Parasha is its triviality.

According to Goffman, Pushkin's original idea for the poem is fully reflected in the initial, openly polemic and metapoetical stanzas: "Initially the Poet even contemplated relinquishing any anecdotal plot [*fabula-anekdot*], but when one was found in the process of creation, Pushkin came to value that anecdote because it was a poetically articulate and poetically significant illustration of the argument he wished to defend" (30–31). A more recent, passing comment by Robert Maguire is symptomatic of received notions about "Little House"; he calls the poem "a deliberate exercise in nonsense, which makes the point that art is absolutely free in its choice of themes" ("The Legacy of Criticism," 26).

10 Vladimir Nabokov credits the verse form of the Onegin stanza to the influence of La Fontaine; he points out that some of La Fontaine's verse tales use this form, and he calls La Fontaine "Pushkin's unconscious source" (introduction to *Eugene Onegin*, 10–11).

11 Write Johnston and Owen, "There is something paradoxical in the way in which the writers of the fabliaux determinedly cudgelled a moral from tales which so often appear deliberately immoral in conception." Further: "No doubt there was a persistent tendency in medieval literature to extract a lesson from any tale, the moral plane being the third on which a work could be judged, after literal and allegorical meanings had been deduced" (xv).

12 See Gershenzon, *Mudrost' Pushkina*, 150.

13 See Way for the self-justification of one translator and editor who "refined" his material (xxxvi).

14 This is also discussed in Stenbock-Fermor, "French Medieval Poetry," 61–62.

15 "The Life of Aesop" may be found in *Aesop without Morals*, 29–90. See pp. 56–58 for this episode.

Semjonow glosses this allusion to Aesop (145).

16 Of course, the opposite situation is also possible, as in an American film comedy from the 1980s where a Parisian waiter smiles, nods, and with the most pleasant gestures verbally insults his monolingual American customers in sweet-sounding French. The key to proper decoding remains a wider perspective on the speech situation.

17 Incidentally, Tynianov notes that "The majority of Katenin's poems have some 'arrière pensée', a hidden purpose" ("Arkhaisty i Pushkin," 160).

18 "[T]he Poet really almost got muddled up" (Goffman, 63).

19 *Slovar' iazyka Pushkina* lists only one other direct reference to Aesop in Pushkin's works: an 1820 epigram on K. Dembrovsky. This makes the appearance of Aesop in "Little House" seem especially meaningful. Interestingly enough, in the epigram the figure of Aesop is presented as a reflection of the poetic persona: "When I look into a mirror / It seems I see Aesop [Когда смотрюсь я в зеркало / Вижу, кажется, Езопа]."

20 Literally: "to knead the dough / boil the kasha thoroughly"; idiomatically: to really get into it, to make one hell of a mess.

21 This may in turn reflect the larger battle between the neoclassical literary system and the romantic literary system, as Pushkin saw it; for, as Lotman and Uspensky write, it is characteristic of neoclassical culture "that the creator of rules stands higher in the hierarchy than the creator of the texts. Thus, for example, within the system of Neo-Classicism the critic commands markedly more respect than the writer" ("On the Semiotic Mechanism of Culture," 219).

22 The poetic contest between two bards is a story line to which Katenin had frequent recourse (Tynianov, "Arkhaisty i Pushkin," 160–61).

23 As Pushkin designates his muse in *Eugene Onegin*, canto VII, stanza III.

24 The theme of cuckoldry, as developed in the medieval French fabliau, may have an even deeper, more fundamental connection with Pushkin's project. M. Bakhtin has discussed the image of woman in the fabliau; he writes that ". . . womanhood performs the functions of debasement and at the same time of renewal of life. Womanhood is shown in contrast to the limitations of her partner (husband, lover, or suitor); she is a foil to his avarice, jealousy, stupidity, hypocrisy, bigotry, sterile senility, false heroism, and abstract idealism. The woman of Gallic tradition is the bodily grave of man. She represents in person the undoing of pretentiousness, of all that is finished, completed, and exhausted" (*Rabelais*, 240).

The notion of cuckoldry is thus intimately related to the natural, necessary replacement of the old by the new; and Pushkin's poem, from the first stanza forward, is about the natural and necessary replacement of old and bankrupt literary systems by new and vital ones.

25 "Sochineniia i perevody v stikhakh Pavla Katenina" was published in *Literaturnye pribavleniia k Russkomu Invalidu*, no. 26 (April 1, 1833), 206–7.

26 Katenin was quite (better, *overly*) sensitive to this sort of treatment, and noted that Pushkin's "The Bridegroom" ("Zhenikh," 1825) had been something of an imitation or parody of his own "Natasha" (1814), some kind of competitive gesture (Rozanov, 111, 123).

27 Harkins has noted the parallel between these scenes; however, he focuses on the common motif of loss and the "working of blind fate" ("The Place of 'Domik v Kolomne,' " 202), while the motif of rebellion (suppressed by the rebellious self in "Little House") is more important for our interpretation of the poem.

Jakobson has already suggested (in passing) that these two stanzas from "Little House" have both metapoetic and political meaning. They refer to the double creative life of the poet under censorship: he writes for publication, censoring himself before the government apparatus censors him; and he writes freely—bitterly, ribaldly, or with democratic sentiment—for his friends ("Pushkin Unrestrained").

28 Letter of December 23, 1829, to N. I. Bakhtin (Katenin, *Razmyshleniia*, 300; see 273 and 283 for similar uses of martial metaphors).

29 However, Katenin himself was not particularly tall, according to Rozanov, who also notes that Katenin was apparently very similar to Pushkin in general appearance; Pogodin, upon meeting Katenin for the first time in 1834, wrote in his diary, "The prototype, in appearance, of Pushkin" (Rozanov, 109).

30 Referring to Pushkin's article on Katenin's works, Rozanov asserts that "... Pushkin had an amazing ability to take on the tone of the person he was dealing with" (156).

31 Marena and Savely Senderovich found a strikingly similar situation in the course of reconstructing the dialogic meaning of a short lyric written by Pushkin fifteen years before "Little House in Kolomna" and addressed to Batiushkov. They write: "Most often the use of another's motif in Pushkin is a polemical and antithetical response to the source-motif; but sometimes it is a broader conception which dialectically incorporates the source-conception as a particular moment in a broader synthesis" (" 'Roza' Pushkina," 38).

See also William M. Todd III's discussion of the aesthetics of Arzamas in respect to the genre of the familiar letter. Especially relevant are the similarities he finds between that genre and the genre of light verse (*The Familiar Letter*).

3 Genre and Incarnation in Dostoevsky's *The Idiot*

1 All citations of Dostoevsky's writings are from F. M. Dostoevskii, *Polnoe sobranie sochinenii v tridtsati tomakh* (henceforth *Pss*). All references to the text of *The Idiot* are to Volume 8 of *Pss*, and are indicated by page number only. All translations from this and other Russian sources are mine unless otherwise indicated.

2 In particular by Robin Feuer Miller, who takes up each instance in which characters in the novel tell stories and analyze the narrator's digressions. She is primarily concerned with the rhetorical strategy that lies behind this overtly self-reflexive aspect of the novel. The more the narrator takes as his theme the problems confronting him as narrator of the tale we are reading, she finds, the greater the divergence between this narrator and the novel's implied author, and the less reliable the narrator, the effect of which is to "force the reader to examine his own notions of responsibility to his fellow man" (*Dostoevsky and "The Idiot,"* 227). See also Goerner.

3 For example, Mochulsky wrote of Myshkin: "And this Swiss Idyll he attempts to transfer into the world of darkness [Petersburg]" (375). A more fully articulated view of this process, and the one closest to my understanding of the Rousseau connection in *The Idiot* (arrived at independently), is advanced by Kovacs in "Poetika romana *Idiot.*" Gus also briefly mentions the Rousseau connection (367–68); Zlochevskaia gives it fuller treatment, but without mentioning preceding scholarship.

4 See for instance Lord, 90.

5 If one were to follow up on Miller's observations regarding questions of truth and falsity in narration and the "reliability" of narrators, this would have to be a crucial moment in the novel: one of Myshkin's first actions in the novel, writing "The humble High Monk Pafnuty signed here" (29), is actually a forgery, a lie.

6 Dostoevsky apparently had in mind a work by Hans Fries (1465–1520), a Swiss painter of the German school, depicting the beheading of John the Baptist. The painting (1514) was in the museum in Basel ("Primechaniia," *Pss* 9:433; see *Cyclopedia of Painters and Paintings*, Vol. II, 93).

7 Robert Louis Jackson returns to this episode several times in *Dostoevsky's Quest for Form*; he also finds it to be a nodal and self-reflexive moment in the novel, although our interpretations vary somewhat. Jackson writes: "What Myshkin sees, of course, is not on the surface of reality; he perceives the inner idea of that reality. Myshkin [is] by nature an artist (as Ganya in the novel correctly notes)" (52).

8 Kovacs writes that Myshkin "gradually develops a 'Swiss'—sentimentalist-Enlightenment—logic of thought, leading, in Dostoevsky's opinion, to 'the Geneva idea,' to Rousseau's concept of man. In this spirit Myshkin idealizes and poeticizes in his 'novella' the 'triumph of virtue,' of 'singular good,' which are based on a personal origin, on the principle of the premoral purity of man, his inherent innocence and the 'natural law of compassion.' Such a conception of man and the world lies at the base of Myshkin's lyrical novella and constitutes the principle by which the events of Marie's tragedy, and the everyday happiness of the children surrounding her, are monologically systematized. Precisely this principle organizes the hero's monologic discourse, and constructs from these events a *sentimental idyll* with a 'moral' which Myshkin then advances as an ideal model for a happy life on this earth, demonstrating meanwhile a high degree of unification with the object of his utterance" (*Critical Essays on Dostoevsky*, 120; in original Russian, *Hungaro-Slavica*, 155).

9 Aleksandr P. Skaftymov's reading of *Idiot* poses such ambivalences very sharply; see his "Tematicheskaia kompozitsiia romana *Idiot*," esp. 32–44.

10 Here I would take issue with Diana Lewis Burgin, who writes (and is echoed by Matich [54]): "Are not all the catastrophes, peripeteias, expositions, and [particularly] denouements of the *Idiot*, in essence, the dreamer-Nastasja 'attempting the pen' and authoring her own life?" (259). As everybody's hero, Nastasya's power in the novel resides not in assuming some imputedly male instrument of power, the pen, but in refusing to assume the roles laid out for her, in being a resistant hero. From this perspective her attitude toward Myshkin is no different than her attitude toward all the other men who would shape her life into a finished, aesthetic whole.

11 M. O. Al'tman has shown that this plot follows the lines of Dumas fils's *La Dame aux Camelias*, to which Totsky alludes in his turn at the confessional parlor game (58–67).

12 Al'tman writes further: "Even before the meeting with Myshkin, Nastasya Filippovna says that she 'would like to be resurrected, if not in love, then in a family.' And having met Myshkin she came to believe in the possibility of her resurrection through Myshkin's love for her. And it is about this that Aglaya says to Myshkin: 'You must, you are obligated to resurrect her.' And Myshkin himself 'sincerely believed, that she could still be resurrected.' And when Myshkin says to Nastasya Filippovna, who is kneeling before him: 'Arise!', we are reminded of Christ's command to the deceased daughter of Jairus: 'Maiden, arise!', that is—arise from the dead, be resurrected!" (70).

To be added to this series are Myshkin's own "resurrection" from idiocy in Switzerland, and Ippolit's reflections on the difficulty of believing in the resurrection of the Christ depicted in Rogozhin's reproduction of the Holbein painting (339).

13 See Kovacs and note 8 above; see also Mochulsky (375), Dalton, 93, and Slattery, 65.

The latter's reading of the novel is rather odd and uneven, however; he calls Marie the "double" of Nastasya Filippovna, which—since these two women can have no relation to one another outside Myshkin's mind—empties the concept of the double of the deep psychological significance it bears in regard, say, to the relationship between Myshkin and Rogozhin (cf. the general definition Bitsilli gives the notion of the "double": "an image, producing in itself to an extreme degree that which the 'prototype' hates and scorns, or that in which he sees his ideal" ["K voprosu," 21]).

14 Myshkin's fixation with the eyes of Nastasya Filippovna fits nicely with Jackson's observations regarding the prince's "artistic vision" (see note 8 above). It reflects a persistent concern of Dostoevsky's dating from before the long sojourn in Western Europe during which he wrote *Idiot* (see "The Meek One" ["Krotkaia"], for example; see also Jackson's discussion of Akulka's eyes in "Akulka's Husband," from *Notes from the House of the Dead* [*The Art of Dostoevsky*, 92–93]). Also characteristic of this opposition between outer form and behavior and inner meaning is Dostoevsky's 1873 article on Leskov's "The Sealed Angel" ("Zapechatlennyi angel"), "Smiatennyi vid" (in *Dnevnik* [*Pss* 21:54–60]), where he criticizes Leskov for attaching a rational explanation for the miracle regarding an icon, instead of underlining the inner meaning of the artel's conversion and adherence to Orthodoxy. I am indebted to Nina Perlina for the last reference.

15 *Ptitsa* = bird; *ivolga* = oriole; *lebed'* = swan.

16 Dalton's psychoanalytical approach has the distinction of showing a great deal of continuity between Dostoevsky's notebooks and the end product (see her appendix, "The Creative Process in *The Notebooks for "The Idiot,"* 185–208).

17 Leatherbarrow associates the proliferation of bird names in *Idiot* with the novel's apocalyptic subtext (discussed below). But the association of Myshkin's children with the bird motif makes Leatherbarrow's interpretation unlikely, as does the fact that the *types* of birds alluded to in character names (oriole, swan) are quite unlike those of the Book of the Apocalypse (crows, ravens); or at the very least, this difference requires interpretation.

A similar point can be made regarding Al'tman's contention that the bird names of the Petersburg characters, all of whom are aspiring capitalists and moneylenders, are derived from the names of two famous Petersburg slum landlords, Voronin and Utin (*Voron* = raven, while *utka* = duck; 73–74). This may well be so, but how does it relate to Myshkin's habit of calling the Swiss children "little birds"?

18 David Bethea, whose *Shape of the Apocalypse* became available during this chapter's revision, also interprets "Belokonskaya" as a talking name: "It seems more than chance that the author, who was sensitive to the nomenclature level of his art, would choose a character with this name to be society's keeper" (84 n; see also 100). Bethea's focus on the novel's apocalyptic imagery leads him to point out all "horsey" names, among which he includes the patronymic of Nastasya Filippovna (related to the Greek for "lover of horses" [83]) and the name of Ippolit, "releaser of horses" (of the apocalypse). Monas, however, gives Ippolit's equine name a diametrically opposite meaning (80).

Leatherbarrow also suggests that Belokonskaya's name may also be associated with the novel's apocalyptic imagery: the fourth horse of the apocalypse, Death, is white ("Apocalyptic Imagery," 46–47). In *The Idiot*, Lebedev discusses the horses of the apocalypse (167–68).

19 The reference is to "Lev sostarevshiisia" (Krylov, 2:163).

20 See the commentary ("Primechaniia") to *Idiot* in *Pss* 9:432, where Shakespeare's *A Midsummer Night's Dream* is also adduced as a possible referent for Madame Epanchin's statement.

21 This method of teaching the classics through paraphrase is portrayed in recollections of the lessons given by the elder Verkhovensky in *The Devils* (*Besy*).

22 On Apuleius's and the ass's place in the tradition of lower-body humor, see Bakhtin, *Rabelais and His World*, 78.

23 This is mentioned by the editors of Dostoevsky's works in *Pss* 9:399. For further discussion of the Rothschild theme in Dostoevsky's works, see Goldstein, 57–67.

24 Vetlovskaia found no evidence in the notebooks or letters of Dostoevsky to prove the importance of St. Francis, but the textual evidence she provides is convincing.

25 See Margaret Ziolkowski, 138–70, for a discussion of "Saintly Personalities in the Novels of Dostoevsky."

26 Dostoevsky adduced Don Quixote as an example of a "positively beautiful person" in literature in the famous letter to his niece, Sofya Ivanova, describing his writing project (*Pss* 28[2]:251). Leonid Grossman made some remarks regarding the significance of Cervantes and *Don Quixote* for Dostoevsky in *Biblioteka Dostoevskogo* (94–95). For an extensive (and overreaching) treatment of the Don Quixote theme in *The Idiot*, see Serrano-Plaja, esp. 28–81; see also Welsh, *passim*; and most recently Eric Ziolkovski, 85–166. For an interesting alternative reading of Dostoevsky's use of the Pushkin poem, see Fiene.

27 Joseph Frank views this capacity as psychopathological; employing the categories of Max Scheler, he writes that Myshkin moves from "completely lucid vicarious fellow-feeling" to "total emotional identification with others that leads to a loss of identity and personality," in "A Reading of *The Idiot*," 306.

28 For discussions of the semantics of the word "idiot," see the editors' commentary (*Pss* 9:394); Holquist, *Dostoevsky and the Novel*, 111–12; and Blackmur, 143–44.

29 See the editors' commentary on this description of Myshkin by Dostoevsky in the letter to his niece S. A. Ivanova of January 1, 1868 ("Primechaniia," *Pss* 9:358).

30 See the discussion in the editor's notes, Bakhtin, *Estetika*, 390–91.

31 See also Anderson, "*The Idiot*: Duality, Paradox, and Dionysos," in his *Dostoevsky*, 66–94. His association of Myshkin with Dionysus makes a great deal of sense when considered in the context of this ass theme, although one is inclined to view the Dionysian subtext he elucidates as assimilated in and mediated by the more relevant myth of Christ.

32 This point is stressed by R. P. Blackmur, who writes: "[I]t was that lack, that incompleteness as a man in Myshkin, which brought on the downfall of the women, and transformed what ought to have been the tragic triumph of the good man into his reduction to complete idiocy" (162). See also Mochulsky (375).

33 On the painting, faith, and Holbein's own ambivalences, see Kristeva, "Holbein's Dead Christ."

34 For instance: "Prince Myshkin is a truly Christlike man—in his notes Dostoevsky once refers to him as 'Prince Christ'—of great moral beauty. But to make him plausible as a human being Dostoevsky found it necessary to mar his moral beauty with certain flaws" (T. Ziolkowski, 104).

35 References are given to both the Liapunov translation ("Author"), cited here, and the Russian text (*Estetika*).

36 Bakhtin writes: "It was the second trend that enabled and gave rise to the idea of transfiguration of the body in God as the transfiguration of that which is the other for God. The Church as the body of Christ, the bride of Christ. [. . .] Finally, the idea of Grace as the bestowal—from outside—of lovingly merciful acceptance and justification of the given, as of that which is in principle sinful and, therefore, cannot be surmounted from within itself. This includes the associated idea of confession (total and utter penitence) and absolution. From within my own penitence there is negation of the whole of myself; from outside myself (God is the other) there is loving mercy and restoration. In himself, a human being can only repent; only the other can give absolution.

"This second tendency within Christianity finds its deepest expression in the phenomenon that is St. Francis of Assisi, Giotto, and Dante" (Bakhtin, "Author," 57; *Estetika*, 52).

37 This echoes Romano Guardini's comment on Myshkin's Platonism, cited above. Bitsilli makes a similar observation regarding Dostoevsky's work in general: "The 'I' of Tolstoy is a real life process. Dostoevsky's is more Platonic, a 'pure idea' emerging outside of space and time" ("K voprosu," 24).

38 Bitsilli relates the paradox of beauty in Dostoevsky and the *distancing* required for aesthetic perception ("pafos distantsii" [38]) to the attempts by Dostoevsky's characters (such as Ippolit) to view their own lives as complete aesthetic wholes: "Actually all attempts to achieve a catharsis of one's own inner [*dushevnaia*] tragedy suffer failure. It is impossible to turn one's life entirely into a work of art" ("K voprosu," 38). Death made aesthetic distancing viable in regard to Marie; with Aglaya and Nastasya Filippovna it is more problematic (see below).

39 The semantic relationship between the figures of Rogozhin and Myshkin is taken up in the editors' commentary (*Pss* 9:406–18), as well as in most treatments of the novel. See for example Peace (91), who takes up the exchange of crosses.

40 The most recent and fullest treatment of the holy fool motif in Dostoevsky is to be found in Harriet Murav, *Holy Foolishness.* For discussions of the motif in *The Idiot*, see Murav, 71–98; Miller, *Dostoevsky and "The Idiot,"* 65–69; Kjetsaa, 221; and Margaret Ziolkowski, 143–46.

See Fedotov for a discussion of the origins and early history of the cultural phenomenon of the holy fool.

41 For a discussion of Bakhtin's understanding of Tolstoy and Dostoevsky that takes up precisely this distinction, see Caryl Emerson, "The Tolstoy Connection in Bakhtin."

See Miller, *Dostoevsky and "The Idiot,"* 59–60, for a discussion of the possible allusions to Tolstoy and the first part of *War and Peace* in the figure of Myshkin (note especially Myshkin's name and patronymic).

The editors of Dostoevsky's collected works also note a connection between Tolstoy's pedagogical ideas and Myshkin's handling of the children in Switzerland ("Primechaniia," *Pss* 9:364); as seen below, the figure of Rousseau is likely a mediating link.

42 "Soul" (*dusha*) here is understood as the outer visage of one's inner life, one's inner life perceived as a whole by the other; "spirit" (*dukh*) is the open-ended, inner lived-experience of the "I-for-myself." See Bakhtin ("Author," 110; *Estetika*, 97–98).

43 This dimension of the plot of *The Idiot* thus serves a function equivalent to the one attributed by Miller to the novel's narrative strategy: the divergence between narrator and implied author, and the increasingly unreliable narrator, "force the reader to examine his own notions of responsibility to his fellow man" (*Dostoevsky and "The Idiot,"* 229).

44 For a discussion of the theme of children in *The Idiot* and in Dostoevsky generally, see Rowe, who states: "Myshkin is probably the adult most repeatedly and unequivocally described as a child in all of Dostoevsky's works" (178), and for whom the notion of redemption in the novel involves rediscovering the child in one's self. Translated into Bakhtin's terminology, the child is recognizable as the predominance of the inner self, the "I-for-myself" discussed above, as yet not fully shaped by the values of the self as perceived in the category of the other.

45 Kovacs has demonstrated the relevance of this genre classification.

46 The Rousseau connection is taken up in the editors' commentary (*Pss* 9:404–5), as well as in Zlochevskaia. For a discussion of Rousseau's importance to Chernyshevsky—a figure very much in Dostoevsky's field of vision and speaking—see Scanlan; for a discussion of *The Idiot* as a polemic with Chernyshevsky, see Lidiia Lotman (243–56). See also Paperno, 124.

47 See Miller's discussion in "Dostoevsky and Rousseau," 95. See also her "Imitations of Rousseau in *The Possessed*," her discussion of the confession game in *Dostoevsky and "The Idiot"* (175–83), and Howard's discussion in "The Rhetoric of Confession."

48 Rousseau as educator and author of *Emile* is taken up explicitly in *Netochka Nezvanova* (*Pss* 2:216–17; see also editors' commentary, 498–99).

49 See Iu. Lotman ("Russo," 557–61) for a discussion of native Russian manifestations of this opposition preceding Rousseau's influence. Dostoevsky's editors note that the handling of Myshkin's disease complicates the parallel Rousseau had set up between health and illness, on the one hand, and natural man and civilized man, on the other (*Pss* 9:405).

50 The Epanchin dacha at Pavlovsk is said to be styled after a Swiss chalet (275), and the editors of the thirty-volume edition of Dostoevsky's works point out that the architecture of the dachas in Pavlovsk was in general very Swiss in style ("Primechaniia," in *Pss* 9:449).

51 For other discussions of this theme, see Guardini, 368; Holquist, 113; Leatherbarrow; and Hollander. For Hollander, apocalyptic vision is the central organizing feature of the second part of the novel. See also Bethea (*Shape of the Apocalypse*, 62–

104), who situates the apocalyptic themes in *The Idiot* within the history of Dostoevsky's artistic, philosophical, and journalistic development, and within the broader context of Russian culture.

52 For a lengthy, wide-ranging treatment of the meaning the illness of epilepsy is likely to have had for Dostoevsky and his milieu, see Rice.

53 See Bakhtin, "Forms of Time," 112–129, for a discussion of the "theme of metamorphosis" and individual crisis time in Apuleius's *The Golden Ass* (and in Christian hagiography), which is extremely relevant to this point.

54 See Hugo, *Last Day of a Condemned.* Dostoevsky probably first read this short novel in 1838, and its lasting impact on him is easily shown: Dostoevsky echoed the words of Hugo's condemned man in an interpolation in French in the well-known letter to his brother describing his own "last day" and last-minute reprieve (*Pss* 28:162); he even alluded to it while on the scaffold (see Frank, *The Years of Ordeal*, 58). Dostoevsky borrows from Hugo's short masterpiece in works other than *The Idiot* (especially *The Devils* [*Besy*]); and he discusses Hugo's narrative technique in a preface to "The Meek One" ("Krotkaia," 1876), where he calls *The Last Day* a masterpiece, "[t]he most real and the most true work of all he has written" (*Pss* 24:6), in spite of the improbability of a condemned man continuing his notes up to the moment he is led away.

For discussions of the relation of this work to Dostoevsky's, see Andrews; see also Brown, *Hugo and Dostoevsky*, esp. 111–34.

55 See Turner, who has found that "Myshkin, Aglaya, Ippolit, and Ivolgin are all explicitly compared to fragile pottery" (173) and who demonstrates how the biblical metaphor is integrated into the novel's major themes, including its treatment of the central hero, Myshkin.

56 Writes Iu. Lotman, "Rousseauism became for him the 'European' idea, in distinction from the 'Russian' idea of Christianity" ("Russo," 604). Recall that Nastasya Filippovna, who should take the same role as that of the Swiss girl Marie, is described by Gania Ivolgin as "an extraordinarily Russian woman" (104).

57 The connection between Myshkin and Akaky Akakievich on this basis has been noted by Iurii Mann ("Gogol and Dostoevsky," 18–20). See Monas for a discussion of the novel in the context of the tradition of the Petersburg tale. See also Terras, " 'Shinel' ' Gogolia" and *The Young Dostoevsky.*

4 Aesthetics and Ethics in Tolstoy's *Anna Karenina*

1 Noted for example in Bem, "Khudozhestvennaia polemika," 207.

2 In 1905 Tolstoy wrote to Bernard Bouvier, founder of Société Jean Jacques Rousseau, "Rousseau was my teacher from the age of fifteen. Rousseau and the Gospels are the two biggest and most beneficent influences of my life" (*Polnoe sobranie sochinenii* [henceforth *Pss*], 75:234–35).

3 See Bem, "Khudozhestvennaia polemika" for a reading of Dostoevsky's *Podrostok* (*Raw Youth* or *The Adolescent*) as a polemical response to Tolstoy.

Of Tolstoy a Soviet critic has written: "Tolstoy took literary influence as a sign of decadence. According to his notions, a work should be never-before-seen, original, and traces of another's perception signify an inhibition, hardening, or temporary closure of the idea" (P. V. Palievsky, cited from Sakharov, 343). This is not to say that Tolstoy never engaged in parody; but when he did, as in his reworking of Pushkin's "Prisoner of the Caucasus" under the same title, it was in a manner fundamentally different from Dostoevsky's: rather than a dialogic response, or the appropriation and reaccenting of another's discourse, Tolstoy acts as an authoritative corrector. What on the surface appears paradoxical — that Tolstoy, considered by Bakhtin to be a "monological" author, can at the same time be engaged in other, more subtle forms of parody, is taken up in Morson, *Hidden in Plain View.*

4 As pointed out in Bethea, 77–79. On a number of further possible allusions to Tolstoy and *War and Peace* in *The Idiot*, see Miller, *Dostoevsky and "The Idiot,"* 59–60; see also George Steiner, 11 and 326–27. In any joint treatment of the two novels, which is not my purpose here, these parallels would have to be a point of departure for discussing the manifold and significant differences between the works.

5 The well-known fact that the idea for this novel came from a true story told to Tolstoy by the jurist A. F. Koni in no way invalidates these structural similarities. Of course, in title (and in the way the narrative is structured syntactically as a series of "business" visits) the novel recalls Gogol's *Dead Souls*; as a "descent" into the Russian legal and penal system, it also continues the tradition begun by Dostoevsky's *Notes from the House of the Dead*, which Tolstoy valued very highly, as well as Chekhov's *The Island of Sakhalin.*

6 Dostoevsky offered high praise for the novel, agreeing with an unnamed interlocutor: "This is an unheard of, outstanding thing. Who among our writers can match him? And in Europe, who can exhibit at least anything of the like?" (*Diary*, 785; *Pss* 25:199). He especially liked the episode when Karenin and Vronsky are prematurely reconciled over what proves not to be Anna's deathbed (*Diary*, 610–11; *Pss* 25:52–53). But the weight of his writing on *Anna Karenina* is sharply critical, in particular regarding the novel's controversial ending. For a discussion of Dostoevsky's Tolstoy criticism, see Sorokin, 125–47.

For a recent discussion of the critical response to *Anna Karenina*, see Babaev, *Lev Tolstoi*, 125–211. See also *Russkaia kriticheskaia literatura*, which contains periodical articles from 1875 and 1876. Some of this material is translated and appears together with Western reviews in *Tolstoy: The Critical Heritage*, 233–370.

7 They were once present in the same room: both attended a lecture by Vladimir Solov'ev, but Tolstoy — who came in the company of Strakhov, also an intimate of Dostoevsky — was of a mood to avoid contacts with others that day and asked Strakhov not to introduce him to anybody; Dostoevsky later reproached Strakhov bitterly for not at least pointing Tolstoy out to him, so that he could see him in the flesh (recounted by Dostoevsky's wife [Dostoevskaia, *Vospominaniia*, 319–20]; see also Bem, "Tolstoi v otsenke," 167).

Among Tolstoy's recorded comments on Dostoevsky are two letters to Nikolai Strakhov, separated by only a couple of years but expressing rather opposite views. After hearing of Dostoevsky's death, Tolstoy wrote: "I never saw the man and never had any direct relations with him, and suddenly when he died I realised that he was the very closest, dearest and most necessary man for me. I was a writer, and all writers are vain and envious — I at least was that sort of writer. But it never occurred to me to measure myself against him, never. Everything that he did (every good and real thing that he did) was such that the more he did it, the happier I was. Art arouses envy in me, and so does intelligence, but the things of the heart arouse only joy. I always considered him my friend, and I never thought otherwise than that we should meet, and that it was my fault that we hadn't managed to do so yet" (*Tolstoy's Letters*, 340; *Pss* 63:44–45).

After Strakhov published a biography and selected notebook entries and letters of the late author, however, Tolstoy wrote that Dostoevsky was overrated, that there had been "an exaggeration of his importance, an exaggeration to fit a pattern, the elevation into a prophet and saint of a man who died in the very feverish process of an inner struggle between good and evil. He is touching and interesting, but one cannot set on a pedestal for the edification of posterity a man who was all struggle" (*Tolstoy's Letters*, 363; *Pss* 63:142).

8 Tolstoy's "conversion" did not assuage Dostoevsky's doubts. Five days before the latter's death in 1881, Count Tolstoy's aunt and correspondent, A. A. Tolstaya, showed Dostoevsky a letter in which Tolstoy's new tendencies were explained. While reading it, Dostoevsky "grabbed his head and in a despondent voice repeated: 'It's wrong, it's wrong [*Ne to, ne to!..*]' " (Bem, "Tolstoi v otsenke," 190).

9 For other discussions of Tolstoy and Dostoevsky, one might begin with Merezhkovskii, *L. Tolstoi i Dostoevskii*; N. N. Apostolov, *Lev Tolstoi i ego sputniki*, 139–55; and George Steiner, *Tolstoy or Dostoevsky*. See also the recent article of Emerson, "The Tolstoy Connection," for some very fine points of comparison.

10 And with *Don Quixote*. The phrase, "pathology of novel reading," belongs to Jauss (7).

11 *Anna Karenina* is found in vols. 18–19 of Tolstoy's *Polnoe sobranie sochinenii* (*Pss*). Citations are taken from the Maude translation (Norton ed.), and are referenced (in roman numerals) by both part (*chast'*) and chapter (*glava*), which correspond in the two sources, and by page number (Arabic numeral) in the Norton edition. Since the chapters are generally quite short, this method should allow readers to find the relevant passages in most editions of the novel.

12 I would not want to reduce this detail to one meaning, however. It is also an index of sensuality — Anna is seeking sensations; and it is a potentially dangerous, self-destructive gesture, perhaps foreshadowing her suicide (as well as recalling the knife by which Nastasya Filippovna of *The Idiot* perishes, a knife that at one time is used to cut the pages of another great nineteenth-century adultery novel, *Madame Bovary*).

13 See Emerson's discussion of death in Tolstoy in "The Tolstoy Connection in Bakhtin," 73–74. See also Morson, *Hidden in Plain View*, 26–32.

14 Eikhenbaum interprets this candle as both a fixed topos, a case of the "mythological symbolism" of an extinguished candle standing for death, which Tolstoy also uses in *War and Peace*, and as a realistic detail from Anna's inner life (158–59).

15 For Tolstoy's observations regarding Kramskoy, who was later to correspond with Tolstoy (see letter of Jan. 29, 1885, to Tolstoy), see the letters to Strakhov (*Pss* 62:50) and to Fet (*Pss* 62:48).

16 By the "Ivanov-Strauss-Renan" attitude toward Christ is meant a scholarly and historical approach to the origins of Christianity, and the realistic representation of Christ in art, rather than the reliance on the tradition of conventional representations. The second of the trio is David Friedrich Strauss, a German philosopher, theologian, historian, and publicist. Strauss was a great influence on Ivanov, who traveled to consult with him but was foiled by insurpassable linguistic barriers (Barooshian, 51–52). The third is Joseph Ernest Renan, author of the *Life of Jesus* (of which more than 60,000 copies sold within months of its first publication). The phenomenon is discussed in general terms by Fuller.

17 Nevertheless, Repin wrote to Stasov that it was a pity Tolstoy "didn't understand Ivanov's painting" (*Tolstoi i khudozhniki*, 72).

18 Richard Gustafson has written: "*Anna Karenina* contrasts the career of the personality [*lichnost'*] and the career of the divine self. The artist Mikhailov's painting of Pilate and Christ embodies and reveals these two modes of being and is the emblem of the book" (142; see also 260–61). This is essentially what E. I. Kupreianova found to be the symbolic significance of Mikhailov's depiction of Christ and Pilate, which is "correlated symbolically with the whole problematic of the novel, that is, with its fundamental antithesis between the evil of 'life for one's self' and the good of 'life for others' " (347–48). She also discusses the opposition that this episode sets up between Mikhailov's painting, which catches the expression of Anna's soul, and Vronsky's unfinished portrait, which "attempts only to render her physical charms" (338).

Others have interpreted this episode as chiefly a reflection on artistic practices. Mack Smith finds that "the painting of Anna's portrait by Mikhailov is symbolic of Tolstoy's creation of her [Anna]" (221), and sees the distinctive difference between Mikhailov's portrait of Anna and the other two portraits of Anna in Mikhailov's ability to go beyond convention, create spontaneously, and reveal something essential about Anna. Eduard G. Babaev situates the three portraits of Anna (the one commissioned by Karenin, Vronsky's, and Mikhailov's) in the context of the theory of art Tolstoy later expressed in *What Is Art* (*Chto takoe iskusstvo*). Only the portrait by Mikhailov possesses that quality of "infectiousness" ("*zarazitel'nost'* ") commended in Tolstoy's theoretical tract. And, writes Babaev, "If one is to speak of the novel as a whole, then Tolstoy's art produces the same effect on the reader as the portrait painted by Mikhailov produced on Levin" (*Tolstoi ob iskusstve*, 33).

Joan Delaney Grossman cites Tolstoy's claim regarding *Anna Karenina* that ". . . I'm proud of the architecture—the arches have been constructed in such a way that it is impossible to see where the keystone is" (*Tolstoy's Letters*, 311; *Pss* 62:377 [letter of January 27, 1878, to S. A. Rachinsky]; see J. D. Grossman, 1). She considers Mikhailov's portrait of Anna to be this keystone. "In a sense by painting Anna he does Tolstoy's work for him. Or more correctly, the process by which he penetrates Anna's character and spiritual state and renders them in his medium suggests parallels with Tolstoy's own creative process" (8). To Grossman it is highly significant that the novel's two plot lines — Levin's and Anna's — meet when Levin and Anna meet, and just when Levin is contemplating Mikhailov's portrait.

Amy Mandelker's "A Painted Lady: *Ekphrasis* in *Anna Karenina*" was published as this chapter was in revision. The similarities and more significant divergences between Mandelker's treatment of the pictorial in *Anna Karenina* and my own will be noted as the chapter proceeds.

19 The issue of "convention" is central to Mack Smith's article.

Nekhliudov of *Resurrection* is also introduced as a gentleman dilettante painter, although this pursuit is already in the past as the novel begins, and the motif is not situated in the context of a plane of metapoetic meaning, as in *Anna Karenina.*

20 Mandelker associates Tolstoy's opposition of Mikhailov and Vronsky with Lessing's differentiation "between works of art that imitate nature directly and those that imitate other works of art (imitations of imitations)" (6–7).

21 He interpreted this lack as a "sign of the times," however, and not a fault in Tolstoy's novel. See also the anonymous review in *Russkie vedomosti* (*Russian News*), attributed to Aleksei Suvorin: "The long-awaited continuation of Count Tolstoy's novel 'Anna Karenina' appeared at last. . . . In reading it, one becomes again convinced of the justice of the regret expressed by the majority of critics that such a great talent was being wasted on absolutely insignificant subject-matter . . ." (*Tolstoy: The Critical Heritage*, 282).

22 See Eikhenbaum, who cites B. Chicherin's dismissal of Tolstoy in this period: "He had no notion of philosophy. He himself admitted to me that he had tried to read Hegel, but that it was all Greek to him. Schopenhauer, recommended to him by Fet, was his sole nourishment"; Eikhenbaum also notes that when Tolstoy pronounced his discovery of Schopenhauer to literary acquaintances, it was cause for humor: "This was one of those 'discoveries,' typical for Tolstoy, over which Turgenev laughed at this time in a letter to Fet: 'Let Tolstoy discover the Mediterranean Sea, as Vas. P. Botkin used to say' " (79–80). See also Sorokin (431), who points out contemporary criticism of Tolstoy's "unscholarly" approaches to history and philosophy in *War and Peace.*

23 In general, Tolstoy held art criticism in low regard. In April of 1876 he apologized to Strakhov for not reading a volume of criticism by Apollon Grigorev, saying ". . . criticism is for me the most boring of everything that is boring in the world. In smart art criticism everything is the truth, but it's not the *whole* truth, while art is art only because it is *whole*" (*V umnoi kritike iskusstva vsë pravda, no ne* vsia *pravda, a iskusstvo potomu tol'ko iskusstvo, chto ono* vsë; *Pss* 62:265; *Tolstoy's Letters*, 295).

24 See for instance J. D. Grossman, 3; and Mandelker, 10.

25 The contrary position, now a critical commonplace, was argued in the early article of Roman Jakobson, "On Realism in Art." He remarked: "Classicists, sentimentalists, the romanticists to a certain extent, and even the 'realists' of the nineteenth century, the modernists to a large degree, and finally, the futurists, the expressionists, and their like have more than once steadfastly proclaimed faithfulness to reality, maximum verisimilitude — in other words, realism — as the guiding motto of their artistic program" (39); every literary movement thus considers adherence to its own conventions "realistic"

and can garner a truth effect from laying bare and repudiating the conventions of previous artistic systems. Mack Smith's article on *Anna Karenina* takes up this issue.

26 "It is clear that Tolstoj had a definite literary genre in mind" (Stenbock-Fermor, *Architecture*, 35).

27 This point is dwelt upon by Gustafson, although rather than emphasizing the artistic significance of Mikhailov's creative process, he makes of it a metaphor for living, with the notion of "unwrapping" and penetrating to the inner person acquiring a metaphysical significance; as part of Tolstoy's "doctrine of person" generally speaking, it derives from Eastern Christian notions of person and sin (Gustafson, 176–77). Where Gustafson is interested in Tolstoy's metapoetic treatment of aesthetics insofar as it represents his religious and ethical beliefs, my study departs from an interest in the metapoetic as such, and finds it necessary to confront Tolstoy's ethics, as well as the complicated interconnection between the "two shoulders."

28 The painting thus falls within the tradition of idealized representation, represented quite well in the following citation from Diderot: "Admit then that there is and can be neither an entire existing animal nor any part of the existing animal that you could take in the last analysis as a primary model. Admit then that this model is purely ideal, and that it is directly borrowed from no individual image of Nature, whose scrupulous copy would have remained in your imagination as one that you could summon back, hold before your eyes and copy slavishly, unless you wanted to be a portraitist. Admit then that when you make something beautiful, you make nothing that is, nothing even that can be" (cited in Todorov, *Theories of the Symbol*, 118). See also Abrams, 35–46; and Hagstrum, 7–8.

29 Gogol's own verbal creations are marked by a striving toward pictorial effects, most notable perhaps in *The Government Inspector*, which is at its climax transformed into a *tableau vivant.* On Gogol and the iconic arts generally, see Judith Robey, *Pictorial Language in Gogol: Metaphor, Tableau, Intertext* (Ph.D. dissertation, Indiana University, 1991). See Iurii Mann, *Komediia*, 68–77, for a discussion of the "dumb scene"; see also his *Poetika Gogolia*, where this moment is discussed in greater detail as an exception to Gogol's general observance of the dramatic convention of the "fourth wall" (255–57).

On the two-way interpenetration of the codes of the theater and painting in Russia of the nineteenth century, see Iu. M. Lotman, "The Stage and Painting."

30 Here I diverge sharply from Mandelker, who claims that the portrait has a positive ethical effect on Levin; instead of viewing Levin's visit to Anna as a *fall*, as I have above, she considers it the start of his moral regeneration. But the crisis with which Levin will struggle in the novel's last part has not even begun yet. Mandelker does offer some very sharp insights regarding Anna's aesthetic self-presentation (9).

Unfortunately, the pun on "painted," which in English associates these two episodes so nicely — the same pun that underlies the title of Mandelker's article, "A Painted Lady" — does not occur in Russian, where the Frenchwoman in make-up is *krashenaia*, and the subject of a portrait would be *narisovannaia* or *napisannaia.* Nevertheless, in these two parallel instances where Levin's attitude toward fallen women is central, the modifiers translated as "painted" are clearly synonymic in their common reference to an aestheticized and alluring self-presentation.

31 Elsewhere Tolstoy referred to Lessing as a fundamental authority in regard to such questions. In 1870 he complained in his notebook that "tens of thousands of artists read and work, and they have never come to terms with even Lessing, let alone the philosophical theories regarding their own pursuits. Ge has painted a picture of the civic Christ excellently. But that is the one thing that cannot be the subject of a painting. That would have been clear from even *Laocoön* of Lessing" (*Pss* 48:118). The reference is to Ge's "The Last Supper" ("*Tainaia vecheria*"; reproduced in *L. N. Tolstoi i khudozhniki*, 1978, 128–29). At the end of *War and Peace* Tolstoy has his character Nikolai wearing a ring with a cameo of Laocoön's head (Epilogue, I, viii).

32 The connection with Lessing, arrived at independently, is also remarked in Mandelker. Mandelker's interesting reading pursues a different set of associations, however, and does not treat the opposition between space and time.

A lengthier treatment of this theme in the novel could find much material beyond the spheres of portrait painting and fiction writing. Levin's half brother, the philosopher Koznyshev, is occupied with yet another world of discourse—that of philosophy. What is true of language and music—that they rely on arbitrary, conventional signs—is certainly the case for philosophical discourse as well. And indeed, throughout the novel stress is placed on Koznyshev's artificial relationship to nature, which culminates in the event proving his artificial relationship to his own inner nature and desires—his failure to propose to Varenka (VI, v; 511–13).

33 Pointed out also by Schultze (107), among many others. In the draft version the artistic principles reflected in this episode are stated more explicitly in free indirect discourse attached to Mikhailov (XX, 399).

34 The painting is reproduced in *L. N. Tolstoi i khudozhniki*, 128–29.

35 The painting had been shown at an exhibition of the Itinerants art movement (*Peredvizhniki*—the art movement to which Kramskoy and Ge belonged), but it caused such a stir that further public displays were prohibited. Tolstoy, who had become personally associated with many of the Itinerant painters, and whose judgment was very highly valued by them, assisted in having this work taken on tour abroad. He also persuaded Tretiakov to buy it. Here is an excerpt from the interpretation of the painting Tolstoy offered in a letter to Tretiakov (June 30, 1890):

> Then Ge took the most simple motif, and one that is intelligible now that he has taken it: Christ and his teaching in conflict with the teaching of the world not just in words but both in words and deeds; i.e. the motif which then constituted and still constitutes the main importance of the phenomenon of Christ, an importance which is not disputable, but something about which churchmen who regard Him as God, and historians who regard Him as an important person in history and Christians who regard His practical teaching as the main thing about Him cannot help but agree.
>
> The picture depicts with complete historical accuracy the moment when Christ, after being led, tormented, beaten and dragged from one jail to another and from one official to

another, is brought before the governor, a very kindly fellow who is not concerned with Christ or the Jews, still less with any truth explained to him, an acquaintance of all the scholars and philosophers of Rome, by this ragamuffin; his only concern is not to be at fault in the eyes of a superior official. Christ sees before him a deluded man bloated with fat, but he decides not to spurn him just because of his appearance, and so begins to express to him the essence of his teaching. But the governor is not concerned with this. He says: what is truth? and goes away. And Christ looks sorrowfully at this impenetrable man. (*Tolstoy's Letters*, 463)

Tolstoy's (misplaced) faith in the moral effect this painting would have on its viewers verges on the Gogolian.

36 Thus, Aleksei Suvorin recorded in his journal a discussion held with Tolstoy and Chekhov in Moscow (February 16, 1896): "A discussion began about the painting of Ge from Christ's life. Tolstoy very heatedly argued that contemporary art has its own tasks, that Christ can be represented differently than did Rafael, with the purpose of showing that we, with our actions, constantly 'crucify Christ' . . ." (*Dnevnik A. S. Suvorina*, 80).

37 A traditional criticism of *Anna Karenina*, dating from the novel's first appearance, is that it is not one novel, but two; that the Anna and Levin lines are not integrated. See Babaev, *Iz istorii*, 192–97.

38 As remarked in Al'tman, *Chitaia Tolstogo*, 20; see also Babaev, *Iz istorii*, 124–27, for a more detailed discussion of the association.

39 Tolstoy often commented on the disgusting, lowly nature of his novel. For instance: " 'The other day Strakhov was at my place,' he writes P. D. Golokhvastov, 'he almost got me interested in my novel again, but I just dropped it. It is terribly disgusting and nasty [*uzhasno protivno i gadko*]' " (*Pss* 62:103; cited in Eikhenbaum, 116); in a letter to A. A. Tolstaya he calls the novel "a frivolous matter [*pustoe delo*]" (*Pss* 62:266; Eikhenbaum, 121); see also *Pss* 62:265.

40 This episode may be another parallel with Dostoevsky's *The Idiot*, where Myshkin is enchanted by the picture of Nastasya Filippovna before he meets her. This moment is also a counterpart to Kitty's perception of Anna at the ball, discussed earlier; there Anna appears to her "framed," as though the live person were a portrait; here a portrait is perceived as a "living and charming woman."

41 "Auditory signs" includes "letters and glyphs," which are "parasitic formations, optional superstructures imposed upon spoken language and implying its earlier acquisition" ("Visual and Auditory Signs," 334). See also Jakobson's "The Relations between Visual and Auditory Signs," which discusses Lessing and points out some of the semiotic traits shared by visual and auditory signs (343–44); and Todorov's treatment of Lessing in *Theories of the Symbol*, 137–46.

42 See Mandelker's discussion of Levin's "flawed nature, which needs to try to preserve moments in a 'frozen,' 'framed' state" (17)—although it appears more an issue of projection than preservation; see also Morson's treatment of this dynamic in Tolstoy's *Sevastopol Sketches* ("The Reader as Voyeur"), as well as his remarks about the idyllic in "Prosaics and *Anna Karenina*" (5).

43 The operation of this antifictional and "frame-breaking" principle in Tolstoy's *Sevastopol Sketches* is analyzed in Morson, "The Reader as Voyeur."

5 Chekhov's "The Steppe"

1 Although the term *povest'* did not have uniform usage in the nineteenth century, here it is applied in its most generally accepted meaning: a narrative fiction longer and more complex than a short story, but without the length and range of characters and events one expects of a novel; the various redactions of "The Steppe" come out to around one hundred pages.

2 For a treatment of the cultural and psychological significance of the theme of the steppe's space in the story, see Jackson, "Space and the Journey: A Metaphor for All Times," *Russian Literature* 29 (1991): 427–38.

3 All references to the text of "The Steppe" are to volume 7 of *Sochineniia* in Chekhov, *Polnoe sobranie sochinenii i pisem v tridtsati tomakh*, and are indicated in this chapter by page number only. Otherwise, "*Soch.* volume number : page number" refers to the first eighteen volumes of *Polnoe sobranie*, which hold Chekhov's works (*Sochineniia*); "*Pis'ma* volume number : page number" refers to the following twelve volumes, which are comprised of Chekhov's letters (*Pis'ma*). Letters referenced to *Anton Chekhov's Life* are taken from that source; all other translations are my own.

4 In a letter to his editor, Aleksei Pleshcheev, Chekhov said that the story's "subject is poetic" and should therefore please "my dear poet" (*Pis'ma* 2:179–80); but three days later he complained to Ivan Shcheglov that "The Steppe" lacked any sort of romantic plot (*Pis'ma* 2:182).

5 D. S. Mirsky called "The Steppe" "a languid, melodious, and tedious lullaby" (86).

6 Nilsson suggests that an inconstant narrative voice is the necessary result of the story's dual theme, "the story of Egorushka and the description of the steppe" (47), and he considers this duality "sometimes rather fatal to the unity he [Chekhov] was eager to achieve" (25).

7 Rufus Mathewson, Jr., after outlining in brief his vision of the composition of motifs in "The Steppe," says, "It would take a symphonic score to reproduce the totality of this [the story's] poetical/musical order" (36).

8 Nilsson writes that Chekhov's "intention was certainly not to write a sort of allegory, but thoughts and reflections on the destiny of Russia and the Russian people are more or less clearly interwoven in the narrative texture. And the steppe and its people did in fact lend themselves easily to symbolic interpretation . . . Chekhov's story has . . . come to be looked on more and more as a symbolic work" (20). See also the discussion of the symbolic meaning of the story's repetition of verbs sharing the root "*makh*," suggestive of circular motion, in Maxwell, 152.

9 See also the discussion in Nilsson, 42–44.

10 This episode is suggestively reminiscent of the famous passage in Dostoevsky's *Diary of a Writer* (*Dnevnik pisatelia*) describing a scene the young Dostoevsky had

witnessed while en route from Moscow to Petersburg (in order to continue his education, like Egorushka, though at a higher level): a courier was whipping his driver, who in turn viciously whipped his horses (Dostoevskii, *Pss* 22:27–29 [Jan. 1876, Chap. 3]).

11 In *Zametki o proze russkikh klassikov*, Viktor Shklovsky sees Varlamov as the story's "chief hero" and "plot's center" (297); but Chekhov "disrobes [*razoblachaet*] Varlamov" in the discourse of Solomon, showing that Varlamov's reign over the "tormentful steppe" is "short-lived," and that "the image of Varlamov is deprived of any poeticity" (298). Superficially, this depiction of Varlamov as a capitalist landowner who will be overthrown seems typical of Soviet criticism and rather trite. But if one sees Varlamov as the center of that aspect of the story in which mystery and suspense are key, then it seems as though Shklovsky means to suggest a vision of "The Steppe" similar to the one being developed here. Varlamov stands as a figure for the very device of suspense, of "things in their proper places"; he is laid bare and discarded, however, in a self-referential story which works more as poetry than prose fiction. Such an interpretation of Shklovsky's use of the term "*razoblachat'*" would be consistent with the way he used it in his earlier, formalist days.

12 The use of etiquette and "accepted" moral principles by the strong and guilty to abuse the weak and innocent is a typical Chekhovian motif (as in "The Chorus Girl" ["Khoristka"], 1886).

13 Cf. Nilsson's point that at times Egorushka's viewpoint is too restrictive for Chekhov, and so he steps out of it (47).

14 Such a use of a print or woodcut motif to refer back to the whole of the narrative of which they are a part is not unique to "The Steppe." See for instance Senderovich's discussion of the prints hanging on the inn wall in Chekhov's "On the Road" (Senderovich, "Poetic Structure"). Also worth noting is the presence of a similar device in Pushkin's prose; see Shaw.

15 "Keeping simply to modern times, the Russian Formalists, Propp and Lévi-Strauss have taught us to recognize the following dilemma: either a narrative is merely a rambling collection of events, in which case nothing can be said about it other than by referring back to the storyteller's (the author's) art, talent or genius—all mythical forms of chance—or else it shares with other narratives a common structure which is open to analysis, no matter how much patience its formulation requires. There is a world of difference between the most complex randomness and the most elementary combinatory scheme, and it is impossible to combine (to produce) a narrative without reference to an implicit system of units and rules" (Barthes, "Introduction to the Structural Analysis of Narratives," 80–81).

16 Not one of Solomon's tales is reported in the text of "The Steppe," and this seems significant; it certainly makes Solomon unique among the storytelling figures in the story. It may be that Chekhov wanted to avoid reflecting anti-Semitic values in his story, though, given his farcical and unattractive characterization of the inhabitants of Moisei's hostel, this seems unlikely. Perhaps Solomon's words are meant to seem so negative, so antinarrational, that their inclusion in the text of "The Steppe" was not even viable.

Chekhov's interest in the author of Ecclesiastes, King Solomon, extended beyond his work on "The Steppe." Sometime during the year or two after writing "The Steppe," Chekhov actually began a dramatic work whose hero was Solomon (see editors' commentary in *Soch.* 17:438). The fragment left to us, a monologue by Solomon, is just the sort of negationist discourse one might expect from the Solomon of "The Steppe," and it also repeats many of the same motifs found in "The Steppe" (such as the flock of sheep, the bird flying one knows neither where nor why, the lone tree, the insect, the dust, the trembling and the cold, and last, the opposition between word and music [*Soch.* 17:194]).

17 The past passive participle describing the floor, "*polit*," is sometimes rendered in translations of the story as "watered," but it apparently refers to some sort of ceramic technique (see "*polivat'* " in Dal').

18 Beyond the fact of Chekhov's use of the adjective *kabalisticheskii*, I can offer only the most circumstantial evidence regarding his awareness of what kabbalah meant. First, there is his relationship with his sister's Jewish friend, Dunya Efros, to whom he (apparently) proposed marriage in January of 1886 (see letters to V. Bilibin, *Pis'ma* 1:183, 190 [Jan. 18, and Feb. 1, 1886], as well as the editors' commentary, *Pis'ma* 1:408). The Chekhovs' landlords in Moscow at the time Chekhov worked on "The Steppe" were Jewish, and the two elder Chekhov brothers were both involved with young women from that family (see Rayfield, "What Did Jews Mean to Chekhov?"). The government's policy of "Russification," which was intensified in the 1880s and led to quotas on Jews at institutions of higher learning, the expulsion of Jews from cities, and horrible pogroms, meant that things Jewish were quite prominent in the press and general cultural consciousness, if often in a very negative way. Chekhov's story "Slime" ("Tina") (1886) and his play *Ivanov* (1886) precede "The Steppe" in their treatment of Jewish themes (and according to Karlinsky are a working through of his anxieties regarding Efros [*Anton Chekhov's Life and Thought*, 55–56]), while the later "Rothschild's Fiddle" ("Skripka Rotshil'da," 1894) is one of Chekhov's finest stories (see Jackson, " 'If I Forget Thee,' " for a discussion of the Jewish theme in that story; see also Etkind).

19 While the animation of scenery was fashionable in nature description during the 1880s (Nilsson, 46), in "The Steppe" such descriptions serve an essential, internally motivated function.

20 Chekhov clearly plays with the biblical story of the Fall in other stories; see for instance one of his earliest, "For the Sake of Little Apples" ("Za iablochki," *Soch.* 1:39–45 [1880]).

21 Of course, this illustration must be understood in a strictly metaphoric sense; and yet, the very choice Chekhov had of expressions meaning "like" or "as though" (one can also say, for instance, *slovno*, *kak*, *kak budto*, and *kak by*) makes his heavy reliance on the ambiguous "*tochno*" seem all the more significant.

22 This sort of juxtaposition of psychological and physiological motivations for illness is a typical Chekhovian device, especially in those stories where the critical manifestation of illness serves as the story's denouement; for two examples, see "Grisha" (*Soch.* 5:83–85) and "The Nameday Party" ("Imeniny," *Soch.* 7:167–98).

23 As Dällenbach suggests in his discussion of the metapoetic device of *mise en abyme*

(taken up in this book's introduction), "[M]ultiple or divided [self-]reflections can, in a fragmented narrative, be a unifying factor" (70–71).

24 It also recalls the saying: "*Iazyk do Kieva dovedët*" ("Your tongue will get you to Kiev").

25 To recall just a few of Chekhov's comments regarding the originality of "The Steppe": "There are many places that will be understood by neither critics nor the public; they will seem trifling to both, not meriting attention, but I anticipate with pleasure the two or three literary epicurians that will understand and value these same places, and that is enough for me" (to Ia. P. Polonsky, *Pis'ma* 2:178); "There have been no stories like 'The Steppe' in the thick journals for a long time now; I'm stepping out originally, but for this originality I'll get the same as I got for *Ivanov*" (to M. V. Kiseleva, *Pis'ma* 2:186). See also the letter to Grigorovich cited at the beginning of this chapter.

26 *Slovar' russkikh narodnykyh govorov*, 8:174.

27 Bitsilli says that the "rhythm" of "The Steppe" is "created not by the alternation of qualitatively different 'events,' but by the alternation of 'themes' in a sense close to the meaning of that word in musical terminology, together with the alternation of tempos and harmonies" (*Tvorchestvo*, 64). He identifies these themes as: "the theme of the life impulse, Bergson's *élan vital*, the thirst for life . . . and the theme of exclusion from life, loneliness . . . death" (65).

Abram Derman says that Chekhov was most interested in "influencing the reader's receptivity," that he sought to create an "atmosphere of agitation" and "heightened emotionality"; Chekhov accomplishes this "with the power of influence inherent in rhythm, where this phenomenon would not explain itself" (123–24).

For a treatment of Chekhov's musicality, see N. M. Fortunatov, "Muzykal'nost' chekhovskoi prozy," in his *Puti iskanii: o masterstve pisatelia* (Moscow: Sovetskii pisatel', 1974), 105–34.

28 Chekhov knew *Frigat Pallada* from his reading as a youth, and recommended it to his little brother Misha in a letter of April 1879. Then he considered the work "first class," although upon rereading it not long after finishing "The Steppe" he altered that opinion.

29 "*Vybivat' svoi 'tochki'*" apparently refers to the marking off of a bird's mating grounds, an activity accompanied by distinctive mating calls. See Dal', "*Tokovat'*"; see same in *Slovar' sovremennogo russkogo literaturnogo iazyka*, 17 vols. (Moscow: Izdatel'stro Akademii Nank SSSR, 1950–65).

30 In the passage contrasting Kuzmichov with Father Khristofor as they nap, the apprehension of the former over finding Varlamov is opposed to the easygoing nature of the latter, who "all his life had never known a single problem which could bind his soul *as though it were a boa constrictor*" (23–24; italics mine); Varlamov, with his anxiety-producing effect on Kuzmichov, is thus indirectly associated with another serpent.

In his commentary to *Eugene Onegin* Vladimir Nabokov notes Pushkin's use of the same pun (vol. 2, 469), and himself plays with it elsewhere in the commentary.

31 This connection between the figures of Egorushka and St. George was pointed out to me by Savely Senderovich. See his "Chudo Georgiia o zmie" for a comprehensive treatment of the "St. George complex" in Chekhov's life and works.

32 Indeed, Chekhov's second published work was the metapoetic spoof, "What Is Most Often Encountered in Novels, Tales, and So On?" ("Chto chashche vsego vstrechaetsia v romanakh, povestiakh i t. p.?").
33 For a recent treatment of the Gogolian subtext of "The Steppe," see Pekka Tammi, "Three Remarks on Čechov's *Step'*."
34 For further discussion of this topic, see my "Chekhov's 'At Sea': A Psychoanalytic Approach to Chekhov's First Signed Story," in *Reading Chekhov's Texts*, ed. R. L. Jackson (Evanston, Ill.: Northwestern University Press, 1993).

Conclusion

1 This interpretation finds support in Nabokov's lectures on Chekhov (Nabokov, *Lectures*): "Chekhov was in the first place an individualist and an artist" (246); "[G]reat kindness pervades Chekhov's literary work, but it is not a matter of program, or of literary message with him, but simply the natural coloration of his talent" (247); and "To conclude: Chekhov together with Pushkin are the purest writers that Russia has produced in the sense of the complete harmony that their writings convey" (250 n).
2 Nabokov's lecture on *The Seagull* (*Chaika*) is quite sensitive to the way the play's overt metaliterary themes reflect back on Chekhov's own poetics (Nabokov, *Lectures*, 282–95).
3 Although Chekhov was studying in Moscow at the time, I have not found any mention in his letters or works of the celebration. His brother Mikhail, however, suggests (rather offhandedly, and with some memory slips regarding dates) that this was an important moment in the process of Chekhov's professionalization: "At that time he [Chekhov] apparently didn't feel bored during the summer in stuffy Moscow. There was the great All-Russia exposition, and in 1881 followed the inauguration of the Pushkin monument, which aroused the whole Russian intelligentsia. He was making new acquaintances then, establishing literary connections, he went all out for the newspaper and magazine business" (M. P. Chekhov, 216). On the role of this event in the Russian literary and social consciousness, see Levitt.
4 See the discussion in Annabel Patterson, *Fables of Power: Aesopian Writing and Political History* (Durham, N.C.: Duke University Press, 1991); see also Laura Wilhelm, "The Aesopic Legacy in Russian Literature," unpublished manuscript.
5 For a discussion of Tolstoy's "absolute language," and of Bakhtin's treatment of it, see Morson, *Hidden in Plain View.*
6 See for instance his discussions of aphasia, where contiguity disorders and similarity disorders, respectively, are shown to create different problems for the encoder (addresser) and decoder (addressee). Thus, for instance, as regards the homonymic and synonymic axes of language, "[T]here are no homonyms for the speaker," who selects among synonyms, ". . . whereas the listener, as long as he is not helped by the context, struggles with homonymy" ("Linguistic Types of Aphasia," 313).

Works Cited

Abrams, M. H. *The Mirror and the Lamp: Romantic Theory and the Critical Tradition.* 1953. Reprint, London, Oxford, and New York: Oxford University Press, 1973.

Aesop without Morals. Trans. and ed. Lloyd W. Daly. New York: Thomas Yoseloff, 1961.

Aksakov, S. T. *Istoriia moego znakomstva s Gogolem.* Ed. E. P. Naselenko and E. A. Smirnova. Moscow: Izdatel'stvo Akademii Nauk, 1960.

Alter, Robert. *Partial Magic: The Novel as a Self-Conscious Genre.* Berkeley, Los Angeles, and London: University of California Press, 1975.

Al'tman, M. S. *Chitaia Tolstogo.* Tula: Priokskoe knizhnoe izdatel'stvo, 1966.

——. *Dostoevskii po vekham imen.* Saratov: Izdatel'stvo Saratovskogo Universiteta, 1975.

Anderson, Roger. *Dostoevsky: Myths of Duality.* Gainesville: University of Florida Press, 1986.

Andrews, Larry R. "Dostoevskij and Hugo's *Le Dernier Jour D'un condamné.*" *Comparative Literature* 29, no. 1 (1977): 1–16.

Anton Chekhov's Life and Thought: Selected Letters and Commentary. Trans. Michael Heim and Simon Karlinsky. Selection, commentary, and introduction by Karlinsky. Berkeley: University of California Press, 1975.

Apostolov, N. N. *Lev Tolstoi i ego sputniki.* Moscow: Komissiia po oznamenovaniiu stoletiia so dnia rozhdeniia L. N. Tolstogo, 1928.

Apuleius. *The Golden Ass.* Trans. Jack Lindsay. Bloomington: Indiana University Press, 1960.

Attridge, Derek. "Closing Statement: Linguistics and Poetics in Retrospect." In *The Linguistics of Writing: Arguments between Language and Literature*, ed. Nigel Fabb et al. New York: Methuen, 1987, 15–32.

Babaev, Eduard Grigor'evich. *Iz istorii russkogo romana xix veka: Pushkin, Gertsen, Tolstoi.* Moscow: M.G.U., 1984.

——. *Lev Tolstoi i russkaia zhurnalistika ego epokhi.* Moscow: M.G.U., 1978.

——. *Tolstoi ob iskusstve.* Tula: Priokskoe knizhnoe izdatel'stvo, 1966.

Bakhtin, Mikhail. "Author and Hero in Aesthetic Activity." Trans. Vadim Liapunov. In *Art and Answerability: Early Philosophical Essays by M. M. Bakhtin*, ed. Michael Holquist and Vadim Liapunov. Austin: University of Texas Press, 1990, 4–256.

——. "Avtor i geori v esteticheskoi deiatel'nosti (fragment pervoi glavy)," *Literaturno-kriticheskie stat'i.* Moscow: Khudozhestvennaia literatura, 1986, 5–25.

——. "Discourse in the Novel." In *The Dialogic Imagination*, trans. Caryl Emerson and Michael Holquist. Austin: University of Texas Press, 1981, 259–422.

——. *Estetika slovesnogo tvorchestva.* Ed. Sergei Bocharov. Moscow: Iskusstvo, 1979.

——. "Forms of Time and of the Chronotope in the Novel." In *The Dialogic Imagination*, trans. Caryl Emerson and Michael Holquist. Austin: University of Texas Press, 1981, 224–36.

——. "The Problem of Speech Genres." In *Speech Genres and Other Late Essays*, trans. Vern W. McGee; ed. Caryl Emerson and Michael Holquist. Austin: University of Texas Press, 1986.

——. *Problems of Dostoevsky's Poetics.* Theory and History of Literature, vol. 8. Ed. and trans. Caryl Emerson. Minneapolis: University of Minnesota Press, 1984.

——. *Rabelais and His World.* Trans. Helene Iswolsky. Bloomington: Indiana University Press, 1984.

——, and P. M. Medvedev. *The Formal Method in Literary Scholarship.* Trans. Albert Wehrle. Cambridge: Harvard University Press, 1985.

Baldick, Chris. *The Concise Oxford Dictionary of Literary Terms.* Oxford and New York: Oxford University Press, 1990.

Barooshian, Vahan D. *The Art of Liberation: Alexander A. Ivanov.* Lanham, Md.: University Press of America, 1987.

Barthes, Roland. *Elements of Semiology.* Trans. Annettle Lavers and Colin Smith. New York: Hill and Wang, 1968.

——. "Introduction to the Structural Analysis of Narratives." In his *Image. Music. Text*, trans. Stephen Heath. New York: Hill & Wang, 1977, 79–124.

——. *S/Z: An Essay.* Trans. Richard Miller. New York: Hill and Wang, 1974.

Behler, Ernst. "The Theory of Irony in German Romanticism." In *Romantic Irony*, ed. Frederick Garber. Budapest: Akadémiai Kiadó, 1988, 43–81.

Belinskii, Vissarion. "*Eugene Onegin*: An Encyclopedia of Russian Life." In *Russian Views of Pushkin's* Eugene Onegin, trans., introduction, and notes by Sona Stephan Hoisington. Bloomington: Indiana University Press, 1988.

Bem, Al'fred Liudvigovich. "Khudozhestvennaia polemika s Tolstym." In *O Dostoevskom: sbornik statei.* Vol. 3. Ed. A. L. Bem. Prague: Petropolis, 1936, 192–214.

——. "Tolstoi v otsenke Dostoevskogo." In *O Dostoevskom: sbornik statei.* Vol. 3. Ed. A. L. Bem. Prague: Petropolis, 1936, 167–91.

Bethea, David M. *The Shape of the Apocalypse in Modern Russian Fiction.* Princeton: Princeton University Press, 1989.

——, and Sergei Davydov. "Pushkin's Saturnine Cupid: The Poetics of Parody in *The Tales of Belkin.*" *PMLA* 96, no. 1 (January 1981): 8–22.

Biblioteka velikikh pisatelei: Pushkin. 6 vols. Ed. S. A. Vengerov. St. Petersburg: Brokgauz-Efron, 1907–15.

Bitsilli, Petr. "K voprosu o vnutrennei forme romana Dostoevskogo." In *O Dostoevskom: Stat'i.* Providence, R.I.: Brown University Press, 1966, 3–71. (Originally published by Sofia Universitet, Istorikofilologicheski fakultet, *Godoshnik* 42 [1945–46]: 1–71.)

——. *Tvorchestvo Chekhova: opyt stilisticheskogo analiza.* Sofia: Imprimerié de l'Universit, 1942.

Blackmur, R. P. "*The Idiot*: A Rage of Goodness." In *Eleven Essays in the European Novel.* New York: Harcourt, Brace & World, 1964, 141–62.

Borges, Jorge Luis. "Partial Magic in the *Quixote.*" Trans. J. E. Irby. In Borges's *Labyrinths: Selected Stories and Other Writings.* Harmondsworth, Middlesex: Penguin Books, 1970, 228–31.

Briusov, Valerii. "Domik v Kolomne." In *Biblioteka velikikh pisatelei: Pushkin.* 6 vols. Ed. S. A. Vengerov. St. Petersburg: Brokgauz-Efron, 1907–15, 3:88–91.

Brodsky, Joseph. "Catastrophes in the Air." In his *Less Than One: Selected Essays.* New York: Farrar, Straus, Giroux, 1986, 268–303.

Brown, Nathalie Babel. *Hugo and Dostoevsky.* Ann Arbor, Mich.: Ardis, 1978.

Burgin, Diana Lewis. "The Reprieve of Nastasja: A Reading of a Dreamer's Authored Life." *Slavic and East European Journal* 29, no. 3 (1985): 258–68.

Chekhov, Anton P. *Polnoe sobranie sochinenii i pisem v tridstati tomakh.* Moscow: Nauka, 1974–83.

Chekhov, M. P. "Vokrug Chekhova." In *Vokrug Chekhova.* Ed. E. M. Sakharova. Moscow: Pravda, 1990, 151–322.

Chernyshevsky [Chernyshevskii], Nikolai. *What Is to Be Done?* Trans. M. R. Katz, annotated by W. G. Wagner. Ithaca and London: Cornell University Press, 1989.

Chistova, I. S. "Vodevil' 1830–1840-x godov." In *Istoriia russkoi dramaturgii xvii-pervaia polovina xix veka.* Ed. L. M. Lotman. Leningrad: Nauka, 1982, 402–25.

Coste, Didier. *Narrative as Communication.* Minneapolis: University of Minnesota Press, 1989.

Cuckolds, Clerics, & Countrymen: Medieval French Fabliaux. Trans. J. DuVal. Introduction, texts, and notes by R. Eichman. Fayetteville: University of Arkansas Press, 1982.

Cunningham, Lawrence S. *Saint Francis of Assisi.* Boston: Twayne, 1970.

Cyclopedia of Painters and Paintings. 4 vols. Ed. John D. Champlin, Jr. New York: Empire State Book Co., 1927.

Dal', Vladimir. *Tolkovyi slovar' zhivogo velikorusskogo iazyka.* 4 vols. Moscow: Gosudarstvennoe izdatel'stvo inostrannykh i natsional'nykh slovarei, 1955.

Dällenbach, Lucien. *The Mirror in the Text.* Trans. Jeremy Whiteley and Emma Hughes. Chicago: University of Chicago Press, 1989.

Dalton, Elizabeth. *Unconscious Structure in "The Idiot": A Study in Literature and Psychoanalysis.* Princeton: Princeton University Press, 1979.

Danilov, S. S. *Gogol' i teatr.* Leningrad: Khudozhestvennaia literatura, 1936.

Davydov, Sergei. "*The Gift*: Nabokov's Aesthetic Exorcism of Chernyshevskii." *Canadian-American Slavic Studies* 19, no. 3 (Fall 1985): 357–74.

Debreczeny, Paul. "Nikolay Gogol and His Critics." *Transactions of the American Philosophical Society* 56, pt. 3 (1966): 5–68.

Derman, Abram. *O masterstve Chekhova.* Moscow: Sovetskii pisatel', 1959.

Dnevnik A. S. Suvornia. Ed. and introduction by Mikh. Krichevskii. Moscow-Petrograd: L. D. Frenkel', 1923.

Dostoevskaia, A. G. *Vospominaniia.* Moscow: Khudozhestvennaia literatura, 1971.

Dostoevskii, Fedor M. *Polnoe sobranie sochinenii v tridtsati tomakh.* Leningrad: Nauka, 1974.

Dostoevsky, Fyodor [Dostoevskii, Fëdor]. *The Notebooks for "The Idiot."* Ed. and introduction by Edward Wasiolek; trans. Katharine Strelsky. Chicago: University of Chicago Press, 1967.

Dostoievsky [Dostoevskii], F. M. *The Diary of a Writer.* Trans. and notes by Boris Brasol. Salt Lake City, Utah: Peregrine Smith, 1985.

Eichman, Raymond. Introduction to *Cuckolds, Clerics, & Countrymen: Medieval French Fabliaux.* Trans. J. DuVal. Fayetteville: University of Arkansas Press, 1982, 1–12.

Eikhenbaum, Boris. *Tolstoi in the Seventies.* Trans. Albert Kaspin. Ann Arbor, Mich.: Ardis, 1982.

Emerson, Caryl. "The Tolstoy Connection in Bakhtin." *PMLA* 100, no. 1 (1985): 68–80.

Erlich, Victor. *The Double Image: Concepts of the Poet in Slavic Literatures.* Baltimore: Johns Hopkins Press, 1964.

——. *Gogol.* New Haven: Yale University Press, 1969.

Ermakov, Ivan Dmitrievich. *Etiudy po psikhologii tvorchestva A. S. Pushkina (opyt organicheskogo ponimaniia "Domik v Kolomne," "Proroka" i malen'kikh tragedii).* Moscow-Petrograd: Gosudarstvennoe izdatel'stvo, 1923.

Etkind, Efim. "Ivanov i Rotshil'd (O rasskaze A. P. Chekhova 'Skripka Rotshil'da')." *Russian Language Journal* 39, nos. 132–34 (1985): 31–49.

Fanger, Donald. *The Creation of Nikolai Gogol.* Cambridge: Harvard University Press, 1979.

——. "Gogol and His Reader." In *Literature and Society in Imperial Russia, 1800–1914*, ed. William Mills Todd, III. Stanford: Stanford University Press, 1978, 61–95.

——. "Influence and Tradition in the Russian Novel." In *The Russian Novel from Pushkin to Pasternak*, ed. John Garrard. New Haven: Yale University Press, 1983, 29–50.

——. "The Russianness of the Nineteenth-Century Novel." In *Art and Culture in Nineteenth-Century Russia*, ed. Th. G. Stavrou. Bloomington: Indiana University Press, 4–56.

Fedotov, G. P. "The Holy Fools." In his *The Russian Religious Mind.* 2 vols. Cambridge: Harvard University Press, 1966, 2:316–33.

Fiene, Donald. "Pushkin's 'Poor Knight': The Key to Perceiving Dostoevsky's *Idiot* as Allegory." *International Dostoevsky Society Bulletin*, no. 8 (November 1978): 10–21.

Finke, Michael. "Chekhov's 'Steppe': A Metapoetic Journey." In *Anton Chekhov Rediscovered: A Collection of New Studies with a Comprehensive Bibliography*, eds. Savely Senderovich and Munir Sendich. East Lansing, Mich.: Russian Language Journal, 1987.

Fomichev, S. A. "K tvorcheskoi istorii poemy 'Domik v Kolomne' (Nabliudeniia nad rukopis'iu)." *Vremennik Pushkinskoi komissii* 15 (1977; pub. Leningrad: Nauka, 1980): 49–57.

——. "Oktavy 'Domika v Kolomne' Pushkina (strofa i siuzhet)." In *Problemy teorii stikha*. Leningrad: Nauka, 1984, 125–31.

——, and E. Ia. Kurganov. "Iz real'nogo kommentariia k poeme 'Domik v Kolomne'." *Vremennik Pushkinskoi komissii* 18 (1980; pub. Leningrad: Nauka, 1983): 122–27.

Frank, Joseph. "A Reading of *The Idiot*." *The Southern Review* 5, no. 2 (1969): 303–31.

——. *Dostoevsky, The Years of Ordeal, 1850–1859*. Princeton: Princeton University Press, 1983.

Freidenberg, Ol'ga. "V"ezd v Ierusalim na osle (Iz evangel'skoi mifologii)." In *Mif i literatura drevnosti*. Moscow: Nauka, 1978, 491–523.

Freud, Sigmund. "Negation." Trans. Joan Riviere. In *General Psychological Theory*, ed. Philip Rieff. New York: Collier Books, 1963, 213–17.

Frizman, L. G. "Paradoks Katenina." Introduction to *Razmyshleniia i razbory* by P. N. Katenin. Ed. L. G. Frizman. Moscow: Iskusstvo, 1981, 9–44.

Fuller, Peter. "The Christs of Faith and the Jesus of History." In his *Images of God: The Consolations of Lost Illusions*. London: Hogarth, 1985, 298–311.

Furst, Lilian R. *Fictions of Romantic Irony*. Cambridge: Harvard University Press, 1984.

Gasparov, M. L., and V. M. Smirin. " 'Evgenii Onegin'; 'Domik v Kolomne': Parodiia i samoparodiia u Pushkina." *Tynianovskii sbornik: vtorye tynianovskie chteniia*. Ed. M. O. Chudakova. Riga: Zinatne, 1986, 254–64.

Gass, William. "Philosophy and the Form of Fiction." In his *Fiction and the Figures of Life*. New York: Alfred A. Knopf, 1970.

Gershenzon, Mikhail. *Mudrost' Pushkina*. Moscow: Knigoizdatel'stvo pisatelei v Moskve, 1919.

Gippius, Vasilii Vasil'evich. *Gogol*. Ed. and trans. Robert Maguire. Ann Arbor, Mich.: Ardis, 1981.

——. "Problematika i kompozitsiia *Revizora*." In *N. V. Gogol, materialy i issledovaniia*, ed. V. V. Gippius. Moscow and Leningrad: Akademiia Nauk, 1936, 2:150–99.

Goerner, Tatiana. "The Theme of Art and Aesthetics in Dostoevsky's *The Idiot*." *Ulbandus Review* 2, no. 2 (Fall 1982): 79–95.

Goffman, M. L. "Istoriia sozdaniia i teksta 'Domika v Kolomne.' " Appendix to A. S. Pushkin, *Domik v Kolomne*. Peterburg: Atenei, 1922.

Gogol', N. V. *Polnoe sobranie sochinenii*. 14 vols. Ed. N. F. Bel'chikov and B. V. Tomashevskii. Leningrad: Izdatel'stvo Akademii Nauk, 1937–52.

Gol'dshtein, Sof'ia N. *Ivan Nikolaievich Kramskoi: zhizn' i tvorchestvo*. Moscow: Iskusstvo, 1965.

Goldstein, David I. *Dostoyevsky and the Jews.* Austin: University of Texas Press, 1981.

Gottlieb, Vera. *Chekhov and the Vaudeville: A Study of Chekhov's One-Act Plays.* Cambridge: Cambridge University Press, 1982.

Grossman, Joan Delaney. "Tolstoy's Portrait of Anna: Keystone in the Arch." *Criticism* 18 (1976): 1–14.

Grossman, Leonid. *Biblioteka Dostoevskogo po neizdannym materialam, s prilozheniem kataloga biblioteka Dostoevskogo.* Odessa: A. A. Ivasenko, 1919.

Guardini, Romano. "Dostoyevsky's Idiot, a Symbol of Christ." *Cross Currents* 6, no. 4 (1956): 359–82.

Gus, Mikhail Semenovich. *Idei i obrazy F. M. Dostoevskogo.* 2d ed., rev. Moscow: Khudozhestvennaia literatura, 1971.

Gustafson, Richard F. *Leo Tolstoy, Resident and Stranger: A Study in Fiction and Theology.* Princeton: Princeton University Press, 1986.

Hagstrum, Jean H. *The Sister Arts: The Tradition of Literary Pictorialism and English Poetry from Dryden to Gray.* Chicago: University of Chicago Press, 1958.

Harkins, William. "The Little House in Kolomne." In *Three Comic Poems*, by A. Pushkin, trans. and ed. William Harkins. Ann Arbor, Mich.: Ardis, 1977, 63–69.

———. "The Place of 'Domik v Kolomne' in Puškin's Creation." *Alexander Puškin: A Symposium on the 175th Anniversary of His Birth*, ed. A. Kodjak and K. Taranovsky. New York: New York University Press, 1976, 196–205.

Harrison, Robert. Introduction to *Gallic Salt: Eighteen Fabliaux Translated from the Old French.* Trans. Robert Harrison. Berkeley: University of California Press, 1974, 1–35.

Hibberd, John. *Salomon Gessner: His Creative Achievement and Influence.* Cambridge: Cambridge University Press, 1976.

Holenstein, Elmar. *Roman Jakobson's Approach to Language: Phenomenological Structuralism.* Trans. Catherine and Tarcisius Schelbert. Bloomington: Indiana University Press, 1976.

Hollander, Robert. "The Apocalyptic Framework of Dostoevsky's *The Idiot.*" *Mosaic* 7, no. 2 (1974): 123–39.

Holquist, J. Michael. *Dostoevsky and the Novel.* Princeton: Princeton University Press, 1977.

Howard, Barbara F. "The Rhetoric of Confession: Dostoevskii's *Notes from Underground* and Rousseau's *Confessions.*" *Slavic and East European Journal* 25, no. 4 (1981): 16–32.

Hugo, Victor. *Last Day of a Condemned. Claude Gueux.* Trans. Eugenia de B. New York: Howard Fertig, 1977.

Hutcheon, Linda. *A Theory of Parody: The Teachings of Twentieth-Century Art Forms.* London: Methuen, 1985.

Immerwahr, Raymond. "The Practice of Irony in Early German Romanticism." In *Romantic Irony*, ed. Frederick Garber. Budapest: Akadémiai Kiadó, 1988, 82–96.

Ivanov, V. V. "Poetika." *Kratkaia literaturnaia entsiklopediia.* 9 vols. Ed. A. A. Tsurkov. Moscow: Sovetskaia entsiklopediia, 1968, 5:835–43.

Jackson, Robert Louis. *The Art of Dostoevsky: Deliriums and Nocturnes.* Princeton: Princeton University Press, 1981.

———. *Dostoevsky's Quest for Form: A Study of His Philosophy of Art.* New Haven: Yale University Press, 1966.

———. " 'If I Forget Thee, O Jerusalem': An Essay on Chekhov's *Rothschild's Fiddle.*" In *Anton Chekhov Rediscovered: A Collection of New Studies with a Comprehensive Bibliography*, ed. S. Senderovich and M. Sendich. East Lansing, Mich.: Russian Language Journal, 1987, 35–49.

Jakobson, Roman. "Langue and Parole: Code and Message." In *On Language*, eds. Linda R. Waugh and Monique Monville-Burston. Cambridge: Harvard University Press, 1990, 80–109.

———. "Linguistics and Poetics." In *Selected Writings,* Vol. 3, *Poetry of Grammar and Grammar of Poetry*, ed. Stephen Rudy. The Hague: Mouton, 1981, 18–51.

———. "Linguistic Types of Aphasia." In *Selected Writings*, Vol. 2, *Word and Language.* The Hague: Mouton, 1971, 306–333.

———. "Metalanguage as a Linguistic Problem." In *Selected Writings*, Vol. 7, *Contributions to Comparative Mythology. Studies in Linguistics and Philology, 1972–1982*, ed. Stephen Rudy. Berlin: Mouton, 1985, 113–21.

———. "Puškin Unrestrained." In *Puškin and His Sculptural Myth*, trans. and ed. John Burbank. The Hague: Mouton, 1975, 68–75.

———. "On Realism in Art." Trans. K. Magassy. In *Readings in Russian Poetics: Formalist and Structuralist Views*, ed. L. Matejka and K. Pomorska. Cambridge: MIT Press, 1971. Reprint, Ann Arbor, Mich.: Michigan Slavic Publications, 1978, 38–46.

———. "Quest for the Essence of Language." *Selected Writings*, Vol. 2, *Word and Language.* The Hague: Mouton, 1971, 345–59.

———. "The Relation between Visual and Auditory Signs." *Selected Writings*, Vol. 2, *Word and Language.* The Hague: Mouton, 1971, 338–44.

———. "Shifters, Verbal Categories, and the Russian Verb." *Selected Writings*, Vol. 2, *Word and Language.* The Hague: Mouton, 1971, 130–47.

———. "Two Aspects of Language and Two Types of Aphasic Disturbances." In *Selected Writings*, Vol. 2, *Word and Language.* The Hague: Mouton, 1971, 239–59.

———. "Visual and Auditory Signs." *Selected Writings*, Vol. 2, *Word and Language.* The Hague: Mouton, 1971, 334–37.

———, and Krystyna Pomorska. *Dialogues.* Cambridge: MIT Press, 1983.

Jauss, Hans Robert. *Aesthetic Experience and Literary Hermeneutics.* Theory and History of Literature, vol. 3. Trans. Michael Shaw. Minneapolis: University of Minnesota Press, 1982.

Johnston, R. C., and D. D. R. Owen. Introduction to *Fabliaux*, ed. R. C. Johnston and D. D. R. Owen. Oxford: Basil Blackwell, 1965, v–xix.

de Jonge, Alex. *Dostoevsky and the Age of Intensity.* London: Secker and Warburg, 1975.

Karcevskii, Sergei. "The Asymmetric Dualism of the Linguistic Sign." Trans. Wendy Steiner. In *The Prague School: Selected Writings, 1929–1946*, ed. Peter Steiner. Austin: University of Texas Press, 1982, 47–54.

Karlinsky, Simon. "Nabokov and Chekhov: The Lesser Russian Tradition." In *Nabokov: Criticism, Reminiscences, Translations, and Tributes*, ed. Alfred Appel, Jr. and Charles Newman. Evanston, Ill.: Northwestern University Press, 1970, 7–16.

———. *Russian Drama from Its Beginnings to the Age of Pushkin.* Berkeley: University of California Press, 1985.

———. *The Sexual Labyrinth of Nikolai Gogol.* Cambridge: Harvard University Press, 1976.

Katenin, Pavel A. *Izbrannye proizvedeniia.* Ed. G. V. Ermova-Bitner. Moscow-Leningrad: Sovetskii pisatel', 1965.

———. *Razmyshleniia i razbory.* Ed. L. G. Frizman. Moscow: Iskusstvo, 1981.

Kharlap, M. "Polemicheskii smysl 'Domik v Kolomne'." *Izvestiia Akademii Nauk* 39, no. 3 (1980): 219–29.

Kjetsaa, Geir. *Fyodor Dostoevsky: A Writer's Life.* Trans. Siri Hustvedt and David McDuff. New York: Viking, 1987.

Knox, Norman D. "Irony." In *Dictionary of the History of Ideas*, Vol. 2, ed. Philip A. Wiener. New York: Charles Scribner's Sons, 1973, 286 n.41.

Kovacs, Arpad. "Poetika romana *Idiot.* K probleme zhanrovogo myshleniia Dostoevskogo." *Hungaro-Slavica* (1978): 149–164; partial trans. by Caryl Emerson in *Critical Essays on Dostoevsky*, ed. Robin Feuer Miller. Boston: G. K. Hall, 1986, 116–125.

Kratkaia literaturnaia entsiklopediia. 9 vols. Ed. A. A. Surkov. Moscow: Sovetskaia entsiklopediia, 1962–78.

Kristeva, Julia. "The Ethics of Linguistics." In *Desire in Language.* New York: Columbia University Press, 1980, 23–35.

———. "Holbein's Dead Christ." In *Fragments for a History of the Human Body*, Pt. 1, ed. Michael Foher et al. New York: Zone, 1989, 238–69.

Krivonos, Vladislav Shaevich. *Problema chitatelia v tvorchestve Gogolia.* Voronezh: Izdatel'stvo Voronezhskogo Universiteta, 1981.

Krylov, I. A. *Sochineniia v dvukh tomakh.* Moscow: Khudozhestvennaia literatura, 1969.

Kulish, Panteleimon Aleksandrovich. *Zapiski o zhizni Nikolaia Vasil'evicha Gogol'ia, sostavlennye iz vospominanii ego druzei i znakomykh i iz ego sobstvennykh pisem'.* 2 vols. St. Petersburg: Aleksandr Iakobson, 1856.

Kupreianova, E. I. "*Voina i mir* i *Anna Karenina* L'va Tolstogo." In *Istoriia russkogo realizma*, Vol. 2, ed. V. P. Gorodetskii and N. I. Trutskov. Moscow: Nauka, 1964.

Lacoue-Labarthe, Phillippe, and Jean-Luc Nancy. *The Literary Absolute: The Theory of Literature in German Romanticism.* Trans. Philip Barnard and Cheryl Lester. Albany: State University of New York Press, 1988.

Leatherbarrow, William. "Apocalyptic Imagery in 'The Idiot' and 'The Devils'." *Dostoevsky Studies* 3 (1982): 43–51.

Lessing, Gotthold Ephraim. *Laocoön: An Essay on the Limits of Painting and Poetry.* Trans., introduction, and notes by Edward A. McCormick. Indianapolis and New York: Bobbs-Merrill (Library of Liberal Arts), 1962.

Levitt, Marcus C. *Russian Literary Politics and the Pushkin Celebration of 1880.* Ithaca and London: Cornell University Press, 1989.

Lodge, David. *The Modes of Modern Writing: Metaphor, Metonymy, and the Typology of Modern Literature.* London, 1977. Reprint, Chicago: University of Chicago Press, 1988.

Lord, Robert. "An Epileptic Mode of Being." In *Dostoevsky: Essays and Perspectives.* Berkeley and Los Angeles: University of California Press, 1970, 181–201.

Lotman, Iu. M. "Russo i russkaia kul'tura." In *Traktaty.* By Zhan-Zhak Russo. Moscow: Nauka, 1969, 555–604.

——. "The Stage and Painting as Code Mechanisms for Cultural Behavior in the Early Nineteenth Century." Trans. Judith Armstrong. In *The Semiotics of Russian Culture*, ed. Ann Shukman. Michigan Slavic Contributions, No. 11. Ann Arbor: Department of Slavic Languages and Literatures, University of Michigan, 1984, 165–76.

——. *The Structure of the Artistic Text.* Trans. R. Vroon. Ann Arbor: Michigan Slavic Contributions, 1977.

——, (Yu.), and Boris Uspensky. "On the Semiotic Mechanism of Culture." *New Literary History* 9, no. 2 (1978): 211–33.

Lotman, Lidiia M. *Realizm russkoi literatury 60-kh godov xix veka* (*istoki i esteticheskoe svoebrazie*). Leningrad: Nauka, 1974.

Maguire, Robert. "The Legacy of Criticism." Introduction to *Gogol from the Twentieth Century: Eleven Essays*, ed. Robert MacGuire. Princeton: Princeton University Press, 1974, 13–54.

Magarshak, David. *Gogol, A Life.* London: Faber & Faber, 1957.

Mandelker, Amy. "A Painted Lady: *Ekphrasis* in *Anna Karenina.*" *Comparative Literature* 43, no. 1 (Winter 1991): 1–19.

Mann, Iurii. "Dramaturgiia N. V. Gogolia." In *Istoriia russkoi dramaturgii xvii-pervaia polovina xix veka*, ed. L. M. Lotman. Leningrad: Nauka, 1982, 426–73.

——. "Gogol and Dostoevsky in the Development of the Comic." *Scottish Slavonic Review* 11 (Autumn 1988): 7–23.

——. *Komediia Gogolia "Revizor."* Moscow: Khudozhestvennaia literatura, 1966.

——. *Poetika Gogolia.* Moscow: Khudozhestvennaia literatura, 1978.

——. " 'Uzhas okoval vsekh...' (o nemoi stsene v *Revizore* Gogolia." *Voprosy literatury* 8 (1989): 223–35.

Mathewson, Rufus W., Jr. "Thoreau and Chekhov: A Note on 'The Steppe.' " *Ulbandus Review* 1, no. 1 (Fall 1977): 28–39.

Matich, Olga. "What's to be Done about Poor Nastja: Nastasja Filippovna's Literary Prototypes." *Wiener Slawistischer Almanach* 19 (1987): 47–64.

Maxwell, David. "A System of Symbolic Gesture in Čexov's 'Step'." *Slavic and East European Journal* 17, no. 3 (Summer 1973): 146–54.

Merezhkovskii, D. S. *L. Tolstoi i Dostoevskii: zhizn', tvorchestvo i religiia.* Vol. 7 of *Polnoe sobranie sochinenii D. S. Merezhkovskogo.* St. Petersburg and Moscow: M. O. Vol'f, 1912. (Translated as Merejkowski, Dmitri. *Tolstoi as Man and Artist, with an Essay on Dostoievsky.* New York & London: G. P. Putnam's Sons, 1902.)

Miller, Robin Feuer. "Dostoevsky and Rousseau: The Morality of Confession Reconsidered." In *Western Philosophical Systems in Russian Literature*, ed. Anthony M. Mlikotin. Los Angeles: University of Southern California Press, 1979, 89–101.

———. *Dostoevsky and "The Idiot". Author, Narrator, and Reader.* Cambridge: Harvard University Press, 1981.

———. "Imitations of Rousseau in *The Possessed.*" *Dostoevsky Studies* 5 (1984): 77–89.

Mirsky, D. S. *Contemporary Russian Literature, 1881–1925.* New York: Alfred A. Knopf, 1926.

Mochulsky, Konstantin. *Dostoevsky: His Life and Work.* Trans. Michael Minihan. Princeton: Princeton University Press, 1967.

Modzalevskii, B. M. "Biblioteka A. S. Pushkina." *Pushkin i ego sovremenniki* 3, nos. 9–10.

Monas, Sidney. "Across the Threshold: *The Idiot* as a Petersburg Tale." In *New Essays on Dostoevsky*, ed. Malcolm Jones and Garth Terry. Cambridge: Cambridge University Press, 1983, 67–93.

Morson, Gary Saul. *The Boundaries of Genre: Dostoevsky's "Diary of a Writer" and the Traditions of Literary Utopia.* Austin: University of Texas Press, 1981.

———. *Hidden in Plain View: Narrative and Creative Potentials in 'War and Peace'.* Stanford: Stanford University Press, 1987.

———. "Prosaics and *Anna Karenina.*" *Tolstoy Studies* 1 (1988): 1–12.

———. "The Reader as Voyeur: Tolstoi and the Poetics of Didactic Fiction." *Canadian-American Slavic Studies* 12, no. 4 (Winter 1978): 465–80.

———, and Caryl Emerson. *Mikhail Bakhtin: Creation of a Prosaics.* Stanford: Stanford University Press, 1990.

Moser, Charles A. *Esthetics as Nightmare: Russian Literary Theory, 1855–1870.* Princeton: Princeton University Press, 1989.

Mukařovský, Jan. "Poetic Reference." Trans. S. Janacek. In *Semiotics of Art: Prague School Contributions*, ed. Ladislav Matejka and Irwin Titunik. Cambridge, Mass., and London: MIT Press, 1976, 155–63.

Murav, Harriet. *Holy Foolishness: Dostoevsky's Novels and the Poetics of Cultural Critique.* Stanford: Stanford University Press, 1992.

Nabokov, Vladimir. *Eugene Onegin, Revised Edition.* By Aleksandr Pushkin. 4 vols. Trans. and commentary Vladimir Nabokov. Princeton: Bollingen Foundation and Princeton University Press, 1975.

———. *The Gift.* Trans. Michael Scammel and Vladimir Nabokov. New York: Popular Library, 1963.

———. *Lectures on Russian Literature.* Ed. Fredson Bowers. New York: Harcourt Brace Jovanovich, 1981.

———. *Nikolai Gogol.* Norfolk, Conn.: New Directions Books, 1944.

The Nabokov-Wilson Letters: Correspondence between Vladimir Nabokov and Edmund Wilson, 1941–1971. Ed., notes and introduction by Simon Karlinsky. New York: Harper and Row, 1979.

Needler, Howard. Introduction to *Fables from Old French: Aesop's Beasts and Bumpkins.* Trans. Norman Shapiro. Middleton, Conn.: Wesleyan University Press, 1982, xi–lix.

Nilsson, Nils Åke. *Studies in Čechov's Narrative Technique: "The Steppe" and "The Bishop."* Stockholm: Almqvist & Wiksell, 1968.

Oksman, Iu. Introduction to "Vospominaniia P. A. Katenina o Pushkine." *Literaturnoe nasledstvo*, nos. 16–18 (1934): 619–34.

Ovid. *Metamorphoses*. Trans. Rolfe Humphries. Bloomington: Indiana University Press, 1955.

Paperno, Irina. *Chernyshevsky and the Age of Realism: A Study in the Semiotics of Behavior*. Stanford: Stanford University Press, 1988.

Peace, Richard. *Dostoevsky: An Examination of the Major Novels*. Cambridge: Cambridge University Press, 1971.

Poliakov, Mark. "Russkii teatr v krivom zerkale parodii." Introduction to *Russkaia teatral'naia parodiia XIX nachala XX veka*, ed. M. Poliakov. Moscow: Iskusstvo, 1976, 6–38.

Pomorska, Krystyna. "On the Problem of Parallelism in Gogol's Prose: 'A Tale of the Two Ivans.' " In *The Structural Analysis of Narrative Texts: Conference Papers*, ed. A. Kodjak, M. J. Connoly, and K. Pomorska. Columbus, Ohio: Slavica, 1980, 31–43.

———. "Tolstoy—Contra Semiosis." *International Journal of Slavic Linguistics and Poetics* 25–26 (1982): 383–90.

Pratt, Mary Louise. *Towards a Speech Act Theory of Literary Discourse*. Bloomington: Indiana University Press, 1977.

Princeton Encyclopedia of Poetry and Poetics. Ed. Alex Preminger. Princeton: Princeton University Press, 1974.

Proffer, Carl R. *The Simile and Gogol's "Dead Souls"*. The Hague and Paris: Mouton, 1967.

Pushkin, A. S. "Domik v Kolomne." In *Biblioteka velikikh pisatelei. Pushkin*. 6 vols. Ed. S. A. Vengerov. St. Petersburg: Brokgaus-Efron, 1907–15, 3:92–99.

———. "The Little House in Kolomna." Trans. Walter Arndt. In *Collected Narrative and Lyrical Poetry* by Alexander Pushkin. Ann Arbor, Mich.: Ardis, 1984, 399–410.

———. *Polnoe sobranie sochinenii v shesti tomakh*. Ed. Iu. G. Oksman and M. A. Tsialovskii. Moscow-Leningrad: Academia, 1936–38.

Raffe, W. G. *Dictionary of the Dance*. New York: A. S. Barnes, 1964.

Rayfield, Donald. "Anton Chekhov and the Literary Tradition." In *A Chekhov Companion*, ed. Toby W. Clyman. Westport, Conn., and London: Greenwood Press, 1985, 35–51.

———. "What Did Jews Mean to Chekhov?" *European Judaism* 8 (Winter 1974): 30–6.

Repin, I. E., and V. V. Stasov. *I. E. Repin i V. V. Stasov. Perepiska*. Ed. A. K. Lebedev. Moscow and Leningrad: Iskusstvo, 1949.

Rice, James L. *Dostoevsky and the Healing Art: An Essay in Literary and Medical History*. Ann Arbor, Mich.: Ardis, 1985.

Rose, Margaret A. *Parody//Meta-Fiction: An Analysis of Parody as a Critical Mirror to the Writing and Reception of Fiction*. London: Croom Helm, 1979.

Rousseau, Jean-Jacques. *The Confessions*. Trans. J. M. Cohen. Middlesex, England: Penguin Books, 1987.

Rowe, W. W. *Dostoevsky: Child and Man in His Works.* New York: New York University Press, 1968.

Rozanov, I. N. "Katenin." In his *Pushkinskaia pleaiada: starshee pokolenie.* Moscow: Zadruga, 1923, 93–183.

Russkaia kriticheskaia literatura o proizvedeniiakh L. N. Tolstogo: khronologicheskii sbornik kritiko-bibliographicheskikh statei. Vol. 8. Ed. V. Zelinskii. Moscow: V. Rikhter, 1902.

Russkii vodevil'. Ed. V. V. Uspenskii. Leningrad-Moscow: Iskusstvo, 1959.

Sakharov, V. I. "Surovyi Naslednik (Gogol' i Lev Tolstoi)." In *Gogol': istoriia i sovremennost'.* Ed. Kozhinov, Osetrov, and Palamarchuk. Moscow: Sovetskaia Rossiia, 1985. 339–47.

Scanlan, James F. "Chernyshevsky and Rousseau." In *Western Philosophical Systems in Russian Literature*, ed. Anthony M. Mlikotin. Los Angeles: University of Southern California Press, 1979, 103–20.

Schlegel, Friedrich von. *Dialogue on Poetry and Literary Aphorisms.* Trans., introduced, and annotated by Ernst Behler and Roman Struc. University Park: Pennsylvania State University Press, 1968.

Scholem, Gershom. *Kabbalah.* New York: New American Library, 1978.

Scholes, Robert. *Structuralism in Literature: An Introduction.* New Haven: Yale University Press, 1974.

Schultze, Sydney. *The Structure of Anna Karenina.* Ann Arbor: Mich.: Ardis, 1982.

Segal, Dmitrii. "Literatura kak okhrannaia gramota." *Slavica Hieroslymitana* 5–6 (1981): 151–244.

Semjonow, Jurij. *Das Häuschen in Kolomna in Der Poetischen Erbschaft A. S. Puškins. Text, Interpretation und Literatur-Historischer Kommentar.* Uppsala: Almqvist & Wiksell, 1965.

Senderovich, Marena, and Savely Senderovich. " 'Roza' Pushkina i ee literaturnoe okruzhenie." *Canadian-American Slavic Studies* 11, no. 1 (1977): 36–61.

Senderovich, Savely. "Chudo Georgiia o zmie: Istoriia oderzhimosti Chekhova odnim obrazom." *Russian Language Journal* 39, nos. 132–34 (1985): 135–225.

———. "The Poetic Structure of Čexov's Short Story 'On the Road.' " In *The Structural Analysis of Narrative Texts*, eds. A. Kodjak, M. Connolly, and K. Pomorska. Columbus, Ohio: Slavica, 1980, 44–81.

Serrano-Plaja, Arturo. *"Magic" Realism in Cervantes: "Don Quixote" as Seen through "Tom Sawyer" and "The Idiot."* Trans. Robert S. Rudder. Berkeley, Los Angeles, and London: University of California Press, 1970.

Setchkarev, Vsevolod. *Gogol: His Life and Works.* Trans. Robert Kramer. New York: New York University Press, 1965.

Shaw, J. Thomas. "Pushkin's 'The Stationmaster' and the New Testament Parable." *Slavic and East European Journal* 21, no. 1 (Spring 1977): 3–29.

Shepherd, David. *Beyond Metafiction: Self-Consciousness in Soviet Literature.* Oxford: Clarendon Press, 1992.

Shklovskii, Viktor. *Lev Tolstoi.* Moscow: Molodaia gvardiia, 1967.

———. *Zametki o proze russkikh klassikov.* Moscow: Sovetskii pisatel', 1953.

Silbajoris, Rimvydas. *Tolstoy's Aesthetics and His Art.* Columbus, Ohio: Slavica Publishers, 1991.

Simpson, Mark S. *The Officer in Nineteenth-Century Russian Literature.* Washington, D.C.: University Press of America, 1981.

Skaftymov, Aleksandr P. "Tematicheskaia kompozitsiia romana *Idiot.*" In *Nravstvennye iskaniia russkikh pisatelei.* Moscow: Khudozhestvennaia literatura, 1972, 23–87.

Slattery, Dennis. "Narcissus Inverted: Fantastic Realism as a Way of Knowing in *The Idiot.*" In *Dostoevsky and the Human Condition after a Century*, ed. A. Ugrinsky, F. Lambasa, and V. Ozolins. New York: Greenwood Press, 1986, 61–69.

Slovar' iazyka Pushkina. 4 vols. Ed. V. V. Vinogradov. Moscow: Gosudarstvennoe izdatel'stvo inostrannykh i natsional'nykh slovarei, 1956–61.

Slovar' russkikh narodnykh govorov. Ed. F. P. Filin. Leningrad: Nauka, 1965– .

Smith, Barbara Herrnstein. "On the Margins of Discourse." In *On the Margins of Discourse: The Relation of Literature to Language.* Chicago: University of Chicago Press, 1978.

Smith, Mack. "Tolstoy and the Conventions of Representation." In *Renascence: Essays on Value in Literature* 37, no. 4: 220–37.

Sobel, Ruth. *Gogol's Forgotten Book: Selected Passages and its Contemporary Readers.* Lanham, Md.: University Press of America, 1981.

Sorokin, Boris. *Tolstoy in Prerevolutionary Russian Criticism.* Columbus: Ohio State University Press (for Miami University), 1979.

Steiner, George. *Tolstoy or Dostoevsky: An Essay in the Old Criticism.* New York: Alfred A. Knopf, 1959.

Steiner, Peter. *Russian Formalism: A Metapoetics.* Ithaca and London: Cornell University Press, 1984.

Steiner, Wendy. *The Colors of Rhetoric: Problems in the Relation between Modern Literature and Painting.* Chicago: University of Chicago Press, 1982.

Stenbock-Fermor, Elizabeth. *The Architecture of "Anna Karenina." A History of Its Writing, Structure, and Message.* Lisse: Peter de Ridder Press, 1975.

———. "French Medieval Poetry as a Source of Inspiration for Puškin." In *Alexander Puškin: A Symposium on the 175th Anniversary of His Birth*, ed. A. Kodjak and K. Taranovsky. New York: New York University Press, 1976, 56–70.

Stilman, Leon. "The 'All-Seeing Eye' in Gogol." In *Gogol from the Twentieth Century*, trans. and ed. Robert Maguire. Princeton: Princeton University Press, 1974, 375–89.

Striedter, Jurij. "The Russian Formalist Theory of Literary Evolution." *PTL: A Journal for Descriptive Poetics and Theory of Literature* 3 (1978): 1–24.

Tammi, Pekka. "Three Remarks on Čechov's *Step'*: Point of View, Subtext, and Their Conjunction." *Scando-Slavica* 33 (1987): 91–107.

Terras, Victor. " 'Shinel' ' Gogolia v kritike molodogo Dostoevskogo." *Zapiski russkoi akademicheskoi gruppy v SShA [Transactions of the Association of Russian-American Scholars in the U.S.A.]* 17 (1984): 69–75.

———. *The Young Dostoevsky (1846–1849): A Critical Study.* The Hague and Paris: Mouton, 1969.

Todd, William M., III. *The Familiar Letter in the Age of Pushkin.* Princeton: Princeton University Press, 1976.

——. *Fiction and Society in the Age of Pushkin.* Cambridge: Harvard University Press, 1986.

Todorov, Tzvetan. "An Introduction to Verisimilitude." In his *Poetics of Prose*, trans. Richard Howard. Ithaca: Cornell University Press, 1977, 80–88.

——. *Genres in Discourse.* Trans. Catherine Porter. Cambridge: Cambridge University Press, 1990.

——. *Mikhail Bakhtin: The Dialogic Principle.* Trans. Wlad Godzich. Minneapolis: University of Minnesota Press, 1984.

——. *Theories of the Symbol.* Trans. Catherine Porter. Ithaca and New York: Cornell University Press, 1982.

——. "Three Conceptions of Poetic Language." In *Russian Formalism: A Retrospective Glance. A Festschrift in Honor of Victor Erlich*, ed. Robert Louis Jackson and Stephen Rudy. New Haven: Yale Center for International and Area Studies, 1985, 130–47.

Tolstoi, L. N. [Tolstoy, Leo]. *Anna Karenina.* Trans. Aylmer Maude; ed. George Gibian. New York: W. W. Norton & Co., 1970.

——. *Polnoe sobranie sochinenii.* 90 vols. Moscow: Gosudarstvennoe izdatel'stvo khudozhestvennoi literatury, 1928–58.

——. *Tolstoy's Letters.* 2 vols. Selected, edited, and translated by R. F. Christian. New York: Charles Scribner's Sons, 1978.

L. N. Tolstoi i khudozhniki: L. N. Tolstoi ob iskusstve. Pis'ma, dnevniki. Vospominaniia. Ed. and introduction by I. A. Brodskii. Moscow: Iskusstvo, 1978.

Tolstoy: The Critical Heritage. Ed. A. V. Knowles. London, Henley, and Boston: Routledge & Kegan Paul, 1978.

Tomashevskii, Boris. *Pushkin i Frantsiia.* Leningrad: Sovetskii pisatel', 1960.

Turner, C. J. G. "Dostoevsky's Idiot: Treasure in Earthen Vessels." *Dostoevsky Studies* 6 (1985): 173–80.

Tynianov, Iurii M. "Arkhaisty i Pushkin." In *Arkhaisty i novatory.* Slavische Propyläen: Texte in Neu- und Nachdrucken, 31. Leningrad, 1929. Reprint, Munich: Wilhelm Fink, 1967, 87–227.

——. "Dostoevskii i Gogol': k teorii parodii." In *Arkhaisty i novatory.* Slavische Propyläen: Texte in Neu- und Nachdrucken, 31. Leningrad, 1929. Reprint, Munich: Wilhelm Fink, 1967, 412–55.

——. "O literaturnoi evoliutsii." In *Arkhaisty i novatory.* Slavische Propyläen: Texte in Neu- und Nachdrucken, 31. Leningrad, 1929. Reprint, Munich: Wilhelm Fink, 1967, 30–47.

——. "O literaturnom fakte." In *Arkhaisty i novatory.* Slavische Propyläen: Texte in Neu- und Nachdrucken, 31. Leningrad, 1929. Reprint, Munich: Wilhelm Fink, 1967, 5–29.

——. "O Parodii." In *Poetika, istoriia, literatury, kino.* Moscow: Nauka, 1977, 284–310.

Uspenskii, V. V. "Russkii klassicheskii vodevil'." Introduction to *Russkii vodevil'*, ed. V. V. Uspenskii. Leningrad-Moscow: Iskusstvo, 1959, 3–50.

Uspensky, Boris. *A Poetics of Composition: The Structure of the Artistic Text and Typology of a Compositional Form.* Trans. V. Zavarin and S. Wittig. Berkeley, Los Angeles, and London: University of California Press, 1973.

"Varianty i kommentarii." Ed. notes to Pushkin, "Domik v Kolomne," *Polnoe sobranie sochinenii v shesti tomakh.* Ed. Iu. G. Oksman and M. A. Tsialovskii. Moscow-Leningrad: Academia, 1936–38, 2:595–98.

Varneke, B. V. *History of the Russian Theatre, Seventeenth through Nineteenth Century.* Trans. Boris Brasol; ed. Belle Martin. New York: Macmillan, 1951.

Vetlovskaia, V. E. "Ob odnom iz istochnikov *Brat'ev Karamazovykh.*" *Izvestiia Akademii nauk SSSR, Seriia literatury i iazyka* 40, no. 5 (1981): 436–45.

Vinogradov, Viktor. "O stile Pushkina" *Literaturnoe nasledstvo*, nos. 16–18 (1934): 135–214.

Vishnevskaia, I. L. *Gogol' i ego komedii.* Moscow: Nauka, 1976.

Vygotsky, Lev. *Thought and Language.* Ed. and trans. Eugenia Hanfmann and Gertrude Vakar. Cambridge: MIT Press, 1962.

Waugh, Linda R. "The Poetic Function in the Theory of Roman Jakobson." *Poetics Today* 2, no. 1a (1980): 57–82.

Waugh, Patricia. *Metafiction: The Theory and Practice of Self-Conscious Fiction.* London: Methuen, 1984.

Way, Gregory L. Introduction to *Fabliaux or tales, abridged from French manuscripts of the XIIth and XIIIth centuries* (2 vols.), by Pierre Jean Baptiste Le Grand d'Aussy. Selected and translated by G. L. Way. London: W. Bulmer & Co., 1796–1800, 1 (1796): i–xxxvii.

Weber, Samuel. "Criticism Underway: Walter Benjamin's *Romantic Concept of Criticism.*" In *Romantic Revolutions: Criticism and Theory*, ed. Kenneth R. Johnston et al. Bloomington and Indianapolis: Indiana University Press, 1990, 302–19.

Wellek, René. "The Poet as Critic, the Critic as Poet, the Poet-Critic." In *Discriminations: Further Concepts of Criticism.* New Haven: Yale University Press, 1970, 253–74.

Welsh, Alexander. *Reflections on the Hero as Quixote.* Princeton: Princeton University Press, 1981.

Wigzell, Faith. "Gogol and Vaudeville." In *Nikolai Gogol: Text and Context*, ed. Jane Grayson and Faith Wigzell. New York: St. Martin's Press, 1989.

Ziolkowski, Eric J. *The Sanctification of Don Quixote: From Hidalgo to Priest.* University Park: Pennsylvania State University Press, 1991.

Ziolkowski, Margaret. *Hagiography and Modern Russian Literature.* Princeton: Princeton University Press, 1988.

Ziolkowski, Theodore. *Fictional Transfigurations of Jesus.* Princeton: Princeton University Press, 1972.

Zlochevskaia, A. V. "Gumanisticheskii ideal i obraz kniaza Myshkina v romane F. M. Dostoevskogo *Idiot.*" *Nauchnye doklady vysshei shkoly. Filologicheskie Nauki*, no. 2 (1989): 18–25.

Index

Michael C. Finke is Associate Professor of Russian at Washington University in St. Louis.

Library of Congress Cataloging-in-Publication Data

Finke, Michael.

Metapoesis : the Russian tradition from Pushkin to Chekhov /

Michael Finke.

p. cm. — (Sound and meaning)

Includes index.

ISBN 0-8223-1556-4. — ISBN 0-8223-1567-X (paper)

1. Russian literature — 19th century — History and criticism.

I. Title. II. Series.

PG3012.F56 1995

891.709'003 — dc20 94-38198 CIP